The Epic of the Crusades

THE EPIC OF THE
CRUSADES

RENÉ GROUSSET

Translated from the French by
NOEL LINDSAY

Orion Press · New York · 1970

To Pierre Benoit
The expression of a lasting friendship

CONTENTS

The Epic of the Crusades

I

THE POPE, DEFENDER OF EUROPE
Urban II

WHEN, in the closing days of June 1095, Pope Urban II passed from Italy into France to preach the First Crusade, no one yet seemed to have guessed the purpose of his journey. Before proclaiming the adventure which was to change the face of the world, he felt the urge to renew contact with his native province of Champagne and to commune with himself beneath the vaults of the monastery of Cluny where he had dreamed the dreams of youth. The voices which breathed from that countryside were eminently destined to confirm him in his resolution, if indeed it was not they which had first inspired it. Was it not from Cluny, with the great eleventh-century movement of pilgrimages, that the first expeditions had set out to deliver Spanish Christendom from the yoke of the Moslem? When Urban, who still bore the name of Odo of Châtillon, was only in his twenties, had he not seen his countryman, Count Ebles of Roucy, with the chivalry of eastern France, take route for the Pyrenees to drive the Arabs out of Aragon? Loyal to these memories, and to the example of his predecessor, Gregory VII, Urban, now pope himself, had in 1089 launched another expedition on the road to Spain, this time made up mostly of knights from the south of France. At this date the Spanish *reconquista* already foreshadowed the great maneuvers of the Crusades.

What decided Urban II to carry into the East the war of liberation started in the far West?   To answer this question we must follow the great pope in his solitary meditations as he looks out on the world from the Lateran Palace, or from his exile at Salerno, or from the windows of Cluny in these dying years of the eleventh century.

Islam, sprung four hundred years earlier from the sands of Arabia, now covered, from Syria to Spain, nearly half the former territory of Rome, and the cradle of Christianity was still under its sway.   At one moment—a century earlier—there had been a breath of hope that the Holy Land would be liberated.   That was when the Byzantine Empire, in an unexpected recovery and a great vengeance against the Arabs, had driven them back as far as Syria itself.   In 969, the city of Antioch had thus been restored to Christendom.   In 975, the Emperor John Tzimisces, one of the most glorious sovereigns of Byzantine history, had victoriously traversed the whole of Syria and held his court under the walls of Damascus.   From there he had penetrated to the sacred land of Galilee.   He had been seen at the head of the "Roman" legions, praying on the banks of the Sea of Galilee, sparing the population of Nazareth in honor of the Virgin, and going on a pilgrimage to Mount Tabor, the mountain of the Transfiguration.   He was not far from thrusting, as he intended, to Jerusalem itself, but the obligation under which he found himself of turning to attack the Arab garrisons, still masters of the ports of the Lebanon, had halted him in his march; and after so nearly reaching his goal, he returned to Constantinople to die, without having liberated the Holy City.   The persecution which the caliph of Cairo shortly afterward launched against the Holy Sepulcher in 1005 made plainer in the eyes of Christendom this failure of Byzantine arms and of the Byzantine Church.   Byzantium had decisively let slip the glory of giving its name to the crusade. . . .

The situation then became worse with the coming of the Turks. Arabs and Persians, the former masters of eastern Islam, had long lost their original fighting spirit under the influence of a refined civilization. The Turks, in contrast, a paramountly military race, toughened by centuries of nomad life and poverty in the bleak solitudes of Upper Asia, were to give the Moslem world a new strength.   The day in 1055—a memorable date in the history of Asia—when the chief of one of their hordes coming from the Kirghiz steppes, Tughril Bey the Seljuk, entered Baghdad and imposed himself on the Arab caliph as temporal vicar and sultan, thus superimposing a Turkish Empire on the

Arab Empire—when, with him, the Turks became the imperial race of the Moslem world, then everything was changed. The Moslem conquest, halted for two centuries, resumed its course. The future Urban II, still a monk at Cluny, must no doubt have heard pilgrims' tales of how the Seljuk Turks, after dreadful ravages, had wrested the ancient Christian land of Armenia from the Byzantine Empire. Soon even more terrible news was to reach him, of the disaster of Manzikert.

A last energetic soldier, the Emperor Romanus Diogenes, had just ascended the throne of Byzantium. In the spring of 1071, with a hundred thousand men, including many Norman mercenaries, he set out to free Armenia from the Turks. The leader of the Turks, Alp Arslan, the "sturdy lion," the second sultan of the Seljuk dynasty, advanced to meet him. The clash came near Manzikert, north of Lake Van, on August 19, 1071. On this decisive day, Romanus was betrayed by his lieutenants. Left alone with a handful of faithful, he defended himself heroically until, wounded and his horse slain under him, he was taken prisoner and led to Alp Arslan who, for the rest, treated him honorably. It was the Byzantines who, when he was restored to freedom, put out his eyes from political hatred.

The defeat of Manzikert, too often glossed over in our history books, was one of the worst disasters in European history. This battle, fought in the heart of Armenia, resulted in the Turkish conquest of three fourths of Asia Minor over the next ten years. It is true that the progress of the Turks was aided by the incredible absence of "Christian patriotism" among the Byzantine generals who disputed the throne. It was one of these pretenders who, in 1078, committed a heinous crime against the Empire by calling in the Turks as allies and establishing them in this capacity at Nicaea, near the Sea of Marmara, across from Constantinople. Three years later, a younger son of the Seljuk house expelled the Byzantines and, with Nicaea as his capital, founded a Turkish kingdom of his own in Asia Minor, the heart of our own historic Turkey. In the meantime, in Syria, other Turkish chiefs had seized Jerusalem from the Arabs of Egypt (1071) and Antioch from the Byzantines (1085). Under the third Seljuk sultan, Malik Shah (1072–1092), the Turkish Empire extended all the way from Bokhara to Antioch. Malik Shah, the grandson of nomads emerged from the depths of Central Asia, came in 1087, in a curiously symbolic gesture, to dip his sword in the waters of the Mediterranean.

These events, the last of which took place during the papacy of

Urban II (1088–1099), had a profound effect upon the West. The collapse of the Byzantine Empire after Manzikert, its failure to react to the taking over of Asia Minor by the Turkish race and by Islam, convinced the West that, faced with such feebleness, the Western nations were in duty bound to intervene to save Europe from a direct menace. Our old chroniclers made no mistake, William of Tyre looked upon the disaster of Manzikert as the final eviction of the Greeks as the protagonists of Christianity and the historical justification of the Franks coming on to the scene to take over from their partners, now out of the fight. It was indeed high time to take counsel. From Nicaea, where Islam had established a firm foothold, it could surprise Constantinople at any moment. The catastrophe of 1453 might have happened as early as the closing years of the eleventh century. As Urban II was to proclaim, this was one of the reasons which decided him, fourteen years after the taking of Nicaea, to set about preaching the First Crusade. There is no need to imagine a direct appeal from the Byzantine Emperor, Alexius Comnenus, in order to explain such a resolution. Urban's sense of his duties as guide and defender of Christianity are enough to throw light on his policy. A farsighted policy, if ever there was one, which from the heights of the papal throne erected at Clermont-Ferrand, embraced both Jerusalem, where the wars between Egyptians and Seljuks had resulted in fresh massacres of Christians, as well as the question of the Straits, "Saint George's Sound," as they were then called, always under the menace of a Turkish assault.

On November 27, 1095, the tenth day of the Council of Clermont, Urban II, then, summoned the whole of Christendom to arms, the pope calling for the defense of the faith threatened by the new Moslem invasion, the true heir of the Roman Emperors calling for the defense of the West, the highest authority in Europe calling for its safeguarding against the Asiatic conquerors, the successors of Attila and the forerunners of Mahomet II. The cry of "Deus le volt." ("God wills it!") rang out from all sides in response to his proclamation and was taken up by Urban himself, who made it the general rallying cry and called upon the future soldiers of Christ to take the sign of the Cross as their badge. The "crusade" was born, an idea on the march which was to launch princes and people to the depths of the East. The crusading idea of the Council of Clermont can only be compared in this respect with the Panhellenic idea of the Congress of Corinth in 336 B.C. which launched Alexander the Great and the whole of Greece on the conquest of Asia.

The appeal of Urban II, the European mobilization orders of 1095, came at the psychological moment. If it had been launched a few years earlier, if the crusading armies had landed in Asia, not as they were to do in 1097, but seven or eight years earlier, when the great unified Turkish Empire of the Seljuks was still standing, their success would no doubt have been less certain. But at the moment when Urban ranged Europe against Asia, the Seljuk Sultan, Malik Shah had just died (November 15, 1092) and his empire, like Charlemagne's empire before it, had been divided, in the midst of enfeebling family quarrels, among his sons, his nephews, and his cousins. The sons of the great sultan had kept only Persia, whose provinces they were to dispute among themselves for many years to come. His nephews—also two enemy brothers—had become kings of Syria, the first at Aleppo, the second at Damascus. Finally Asia Minor, from Nicaea to Konya, formed a fourth Turkish kingdom under a cadet of the Seljuk house. All these princes, in spite of their kinship, were too divided among themselves to unite against an external peril. When the crusade came, they faced it in isolation and, instead of helping one another in time, allowed themselves to be defeated one by one.

No doubt Urban II did not know all the details of these quarrels; but informed as he was by the pilgrims, he cannot have been ignorant of the broad picture. In any event, it must be recognized that the moment was singularly opportune for the realization of his great project. The crusade, falling upon an Islam in utter disorder, in the midst of a dissolving empire, was to enjoy the same advantages that the Norman invasions had formerly experienced in the West when they fell upon the Carolingian Empire in the depths of its decadence.

What immediate support could Urban II count upon?

Unable to leave Rome to head the crusade himself, his choice of leader fell upon a prelate who had himself made the pilgrimage to the Holy Land and was therefore familiar with the Eastern question, Adhemar of Monteil, bishop of Le Puy. It was an excellent choice. As we shall see, Adhemar's great wisdom was able to preserve the cohesion which was essential between so many turbulent nobles. Adhemar's counsels, no less than the pope's own experience at Cluny, next made him turn his eyes to those barons of the south of France who had already waged the Holy War in Spain. Among their number was Raymond of Saint-Gilles, count of Toulouse, who had taken part in the expedition against Tudela in 1087. Raymond's piety, his deference to the ecclesiastical authorities, made him respond with fervor to the pope's appeal. After the Council of Clermont, Urban stayed with him, in the county of Toulouse, from May to July 1096, and a last council, then held at Nîmes, completed the work begun at Clermont. Thereby, as already indicated, the crusade was directly linked with the *reconquista*.

As well as the barons of the South, already accustomed to fighting the Moors in Spain, Urban II could count on the Normans of the Two Sicilies, already his long-standing friends, since it was among them that he had formerly taken refuge, at Salerno, in his quarrels with the Germanic Empire. The story of the establishment of these astounding adventurers in southern Italy for more than a century had indeed, in many respects, been little more than a crusade before its time, a crusade full of profit, as well as full of heroism, since it was as much from the Arabs as from the Byzantines that they had conquered the land. This was fairly recent history, since it was only in 1072 that the Norman leader, Robert Guiscard, had succeeded in driving the last Arabs out of Palermo. The Normans here therefore represented the vanguard of the Latin world both against the infidel and against the Greek heretic. Already, moreover, they had crossed the Straits of Otranto to pursue the Byzantines in the Balkans before driving the Moslems back into Asia. From 1081 to 1085, Robert Guiscard and his son Bohemund had carried the war into the heart of Byzantine territory, conquered part of Epirus and Macedonia, and carried their arms from Durazzo to the hinterland of Salonika. The death of Robert had meant their withdrawal, but Urban II was to find them eager auxiliaries. For Bohemund, the inheritor of the Eastern dreams of his father, Robert Guiscard, the crusade, in which he was to join with joy, was indeed merely the resumption, under a pious pretext, of the abortive expedition of 1081.

Urban II found other supporters in Italy, ready to his hand, namely Pisa and Genoa. The life of these two maritime communes had for two centuries been a daily battle against the Arab fleets. Pisa had been twice pillaged, in 1004 and 1011, by the Arab corsairs. With the aid of the Genoese, the Pisans had reacted energetically. In 1015, they had driven the Arabs out of Sardinia. In 1087, on the signal given by Pope Victor III, the predecessor of Urban II, their squadrons, united with those of the Genoese, had set sail to attack Tunisia. The Pisans and the Genoese had then taken the Tunisian capital, Mehdia, where they had freed a multitude of Christian captives. We shall see the decisive support which the Pisan, Genoese, and Venetian fleets were to lend the crusade when they revictualed the armies on the coast of Syria and helped to conquer the ports. Urban II, who must have understood the importance of this factor, had taken with him to the Council of Clermont Daimbert, archbishop of Pisa, who four years later was to lead a fleet to Italy and to become the first patriarch of a liberated Jerusalem.

Such was the immediate support which Urban II counted upon to conduct the crusade. His initial plan was that there should be only one army on the move, consisting mainly of the chivalry of southern France, under the leadership of Adhemar of Monteil and Raymond of Saint-Gilles. But already the excitement caused by the preaching of the crusade was becoming infectious, especially in the north of France, where Hugh the Great, count of Vermandois and brother of King Philip I of France, Robert Curthose, duke of Normandy and son of William the Conqueror, and Robert II, count of Flanders, all took the Cross. In the Low Countries, in imperial territory, Godfrey of Bouillon, duke of Lower Lorraine, that is to say of Brabant, also took the Cross, in company with his brother Baldwin of Boulogne, who still owed allegiance to France. The number of crusaders soon became so great that they had to be allowed to organize themselves in four distinct armies, by regional groups. On top of this, the enthusiasm of the mob got out of hand, and long before the regular troops were ready, launched a People's Crusade on the road to Constantinople, which will always be associated with the name of Peter the Hermit.

This last movement hardly fell in with the ideas of Urban II, whose whole activity bespeaks a maturely reflected plan, profound statesmanship and, as well as a powerful intellect, an innate sense of organization; but you cannot stir up Europe, you cannot revolutionize the face of the world, without causing some backwash. . . . What stands to Urban's credit is first, the idea of the crusade, and secondly, its success. Around 1090, Turkish Islam, having almost entirely driven the Byzantines out of Asia, was preparing to pass over into Europe. Ten years later, not only was Constantinople relieved from pressure, not only was half of Asia Minor restored to Hellenism, but seaboard Syria and Palestine had become Frankish colonies. The disaster of 1453, which had been on the brink of happening ever since 1090, was postponed for three and a half centuries. And all that was the deliberate and conscious work of Urban II. At the gesture of the great pope, damming the rising flood, the course of destiny was to be halted and suddenly reversed.

2

THE PEOPLE'S CRUSADE

Peter the Hermit

O F ALL the preachers who popularized the idea of the crusade among the masses, the best known is certainly Peter the Hermit.
We can see him still, as the chroniclers have described him, with his
shortness, his thinness, his dark complexion, clad in a homespun gown,
going on his donkey from town to town, from hamlet to hamlet, to
adjure the population to take the Cross. His rough and ardent eloquence aroused the crowds, and his outward appearance was already
distorted by legend. Was it not told that he had erstwhile gone on a
pilgrimage to the Holy Sepulcher, where in a dream Christ had bade
him go seek the pope for the deliverance of Jerusalem? Thus, the
image of the humble hermit who, in his zeal and enthusiasm, gave
himself up heart and soul to the realization of the papal project,
somewhat ousted the image of Urban himself. The danger was that
his action would also replace that of the pope. We have seen how
maturely reflected Urban's decisions had been, how all his conduct
disclosed a profound sense of politics. Yet now, at the voice of Peter
the Hermit, behold the masses of the people, men, women, and children, without any preliminary screening of noncombatants, without
waiting until Urban II had had the time to organize them and give
them some leadership, without waiting for the barons' army, were on
the march for Constantinople. From Berry, where Peter had started
his preaching, from the Orléanais, Champagne, and Lorraine, where he

had continued it, the movement reached the Rhine.   On April 12, 1096, some fifteen thousand pilgrims reached Cologne with him, poor folk who, every time a town appeared on the horizon naïvely asked if it were Jerusalem.   Such was their haste to see the Holy City that many of them set off as an advance guard, under the leadership of a simple knight surnamed Walter Sans-Avoir, as far as Constantinople where moreover, they awaited the arrival of their companions.

Peter the Hermit, with the bulk of the People's Crusade, in his turn traversed Germany, Hungary, and the Byzantine Empire, but in the course of this long march he could not impose even the minimum of discipline upon his people.   With more charity than caution, he had accepted in his troops many vagabonds, many men of no allegiance, even old criminals who sought, by taking the Cross, to obtain the remission of their faults.   These ill-converted sinners were not long in reverting to their evil instincts.   Looters they were, looters they remained.   Thus, they pillaged Semlin in Hungarian territory and Nish in Byzantine territory.   They soon provoked a severe reaction from the Byzantine authorities, who massacred several thousand of them and kept a close control over the rest as they went down from Nish to Constantinople.

Peter the Hermit reached Constantinople on August 1, 1096.   The Byzantine Emperor, Alexius Comnenus, who received him in audience, counseled him with great wisdom not to cross the Bosphorus to fight the Turks before the arrival of the Barons' Crusade.   He made Peter's companions camp under the walls of the great city and provided them with the victuals they needed.   But here again, the dubious elements admitted by the too trusting Hermit could not refrain from pillage.   In the face of their excesses, Alexius Comnenus, fearing for the safety of his capital, conveyed all the pilgrims over into Asia, where he quartered them, pending the arrival of the barons, in the fortress of Cibotos, or Civetot, on the southern shores of the Gulf of Nicomedia, near the Greek-Turkish frontier.   Once there, unfortunately, they were strongly tempted to start the Holy War without delay.   Peter the Hermit and Walter Sans-Avoir, who had learned a lot from their contact with reality, tried to stop this folly.   But the two of them were completely overwhelmed.   On October 21, 1096, the pilgrims, profiting from the absence of Peter on a visit to Constantinople, marched on Nicaea, the Turkish capital.   The march was conducted in the utmost disorder and had the sequel which might have been foreseen. A couple of miles from Hersek, the unhappy pilgrims were surprised and massacred in mass by the Turks. Walter Sans-Avoir was among the slain. Out of 25,000 men only 3,000 regained Byzantine territory.

In spite of the pitiful end of his expedition, Peter the Hermit, by his zeal and faith, has earned a place as one of the popular figures of the history of the Crusades. The same cannot be said of his German emulators, Volkmar, Gottschalk, and Emich of Leisingen. The latter was no more than a brigand-knight, and all three had a strange fashion of preparing for the holy war. Before starting off, Emich set about massacring the Jews of the Rhineland. The Rhenish bishops having taken these unfortunates under their protection, Emich's bands attacked the bishops' palaces in Mainz and Worms. These misdeeds met with the punishment they deserved. The so-called pilgrims having continued their pillage in the journey across Hungary, the king of Hungary had a great many of them executed and the rest then dispersed.

But let us leave the foam thus raised by the crusading wave and follow the fortunes of the crusade itself, the only one worthy of the name, that of Godfrey of Bouillon and his peers.

3

THE FIRST CRUSADE
Godfrey of Bouillon, Raymond of Saint-Gilles, and Bohemund

WHILE the People's Crusade, wrecked by incompetent or unworthy chiefs, ended in this lamentable failure, the Crusade of the Barons, organized in great regular armies, was on the march for Jerusalem.

The chief of the first group was Godfrey of Bouillon, duke of Lower Lorraine (Brabant). At the moment when the historic personalities of France and the future Belgium were beginning to take shape, Godfrey appears as the first embodiment of Franco-Belgian friendship. His mother was the heiress of the dukes of Brabant, while his father was count of Boulogne-sur-Mer, in the kingdom of France. Physically, he was the typical northern knight. Very tall, broad-chested with strong limbs, but a high narrow waist, and bright gold hair and beard. A doughty warrior, if ever there was one, it was he who, at the battle of Dorylaeum was to restore the desperate situation by arriving, hell bent for leather, to fall upon the Turks with fifty knights. A great hunter, like his cousins of the Ardennes, he was nearly killed in Cilicia wrestling single-handed with an enormous bear. His strength was stupendous. One day, in Syria, some Arab sheiks, to test it, challenged him to decapitate a full-grown camel with a single sword stroke, and in an instant the beast's head was rolling at their feet.

His loyalty is proverbial. Though long maltreated by his sovereign, Henry IV, emperor of Germany, he remained faithful to him in his struggle against the anti-emperor raised up by the papacy. This obedience must have cost Godfrey a pang, for his piety was exemplary. The clerics in his entourage used to complain that his interminable prayers left them to face a cold dinner. During the crusade he was to prove a pious pilgrim, full of good grace, gentleness, charity, and Christian humility. Tradition, as we shall see, has it that he refused to wear the royal crown in that city of Jerusalem where Christ wore only the Crown of Thorns. It is certain, as we shall also see, that it was out of respect for the rights of the Church over the Holy City that he modestly contented himself with the title of Advocate of the Holy Sepulcher. This uncrowned king of Jerusalem retained to the end a legendary simplicity of life. The Arab sheiks who came to salute him were astonished to find him seated in his tent, on the very ground, without carpet or silken coverings, resting on a wretched sack of straw. No doubt this great blond knight, who seems to have lived only for his duty, does not display in secular eyes the powerful personality of his brother Baldwin, or of Bohemund of Tarentum. The fact remains that his high moral qualities were to enable him, among so many barons of stronger character, to play the role of conciliator and arbitrator; and it was this very role which, in the hour of final victory, caused him to be chosen by his peers for the supreme dignity in the delivered Jerusalem.

The superior wisdom of Godfrey of Bouillon early made itself felt on the journey across Hungary. The Hungarians were still feeling the resentment caused by the pillages of the People's Crusade. Godfrey contacted their king, and the army marched through without incident. The next stage was Byzantium; and relations with the Byzantines were to be more delicate, and that not only because of the confessional rift between the Greek Church and the Roman Church. No doubt the Byzantine Emperor, Alexius Comnenus, one of the most adroit politicians of his time, caused Godfrey's army to be welcomed courteously at his frontier and revictualed on its march through his empire. Even when some detachments, evading the control of their chief, pillaged Selymbria on the Sea of Marmara, west of Constantinople, the emperor, without anger, invited Godfrey to camp under the walls of the capital, which he reached on December 23, 1096. But if Alexius

Comnenus received the crusaders so well, it was precisely because he regarded them as benevolent auxiliaries, come to help him recover from the Turks his lost provinces from Nicaea as far as Antioch. Had not the old Christian lands which they were thus going to liberate in Asia Minor, in Syria, and in Palestine, all once been part of the Byzantine Empire, either in the distant past like Jerusalem or more recently like Antioch and Edessa? The whole policy of Alexius Comnenus, with its alternating flattery and constraint of the crusaders, was solely designed to enroll the crusade in his service. In this spirit he immediately called for Godfrey's oath of homage.

For a long time Godfrey refused. As a prince of the Holy Roman Empire, marching in obedience to the pope, how could he enter the service of the Byzantine government, almost of the Greek schism? Alexius then cut off supplies to the crusaders and attacked their camp with superior forces. Godfrey, who had not come East to make war on Christians, decided to yield. Cost what it might, he sacrificed himself in the interests of the crusade. He went in ceremony to the palace of Blachernae, and there, in the great audience chamber, before the emperor, enthroned in majesty, he knelt and took the prescribed oath. In advance, he bound himself to restore to the Byzantines all the territories formerly belonging to them which he might conquer back from Islam. Alexius then bent towards him, embraced him and declared his adoption. This reconciliation was sealed by magnificent gifts from the "father" to the "son"—sumptuous ceremonial garments, precious fabrics, chests full of golden bezants, highbred horses.

At this juncture a second crusading army landed in Epirus, the army of the Normans of southern Italy, led by Bohemund of Tarentum. As we know, Alexius Comnenus was only too familiar with these crusaders, from having had to wage terrible war against them from 1081 to 1085. It was in fact this same Bohemund who, fifteen years earlier, with his father, Robert Guiscard, had invaded the Byzantine Empire, conquered part of Macedonia and directly threatened Constantinople. The excitement in that town was great when it was learned that, in the guise of a crusade, these hereditary enemies were making a reappearance. The route which they were following today, as crusaders, from their landing at the port of Avlona to Upper Macedonia, was precisely the same route which they had formerly taken as invaders.

The anxiety of the Byzantines can well be imagined, especially when one remembers Bohemund's personality. There can be no doubt (as the event was to prove clearly enough) that in the crusade the Norman prince, a devoted son of the Roman Church, but with boundless ambition and completely unscrupulous, saw nothing but an unhoped-for opportunity to realize the Oriental dreams of his ancestors. For Bohemund was well and truly of the race of those Vikings who came down at the end of the ninth century from the Norwegian fjords to settle in Normandy, and who, from there, once baptized and French-ified, ventured out to conquer the blessed shores of Naples and Sicily. And now with him the adventure, more marvelous still, was to rebound onto the shores of Asia. And to back these ambitions what a wealth of temperament, what an informed intelligence! An epic warrior, still burning with all the passion of the old sea kings, and, like them, of incredible courage, Bohemund was to prove himself, from the very first combats, a captain full of resource, and even the best strategist in the army. But into the bargain, this great Nordic was already steeped in Sicilian cunning. With his twofold Italian and Norman astuteness, he was to feel as much at ease in the face of the Byzantine diplomats as he was with his invincible sword in face of the Turks.

The Byzantines, when they saw him arrive at Constantinople, were afraid that he was plotting some mischief against the town. In this they were mistaken in their man. It was true that his long-range ambitions remained boundless, but he was too astute to put them in peril, and with them the chances opened up to him by the crusades, by starting off with ill-considered acts of violence. What did the Byzantines want? Diplomatic guarantees, assurances on parchment, oaths of fidelity? They would have their fill! And from the moment of his arrival at Constantinople, to the general surprise, whereas the loyal Godfrey of Bouillon had shown so much resistance to the oath of homage, he finessed without scruple and unhesitatingly agreed to all the formalities and promises desired, accepted all the commitments asked of him, and became in an instant more Byzantine than the Byzantines. What was an oath, provided that at that price, as a theoretical vassal of the *basileus,* he could carve himself some vast principality in Asia—say, Antioch? In this role the Byzantines, at first mistrustful and incredulous, saw him redouble himself in their service with the other crusaders and claim for Alexius Comnenus the homage

of the newcomers, especially of Raymond of Saint-Gilles, count of
Toulouse, who had just arrived, in April 1097, by way of northern
Italy, Serbia, and Macedonia, to join the headquarters of the crusaders
before Constantinople.

Raymond of Saint-Gilles was a highly complicated personality.
Already in the course of the crusade he had his fervent admirers and
his pitiless detractors. This passionate southerner with his restless,
inconsistent, high-strung character, alternating between enthusiasm and
discouragement, between romantic ambitions and sudden withdrawals,
between fits of caprice and ultimate tenacity, defies all ready-made
definitions. As a soldier, he will be judged very differently, for his
conduct varies greatly from battle to battle. After bearing himself
excellently during the First Crusade, he lost heart during the campaign
of Anatolia in 1101, and fled by night, abandoning his army, which
Godfrey of Bouillon or Bohemund would assuredly never have done.
In contrast, after this lapse he behaved admirably in Lebanon, besieging
Tripoli "singlehanded."

What cannot be doubted is the ardor of his faith and his devotion to
the crusade. Perhaps no one had made so great a sacrifice in taking the
Cross. Bohemund and Godfrey were each to conquer a kingdom. He
risked losing one by his absence, the fair kingdom of southern France,
then in the full process of construction, which he abandoned to the
covetousness of his rivals, the counts of Poitiers. This devotion of
Raymond to the Christian ideal was to survive all disillusionment, all
rancor. When Jerusalem had been delivered and another man had
been proclaimed chief in his place, when at least he could have returned peacefully to his Languedoc, his vows well and truly fulfilled,
he refused with stoicism and, although thus far thwarted of the fruits
of his labor, stayed on in Syria, wishing, as he said, to wear the Cross
until his death "after the example of Christ, Who refused to descend
from the Cross."

At the beginning of the crusade, it is true, his religious enthusiasm
was perhaps strengthened by vast temporal hopes. Was he not the first
baron to whom Urban II had disclosed his projects? Could he not
therefore count on a sort of pre-eminence among the other lords? But
Urban II, with his knowledge of men, while appreciating his zeal, no
doubt feared that the primacy of a lay chief would give umbrage to the

other barons. Raymond had therefore not obtained the chief command which was his ambition, since the pope assigned the responsibility for coordinating the views of the different army chiefs to an ecclesiastical dignitary, the sage Archbishop Adhemar of Monteil. Raymond had, moreover, enough spirit of faith to show no bitterness as a result. Quite the contrary, the Catholic faith continued to have no more zealous defender. When, on his arrival in Constantinople he, in turn, was invited to do homage and to abandon his prospective conquests to Alexius Comnenus, he refused outright. His Roman faith rebelled, his pride as a French baron revolted; the Holy Land, once delivered on the initiative of Urban II, should belong to the papacy, not to a schismatic sovereign. The only oath which could be obtained from Raymond was to respect the emperor's life and property.

Other groups of crusaders had arrived at Constantinople, especially Frenchmen, speaking the language of the North. Count Hugh of Vermandois, brother of King Philip I of France, had preceded them. This great lord, who appreciated the magnificence of the imperial hospitality, was a valuable intermediary with his companions in favor of Frankish-Byzantine agreement. But after bearing himself stoutly under the walls of Antioch, he was to weary of the campaign and to return to France before the capture of Jerusalem. Count Stephen of Blois was to tire of the war even faster, but he soon redeemed this lapse by returning to the Holy Land to find a hero's death. Robert Curthose, duke of Normandy, the son of William the Conqueror, and Robert II, count of Flanders, on the other hand were to accompany the expedition to the very end, displaying the greatest military qualities without remission.

Thus, the crusading army, made up of contingents from northern France and southern France, from Flemish Belgium and Walloon Belgium, from the Holy Roman Empire, and from the Norman Kingdom of the Two Sicilies, was an international army. As a common denomination, the crusaders adopted the name of Franks, giving this word the meaning it had at the time of the Carolingian unity, when Gaul, Germany, and Italy had formed a single empire under the aegis of the Roman Church.

As soon as they had crossed into Asia Minor, the crusaders, in conformity with the pact made with the Emperor Alexius Comnenus, began the Holy War in May 1097 by laying siege, in concert with the Byzantines, to the town of Nicaea. It was a self-evident objective; Nicaea, which had been captured from the Byzantine Empire by the Turks sixteen years earlier, had ever since remained the capital of the Seljuk sultanate of Anatolia, whose power extended from there as far as the Taurus and which had to be crossed from frontier to frontier to get to Syria. The cooperation of the "Frankish fury" and the Byzantine siege engines, together with the appearance of a Byzantine fleet on the waters of the Ascanian lake to take the city in the rear, drove the defenders of Nicaea to capitulate. At the very moment when the Frankish army was preparing to mount the final assault, the Turkish chiefs surrendered the stronghold to the Byzantines (June 26, 1097). At the sudden sight of the Byzantine standards floating above the walls, many crusaders, like Raymond of Saint-Gilles, voiced a bitter disappointment: they were being cheated of their victory! It must nevertheless be admitted that the handing over of Nicaea to the Byzantines was in accordance with the stipulations of the agreement of Constantinople.

After the fall of Nicaea the crusaders set out to cross Asia Minor diagonally from the northwest to the southeast, the shortest overland route from the straits to Syria (it is the route followed today by the Orient Express). It was a rough passage. The Anatolian plateau, on which they were entering, is a zone of arid steppes, culminating in the middle in a salt desert, where the question of supplies has always been difficult. To cope with it, the army divided into two echelons, the first traveling with Bohemund, his nephew Tancred, and Robert Curthose, the second with Godfrey of Bouillon and Raymond of Saint-Gilles. The Turks of Asia Minor, who had concentrated all their forces under the orders of their sultan, the Seljuk Kilij Arslan, sought to profit from this division. On the morning of July 1, opposite Dorylaeum, the modern Eskisehir, they fell in mass on Bohemund's army corps. So sudden was the onslaught that Bohemund, surprised in full march, barely had time to regroup his troops in haste to meet the charges of the Turkish cavalry which surrounded them on all sides. Following the tactics of their nomad ancestors, the Turkish squadrons advanced to within bowshot, emptied their quivers, and then wheeled about to give place to fresh bands of mounted archers. The Franks, decimated by this hail of arrows, charged in vain in an attempt to pin down the adversary, who avoided contact and withdrew each time. It was only when the Norman army began to be visibly exhausted by this murderous game that the Turks unsheathed and charged in their turn. The Normans, driven back on their baggage convoy, protected themselves as best they could and resisted with stubborn determination. . . . Was the crusade, at the first encounter, to end in disaster?

But Bohemund, before he was encircled, had had the time to warn the other Frankish division of his peril. At the call, the chiefs hastened to his aid. Godfrey of Bouillon was the first to arrive, with only fifty knights, the rest of the Brabanters following him at the gallop. Almost at the same time there appeared on the battlefield Hugh of Vermandois, followed by the legate Adhemar of Monteil and Raymond of Saint-Gilles. At two in the afternoon they were all in the battle. The arrival of these Frankish masses in itself changed the issue of the day, from the tactical point of view; but in addition, Adhemar de Monteil, defiling under the protection of a line of heights, debouched from the left on the Turkish flank. The movement was duplicated on the right wing by Godfrey of Bouillon, the count of Flanders, and Hugh of Vermandois who, on this side also, began to overrun the Turkish army. Threatened with encirclement, crushed under the furious charge of the heavy Christian cavalry, the Turks took flight, without even having time to safeguard the wealth of their baggage train. "They fled through the defiles, by mountain and by plain, and we took their tents with great booty in gold and silver, beasts and camels."

The battle of Dorylaeum settled the question of power in the Near East for more than a century. Since the day of Manzikert, and the capture of a Byzantine Emperor by a Turkish Sultan in 1071, the Turkish power had dominated the East. The day of July 1, 1097, announced to the world that a new power had now arisen, the Frankish power, which would henceforth prevail. In this respect, the day of Dorylaeum, redeeming the day of Manzikert, assumes equal importance in the history of Asia with the days of the Granicus or Arbela. Two centuries of European hegemony in the Levant were to be the result, two centuries during which the Turkish advance recoiled not only before the Frankish conquests in Syria and Palestine, but also before the Byzantine reconquests in Asia Minor.

It is interesting to note that the Franks and the Turks, the military race of the West and the military race of Asia, learned in this very first encounter to esteem each other. The chronicler of the *Gesta Franco-rum* speaks to us out of his own experience: "We are bound to recognize the military qualities and the valiance of the Turks. They thought to frighten us with their hail of arrows, as they had frightened the Arabs, the Armenians, the Syrians, and the Greeks. But, with the grace of God, they shall not prevail over us! In verity, they recognize, on their side, that none save the Franks and themselves has the right to call himself knight."

After conquering the men, the task remained of triumphing over the opposition of the land, that Anatolian steppe, intersected by bleak mountains, with scarcely any water except in the form of swamps. It was mid-July, with an average temperature of some 80 degrees. The Turks had left a desert before the Frankish army. Their main capital, after the fall of Nicaea, was the town of Iconium, the modern Konya. The Franks hoped to refit themselves there; they found it evacuated, without supplies of any kind. At least, after passing Heraclea, they were entering a less desert zone as they neared the mighty wooded chains of the Taurus and Anti-Taurus Mountains. It is true that the passage through the gorges, in the midst of these "devilish mountains," faced the army with difficulties of a different kind. At this point in their march (it was now mid-September) and in order to advance more easily, they separated. Tancred, Bohemund's nephew, and Baldwin of Boulogne, brother to Godfrey of Bouillon, descended with one detachment into the plain of Cilicia, while the bulk of the crusade skirted the Anti-Taurus in the northeast, through the mountainous region of Caesarea, in the ancient Cappadocia. In both directions, moreover, the Franks discovered unexpected allies—the Armenians.

At the moment of the conquest of Greater Armenia by the Turks in the last quarter of the eleventh century, part of the Armenian population, fleeing the Moslem domination, had flowed back toward Cappadocia, Cilicia, and as far as the region of Edessa in the Jezireh, in the northeast of Syria. If, in the Cilician plain and in Cappadocia, this Armenian immigration had not saved the country from undergoing, in its turn, the Turkish domination, energetic Armenian chieftains had solidly established themselves in the eyries of the Taurus as well as at Melitene, the modern Malatya, and as far as Edessa, the modern Urfa, where, by a prodigy of skill as much as of valiance, they had preserved, together with their Christian faith, their political independence. The arrival of the crusaders was to furnish these heroic Christian communities with unlooked-for succor.   Conversely, the crusade was to find among the Armenians an inestimable aid, not only because they were natural allies against the Turks—allies familiar with the country, capable of providing the Franks with first-class intelligence—but also because, of all Oriental Christendom, the Armenian mountaineers represented the stoutest military element.

Tancred and Baldwin, on arriving in Cilicia, were the first to benefit from this support.   The Armenian population of Tarsus collaborated with them against the Turkish garrison, which evacuated the fortress in panic.   Similarly, it was the Armenians who welcomed Tancred at Adana and in September 1097 opened to him the gates of Mamistra, the modern Missis.   Unfortunately, Baldwin and he quarreled over the possession of Cilicia, and their discord prevented the effective occupation of the province.   Meanwhile, the rest of the crusade was skirting the massif of the Anti-Taurus on the northeast as far as Caesarea, whence they dropped down to Marash, everywhere received with touching enthusiasm by the Armenian element.   On October 16 they left Marash to penetrate into Syria.   On the twenty-first, Bohemund, pushing forward as the advance guard, arrived before Antioch.

Antioch, on the arrival of the crusaders, belonged to the Turkish Emir Yaghi-Siyan, vassal to the Seljuk King of Aleppo, Ridwan.   If Ridwan had resolutely come to the aid of his vassal, if he had been immediately seconded by the other Seljuk princes, his kinsmen, who reigned at Damascus and in Persia, the task of the invaders would no doubt have been difficult indeed.   Medieval Antioch, with its four hundred towers or bastions, and its immense fortifications, protected on the west by the course of the Orontes, on the east by the massif of Mount Silpios, and on the north by a chain of marshes, was one of the strongest fortresses in the East.   So big was the circumference of the fortifications that the crusaders abandoned the idea of an effective blockade.   They satisfied themselves at the outset with keeping watch on the northwest sector, opposite which they pitched their camp.   The garrison could therefore communicate freely with Moslem Syria on the side of the mountains and supply the town by that route, while the Christian camp was beginning to suffer from shortages.

Most fortunately for the besiegers, the Turks were paralyzed by their own quarrels. The emir of Antioch, Yaghi-Siyan, was on bad terms with his neighbor and suzerain, Ridwan, king of Aleppo, who in turn had quarreled with his brother, Duqaq, king of Damascus. The result was that the natural defenders of the city could not agree to save it. The Damascenes were the first to move, but they fell in with a strong Christian patrol which was scouring the countryside under the orders of Bohemund and the count of Flanders and were driven back. A month later, the Aleppans tried in turn to relieve Antioch. Bohemund went to meet them between the course of the Orontes and the lake of Antioch, a very skillfully chosen position to prevent the Turkish mounted archers from deploying and using their usual whirlwind tactics. Obliged to accept hand-to-hand battle in a confined space, the Turks were crushed beneath the weight of the heavy Frankish chivalry.

In spite of this success, the shortages in the Christian camp grew worse, demoralizing the troops. The ranks were thinned by desertion and disease. It was then that Bohemund asserted himself as the strong man, the only one capable of bringing the army back under his control. Having fixed his aim on Antioch, he was more anxious than anyone for the capture of the city. But before making his full effort, he was determined to wring from the other barons a formal promise as to their future conquest. In the worst days of the siege, when everyone had formed the habit of regarding him as the soul of the army, the astute Norman chief suddenly announced his intention of returning to Europe. He saw, he said, his people and his horses dying, and he was not rich enough to stand the cost of a long campaign. This veiled threat produced the desired result. If the barons allowed a man like Bohemund to leave when the army found itself in such a critical state, they were dooming the crusade to disaster. In order to keep him, most of them, in spite of the opposition of Raymond of Saint-Gilles, gave him to understand that as soon as Antioch was taken, they would leave him in possession of it. These were the words he was waiting for. He stayed, and from then on set about laying his hands on Antioch with a personal ardor which was to overcome all obstacles.

There was still one shadow on the picture for him: the paramount rights of the Byzantine Empire. Under the terms of the pact of Constantinople, the Franks had undertaken to remit Antioch to the emperor as soon as they had driven out the Turks. The presence of an imperial division with the besieging army was a perpetual reminder of this promise. Once again Bohemund resorted to ruse. Professing to be the best friend of the Byzantine officers, he came to warn them, in the utmost secrecy, of an alleged plot being contrived against them among the Franks. The Byzantine commander took fright, and thanking Bohemund for his zeal, departed precipitately with his troops. As soon as he had disappeared, Bohemund stirred up the Frankish army against this "defection": the Byzantines having "dishonored themselves," having "betrayed Christendom," the crusaders found themselves released from their vows to the empire. The imperial mortgage over Antioch was thus discharged, to the greater profit of the joyous Norman chief.

We see in him, moreover, a man of exceptional vitality. Some of his stratagems of war look like enormous, if somewhat rough, pleasantries. The Frankish army was infested with Turkish spies disguised as Armenians. No one knew how to get rid of them. Bohemund took on the task. Once evening, at dinner time, he bade his cooks prepare a batch of Turkish prisoners for the table. "Their throats were cut," says the chronicler," they were spitted, and the cooks set about roasting them." On being questioned about these strange preparations, Bohemund, with the most natural air in the world, said that the headquarters mess was being regaled with spies on the spit. The whole camp came running up to see if it was true. Nothing could be more true: the Turks, duly basted, were cooking over a hot fire. The next morning, all the spies had disappeared in horror, without waiting for their quittance.

Apart from these displays of somewhat ferocious humor, the crusaders followed a very wise and flexible policy toward the Moslems. The situation lent itself to this. Islam at that time was divided between two religious obediences, between two enemy "papacies," the Abbassid caliphate of Baghdad and the Fatimite caliphate of Cairo. The first was recognized by the Turks, masters, as we have seen, of Hither Asia, the second in the Arab kingdom of Egypt. This religious "Great Schism" was therefore aggravated by a veiled clash of races, Arabs against Turks, Moslem Africa against Moslem Asia. One of the main points at issue between the two adversaries was Palestine. The Egyptian government could not forgive the Turks for having deprived it of that province. When it saw them at grips with the Frankish invasion on the Antioch front, it thought that the moment was propitious to take them in the rear on the side of the Isthmus of Suez and regain the coveted zone. This was obviously treason to Islam, but the office of grand vizier at Cairo was then held by a converted Armenian, whose Moslem zeal was naturally somewhat lukewarm. This renegade had no better understanding of the religious enthusiasm which impelled the Franks toward Jerusalem. He sent an embassy to the Franks before Antioch to propose a tacit alliance, with the partition of the Turkish possessions of Syria and Palestine: Antioch and Syria to the Franks; Jerusalem and Palestine to the Egyptians.

The crusaders refrained from rejecting the proposal. Although Jerusalem naturally remained their main objective, they gave a great welcome to the ambassadors and encouraged them in their schemes. The main thing was to encourage divisions in the heart of Islam, and so long as Antioch was not taken, to demoralize the Turks by an opportune Egyptian diversion from the side of Judaea. Gallantly, the crusading chiefs presented the Egyptian embassy with the heads of three hundred Turks massacred near the Lake of Antioch: slight gifts to cement the alliance. The Egyptians no longer hesitated. They attacked the Turks on the side of Palestine and in August of the same year (August 26, 1098) captured Jerusalem from them.

To have done with Antioch, however, the crusaders had to convert this desultory siege into an effective blockade. A Genoese squadron, at last bringing siege engines, had just anchored in the mouth of the Orontes. Bohemund and Raymond of Saint-Gilles went to establish contact with it, but the garrison of Antioch profited by their absence to make a murderous surprise sortie against the camp. Panic spread among the defenders of the camp: it was rumored that the companions of Bohemund and Saint-Gilles were slain. Godfrey of Bouillon was admirable: "Sweet lords, if these rumors be true, if these infidel dogs have slain our companions, nothing remains for us but to die with them, like good Christians and men of honor. Or if Christ wills it that we shall continue to serve him, let us avenge the passing of these brave men!" Fitting the example to the word, he hurled himself against the Turks and drove them back into the river. It was in the course of this melee that the same Godfrey, as the chronicler tells us, "did a feat of prowess which will be spoken of forever": with a single stroke of his sword he clove a Turk in twain so that "the trunk fell to earth, while the haunches and the legs clung to the horse as it went off at a gallop."

The arrival of the siege engines allowed a certain number of bastions to be constructed around Antioch, thanks to which the blockade became effective. It was then that Bohemund received personally and in great secrecy the propositions of a resident of Antioch, an Armenian renegade called Firuz who, having been maltreated by the Turks, offered to usher the Franks in. Bohemund, full of joy, nevertheless did not forget his personal ambitions. He called the other barons together and announced to them coldly that he had the means of delivering Antioch into their hands on condition that all of them, once and for all, solemnly and in advance abandoned to him all their rights in the city: "If you reject this condition, find another way of taking Antioch; I will very gladly yield my share to the man who succeeds!"

This speech, full of sarcastic irony, was all the more biting as the news spread of the approach of an immense Turkish army. If it arrived before the fall of the city, the crusaders were lost. Bohemund's offer was their last hope of salvation. Even the most recalcitrant accepted.

Bohemund, in agreement with the mysterious Firuz, then settled all the details of the surprise attack. On the evening of June 2, the besieged were distracted by a feint on the river flank, after which the army regrouped during the night in front of the tower of Mount Silpios, where Firuz was waiting for Bohemund. A little before four in the morning the scaling of the tower began. All the neighboring towers were similarly occupied gropingly in the first light of false dawn. As day broke, the Franks, clambering down the slopes of Mount Silpios, rushed in mass through the city, welcomed as liberators by the Armenian, Greek, and Syrian elements of the population, who joined them in massacring the Turks. As for the emir, Yaghi-Siyan, as soon as he saw Bohemund's purple standard floating over the walls, he lost courage and fled cross-country, where he was thrown by his horse and broke his leg. An Armenian finished him off.

Antioch was taken, but only in the nick of time. The following day, the great Turkish army, dispatched by the Seljuks of Persia and commanded by Kerbogha, the emir of Mosul, appeared on the Orontes.

The situation of the Franks was desperate. Besiegers turned besieged, they were now blockaded in Antioch by the Turks, who allowed no supplies to pass. The famine in the city became atrocious.

"Whoever found a dead dog or a cat ate it ravenously." The worst was that, weakened by lack of food, the Franks neglected to guard the walls. Only Bohemund, with bitter fury, remained unshakable. At night, by torchlight, he scoured the streets to surprise deserters and traitors. The soldiers, collapsing from hunger and fatigue, remained prostrate indoors instead of manning the ramparts. One night, when the alarm had sounded, the terrible Norman chief did not hesitate to set fire to the town to force them to their guard posts. Before the threatening flames the unfortunate troops were driven to crowd into the streets, where they found Bohemund, sword drawn, who forced them on to the battlements. Several quarters of the town were razed to the ground, but the Turkish assault was halted in its tracks.

Nevertheless, to raise the morale of the army, a miracle was needed. The miracle happened. It was the discovery of the Holy Lance. As a result of a vision, a Provençal pilgrim, Peter Bartholomew, unearthed it on June 14 from under the paving stones of one of the churches of Antioch. The Franks who the day before had hardly been capable of defending themselves behind the walls, suddenly felt themselves animated by such ardor that they took the offensive. On June 28, at dawn, Bohemund brought his army out through the gate of the bridge and began to deploy it in the plain. If Kerbogha had attacked while this maneuver was still going on, things might have turned out badly. But the Turkish captain, in his folly, preferred to deal with the whole Frankish army, in order to destroy it at one blow.

Bohemund, rejoicing at this error, had the time to deploy his squadrons methodically, the first corps consisting of the French and Flemings with Hugh of Vermandois and Count Robert, the second of the Lorrainers with Godfrey of Bouillon, the third of the knights of Normandy with Robert Curthose, the fourth of the southern French with Adhemar of Monteil, and the fifth of the Normans of Italy with Tancred and Bohemund himself. Increasingly ill inspired, Kerbogha, instead of resorting to the usual Turkish tactics of harassing by a whirlwind of mounted archers, waited for the massive charge of the ironclad knights which crushed all before it. For an instant, he thought of restoring the situation by outflanking the French army. Bohemund, divining his scheme, immediately formed a sixth corps from the Norman and Lorraine troops, which galloped to take the Turkish army in the rear. The Turkish disaster became general.

Kerbogha fled hell bent for leather, first to Aleppo and then as far as Mosul. In order not to give the bulk of the Turkish army time to get away too, Bohemund, without allowing the crusaders to pillage the enemy camp, gave chase to the fugitives in a relentless hunt to the death. It was only on returning from this furious ride that he released his men to pillage the Turkish tents. The booty was enormous.

The defeat of the Turks, which confirmed the final conquest of Antioch by the Franks, was, as we have seen, on June 28, 1098. But it was not until January 13, 1099, that the crusaders resumed their march toward Jerusalem. This long delay has been criticized. In reality, the army, exhausted by so many trials, had to be reconstituted. And then the disputes for the possession of Antioch started again. While the other crusading chiefs, according to their promise, had handed over to Bohemund without difficulty the various quarters of the city occupied by their troops, while the loyal Godfrey found it quite natural that the Norman chief, after rendering so many services, should become prince of Antioch, Raymond of Saint-Gilles refused to give up the quarter where his Toulousains were installed. On several occasions, Toulousains and Normans nearly came to blows.

These dissensions paralyzed the crusade. The army had long been rested, time passed and the barons were still quarreling. After Antioch, it was now a question of Maarat-al-Numan, another Syrian stronghold which had just been taken and the possession of which was disputed between Bohemund and Saint-Gilles. Faced with such a display of feudal cupidity, the mass of pilgrims ended by rebelling. On January 5, 1099, a veritable riot broke out in Maarat-al-Numan. The chronicler has transmitted to us in striking phrases the indignation of these "poor folk," these "simples," who alone retained the ideal of the early days: "Forsooth! quarrels over Antioch, quarrels over Marra, in every place God delivers to us, disputes between our princes! For Marra, let us do away with the bone of contention by razing the town!" And forthwith, in spite of the officers of the count of Toulouse, the pilgrims fell upon the town and demolished it.

This righteous indignation achieved its object. On January 13, Raymond of Saint-Gilles, deeply moved by this reminder of the oath of Clermont, and in order to show clearly that he was resuming the interrupted pilgrimage, left Maarat-al-Numan by the southern road—

the road to Jerusalem. With his southern changeability, he now shifted from the worst feudal chicanery to the most ardent religious zeal. Moreover, the role of a leader of the masses, communicating with them in the same ideal, suited his temperament. Finally, his ambition, disappointed before Antioch, found its outlet here and his imagination was already taking fire. Bohemund, in his Norman greed, in order not to risk losing Antioch, refused to follow the crusade. Godfrey of Bouillon himself, out of patience with all these quarrels, for which he was not made, had withdrawn to Edessa with his brother Baldwin and Robert of Flanders. This default of his companions played into the hands of the count of Toulouse. He already saw himself entering Jerusalem, alone of all the crusading chiefs and earning immortal glory.

The march of the crusaders from Maarat-al-Numan to Jerusalem was relatively easy. The country was divided among small Arab emirs who could not withstand the Frankish army and sought to win its favor by contributing to its supplies. This was the case, in particular, at Shaizar and Tripoli, which did not, however, prevent the outburst of hostilities around some of the minor strongholds of the emirate of Tripoli. These deeds of war brought an unexpected advantage. Godfrey of Bouillon and the count of Flanders, learning that fighting was going on, rejoined immediately. They arrived at the right moment, for Saint-Gilles, on the beautiful Lebanese riviera, where Tortosa had just been occupied, again felt himself a prey to territorial ambitions. It was with the utmost difficulty that Godfrey of Bouillon tore him away from the conquest of Lebanon, to resume with him the march to Jerusalem along the coast road of Phoenicia.

Before Beirut, before Tyre, before Saint-Jean-d'Acre, the local emirs, terrified by the approach of the crusaders, provided them with the necessary supplies without difficulty. Between Arsuf and Jaffa the crusaders left the coast to follow the track which climbs to Jerusalem across the arid plateau of Judaea. Gaston of Béarn and Robert of Flanders, sent ahead as scouts, were the first to enter Ramleh, evacuated by the Moslems. On reaching Emmaus, Godfrey of Bouillon sent his cousin Baldwin of Le Bourg and Tancred with a hundred horsemen to make a thrust toward Bethlehem.

After galloping all night, the little troop reached Bethlehem at dawn. When the native Christians recognized the Franks, there was an explosion of joy. All of them, Greek rite and Syrian rite alike, marched out in procession with their crosses and their gospels, intoning triumphal psalms to welcome these liberators from the farthest West. The unhoped-for day of the triumph of the Cross over the Crescent had at last dawned! All these poor people, after more than four centuries of oppression, tearfully kissed the hands of these rough knights. Led by a joyful crowd, Tancred and his companions went to the Church of the Nativity. "They saw the crib where the sweet child rested by Whom were created Heaven and Earth. The people in their gratitude took Tancred's banner and planted it on the summit of the Basilica of the Virgin."

On leaving Bethlehem, Tancred encountered Gaston of Béarn, who, with thirty horsemen, had come to reconnoiter the approaches to Jerusalem. On Tuesday, June 7, the whole Frankish army saw the domes of the Holy City. "When they heard that name, Jerusalem, they could not contain their tears, and falling upon their knees, they returned thanks to God for allowing them to reach the goal of their pilgrimage, the Holy City where Our Lord had deigned to save the world. What a moving thing it was to hear the sobs that arose from all that people! They continued to advance until the walls and towers of the city became quite distinct. They raised their hands in gratitude to the skies and humbly kissed the earth."

Jerusalem, as we have seen, had been captured from the Turks some months earlier by the Arabs of Egypt. When they learned of the approach of the crusaders, they had hastily put the city into a state of defense, with a strong garrison, consisting partly of Sudanese. The crusader chiefs divided up the sectors of attack, Robert of Normandy in the northern sector, before Saint Stephen's Gate (the modern Damascus Gate), Robert of Flanders in front of what is now Notre Dame de France, Godfrey of Bouillon and Tancred in the western sector, before the Jaffa Gate and the citadel, and finally Raymond of Saint-Gilles in the south, on Mount Zion. The siege was exceptionally painful. It was mid-June. The heat was torrid. Water was short, so were supplies, and how could such a strong fortress be attacked without siege engines? Finally a Genoese squadron arrived at Jaffa with supplies and equipment. William of Sabran, with a few horsemen, made contact with it, and they were able to set about building giant ladders and mobile wooden scaling towers from which they could dominate the ramparts. Gaston of Béarn distinguished himself as an engineer on this occasion. On the night of July 9–10, Godfrey, Robert of Flanders, and Robert of Normandy transported their engines opposite the north-east sector, from Saint Stephen's Gate to the brook Kedron. On the fourteenth the assault began, at first without any result. The Egyptian garrison had the terrible Greek fire which they poured down on the wheeled towers of the attackers.

The attack began again on the morning of the fifteenth, a Friday. Godfrey had covered his wooden tower with newly flayed animal hides, to protect the beams against fire, and was able to bring it up under the walls themselves. He took his stand on the upper platform with his younger brother, Eustace of Boulogne. About noon he succeeded in grappling a footbridge to the wall. He dashed across with Eustace and two knights of Tournai. At the same moment, the scaling ladders, in place on all sides, yielded passage to groups of Frankish soldiers, to such effect that the wall, on that side, was entirely won, while the defenders fled to the Mosque of al-Aqsa, the "Temple of Solomon," where they entrenched themselves. The mosque was conquered, at the cost of an even more bitter struggle; "they waded in blood up to their ankles." Tancred and Gaston of Béarn hastened to seize the neighboring Moslem sanctuary, the Qubbat es-Sakhra, or Mosque of Omar. There they found fresh throngs of Moslem refu-gees, who this time pleaded for mercy, *aman*. A chivalrous victor, Tancred took these unfortunates under his protection, leaving them his own banner as safeguard. Unfortunately, during the night or the next morning, fresh waves of the Frankish assault massacred these captives. Great was the fury of the Norman chief when he learned of the outrage done to his banner, and the breach of his pledged word, no less than the loss he suffered by the slaughter of these prisoners for whom he rightly expected a noble ransom.

In the southern, and certainly the most difficult, sector, the count of Toulouse had met with greater resistance. It was not until the after-noon of the fifteenth, when the defenders of the temple, fleeing before Godfrey, flowed back on that side under the protection of the citadel, that Raymond of Saint-Gilles in his turn was able to penetrate the stronghold. The Egyptians, caught between the Frankish masses, who from the northeast flowed down from the temple, and those who with

Saint-Gilles came up from the south, circled around hopelessly. Saint-Gilles hastened to the citadel, the "Tower of David" as it was called, which the governor handed over to him on the promise of a safe-conduct for himself and his garrison. Saint-Gilles kept his promise nobly and provided the emir with an escort as far as Ascalon.

Unhappily, this example was far from being followed everywhere. The blood shed in the streets is understandable, and even the terrible scenes in the temple, which the Moslems had transformed into their last redoubt. But even if the number of Moslem victims has been greatly exaggerated, the furies inherent in any capture by storm went on far too long. "The city showed the spectacle of such carnage of the enemies, such a shedding of blood, that the victors themselves were struck with horror and disgust." The speaker here is none other than the great archbishop, William of Tyre, incapable of dissimulating his reprobation as a Christian or his blame as a statesman. For, from this last point of view, the excesses of July 15 constituted a grave error. The coastal towns, from Beirut to Arsuf, had been, up to the very eve, on the point of negotiating their submission. Terrified now by the fate of the Moslems of Jerusalem, they stiffened into a desperate resistance.

And yet, under the terrible conquerors of July 15, the Christians finally came to themselves. On the very evening of the same day they went up to the Holy Sepulcher. "They bathed their hands and their feet, they changed their bloodstained garments for new robes and, barefoot, visited the Holy Places." The fury of the combat had died down. Among these rough men, after so many trials and perils, nothing remained but an immense religious emotion. They pressed, in tears, along the Via Dolorosa "and gently kissed the place where the Saviour of the world had set His feet." The native Christians, who had gone in procession to meet them, led them into the Holy Sepulcher to the sound of hymns of grace. There they all flung themselves prostrate, their arms outstretched in the form of the Cross. "Each man thought he could still see before him the crucified body of Jesus Christ. And it seemed to them that they were at the gates of Heaven."

They came down to earth again to organize the conquest. Who was to be the chief of the new Frankish state? Among the great barons who had helped to take Jerusalem, the count of Flanders and the duke of Normandy wanted to return to Europe. The only competitors remained Raymond of Saint-Gilles and Godfrey of Bouillon.

There is no doubt that Raymond was what we would nowadays call the most brilliant candidate. He had his own personal policy, based (he had completely changed in this respect) on the Byzantine alliance. The final result was largely his doing, since it was he who, six months earlier, before Maarat al-Numan had set the crusade on the march again. It appears that this king of southern France, if he had won the crown of Jerusalem, would immediately have constituted a solid Syrian monarchy, though vassal to the Byzantines. No doubt this is precisely what frightened the other barons. Perhaps they offered him the throne, but with such restrictions that, high-strung as he was, he refused it. We know, moreover, that Robert of Flanders and Robert of Normandy favored Godfrey of Bouillon against him.

Godfrey was much less ambitious for power than Raymond, and it was very much against the grain that he was elected. But everything about him was made to attract the suffrages. His bravery, in the assault on Jerusalem, had been prodigious; at a moment when most of the crusaders were thinking of the return to Europe, who better than this great soldier could preserve the conquest with diminished forces? Moreover, he was as conciliatory, patient, and easygoing as Raymond was headstrong, impulsive, and vindictive. Before deciding, William of Tyre tells us, the barons made discreet inquiries among Godfrey's entourage about his character and tastes. Thus interrogated, the clerics of his chapel complained solely of his excessive devotion, of his interminable church sessions, after which they found their meals either cold or overcooked. In the mouths of the duke's chaplains, this was evidently a very serious reproach. The barons, on the contrary, were edified by it, and the archbishop of Tyre assures us with a smile that it was one of the reasons which decided the election of Godfrey. It was no doubt thought that this crowned monk would be a good-natured monarch.

In fact, on his election, he did not even take the royal title. With magnificent humility, he refused, according to tradition, to wear a crown of gold where Christ had worn a crown of thorns. He contented himself with the dignity, singularly more modest, of "Advocatus Sancti Sepulcri," Advocate (or Defender) of the Holy Sepulcher.

For this great Christian, the only king of Jerusalem was Christ, or the Vicar of Christ, the Roman pontiff. He himself was no more than the regent of Jerusalem on behalf of the Church.

But on the battlefield, this respectful son of the Church became a raging lion, and those who chose him as the fittest to defend Jerusalem against the counterattacks of Islam knew what they were doing. Barely three weeks had elapsed after the capture of the city when a powerful Egyptian army, led by the vizier in person, broke into Palestine. The situation was very serious for the Franks; their troops were dispersed; Tancred was campaigning toward Nablus; Raymond of Saint-Gilles, furious at his eviction, had gone to sulk in the direction of the Jordan. What would have happened if the Egyptians had thrust straight for the Holy City? But they delayed before Ascalon, while Godfrey acted with speed, rallying around him all his comrades in arms. Raymond of Saint-Gilles was reluctant at first but then, in the face of imminent danger, rallied the Christian army; the common peril knit the Frankish forces together again, and whether they willed it or not, created the monarchy. But the Franks had only 1200 horsemen and about 9,000 foot soldiers in all, while the Egyptian army was five times the size.

Godfrey of Bouillon nevertheless advanced on the enemy. On August 12, at dawn, he found himself in sight of the Egyptian camp, between Ascalon and the sea. He at once moved into battle order. He commanded the left wing, toward Ascalon, in person. Tancred, Robert of Normandy, and the count of Flanders spanned the center; and Saint-Gilles held the right wing, next to the sea. Before the suddenness of the attack the Egyptians were completely taken by surprise. "They set about girding their arms and mounting their steeds, but the Franks allowed them no time." Robert of Normandy, seeing the vizier's standard, threw himself upon the standard-bearer and cut him down. Tancred forced the Egyptian camp. In a few minutes the rout of the Arab army was complete. Part of the fugitives took shelter in a sycamore wood which was set afire. The rest were driven into the sea.

After a victory like this the Franks could have seized the coast towns. Once again they were paralyzed by their own discords. The defenders of Ascalon were ready to yield; rather than see the conquest go to the profit of Godfrey, Raymond of Saint-Gilles passed them the word to hold on. This stronghold of paramount importance, the key to Palestine on the Egyptian side, which the Franks could have annexed without effort as early as 1099, was not to be conquered by them until 1153, after doing them untold harm. Godfrey, for all his patience, was so exasperated that he was within an ace of attacking the Toulousain camp. The count of Flanders succeeded in pacifying him, but it was high time for the barons to separate. The count of Toulouse, full of rancor after so many unavowed disappointments, went back north up the Lebanon coast, as far as Laodicea (the modern Latakia), where we shall hear of him again. Robert of Normandy and the count of Flanders took their leave, not without emotion, of Godfrey, whom they were never to see again. He remained alone, with a handful of men, in an only partly subdued Judaea, in the midst of a world of enemies. He prayed the two princes not to forget him on their return to France and to send him speedy reinforcements.

Of the whole host of barons who had set out from Europe to deliver the Holy Places, Godfrey of Bouillon was left to defend his conquests with only the Norman-Italian prince, Tancred. Although he was a match for his uncle, Bohemund, as a fiery soldier and a hardy captain, Tancred's passion for conquest was tempered with greater relative morality and loyalty than Bohemund's. Much younger than Godfrey, he consented to serve under his orders and served faithfully. It was Tancred who subdued Galilee, starting with the stronghold of Tiberias, which Godfrey granted to him in fee. "He held the land so wisely and so well" the chronicler tells us, "that he won the praise of God and the century." Borrowing their own tactics from the Arabs, he conducted veritable *razzias* into the enemy country and on each venture brought back considerable booty to Tiberias and Jerusalem. He even carried his arms east of the Sea of Tiberias into the province of Sawâd, dependent on the Turkish kingdom of Damascus, and subjected it to tribute. Between two campaigns he ornamented with magnificence the sanctuaries of Nazareth. A little later he was to seize from the Egyptians the port of Haifa.

Godfrey's personality seems to have impressed the Arabs as much as Tancred's. First, by his simplicity, which reminded them of the first companions of the Prophet. During the siege of Arsuf (we have already alluded to this episode) a number of sheiks came to bring him in tribute the products of their lands, bread, olives, figs, raisins. They found Godfrey in his tent, sitting on the ground. "When they saw him thus, they marveled, 'How could this redoubtable prince who had come from so far to sow havoc among them, who had annihilated so many armies and conquered so many lands, be satisfied with such a modest array, without carpets or silken couch, without royal raiment or guards?' " When this was interpreted to him, the Advocate of the Holy Sepulcher replied by the verse from the Scriptures. "Man must remember that dust he is, to dust he shall return." They departed, says the chronicle, filled with admiration. The first contacts between Catholic asceticism and Moslem asceticism—as Père de Foucauld was to prove one day much later—showed that they were much nearer than they had thought.

The spirit of chivalry, so keen among the Arab sheiks, also began to bring them closer to the Franks. Men spoke under the great tents of Godfrey's prodigious strength. A desert lord was curious to find out for himself. He asked and obtained a safe-conduct and was led into the presence of the duke. "He saluted him and bowed, according to the Arab custom, and asked him whether he was really able to sever a camel's neck by a single sword stroke as men said" (see above). And he presented an enormous full-grown beast which he had brought for the purpose. "The duke drew his sword, struck the camel at the thickest of the neck, and severed it in twain as easily as if it had been the neck of a goose." The Bedouin, dumbfounded, presented the Frankish chief, before his departure, with his richest trinkets.

While Godfrey of Bouillon in Palestine was laying the foundations for the future kingdom of Jerusalem, Bohemund in Syria was firmly establishing the principality of Antioch. The great city on the Orontes was finally in his hands, tenaciously coveted, won from the Turks in grim battle, the city from which he had cunningly expelled the Greeks and which, at the last, he had had to dispute against the jealousy of the count of Toulouse. The departure of the other crusaders for Jerusalem in January 1099 had left him in peaceful possession. To complete his work, he now needed a great seaport, specifically the town of Laodicea (Latakia). But Latakia had shortly before been occupied by his ancient adversary, Raymond of Saint-Gilles, and handed over by him to the Byzantines. Bohemund had no hesitation in going to besiege the Byzantine garrison. A powerful Pisan squadron had just anchored off Syria under the command of the energetic Daimbert, archbishop of Pisa. Bohemund proposed that the Pisans should attack Latakia by sea while he invested it by land. The Pisans, already in dispute with the Byzantines, were happy to accept. But the allies had counted without Raymond of Saint-Gilles. The siege was in progress when, in September 1099, Raymond, returning from Jerusalem appeared before Latakia.

The count of Toulouse almost choked with rage. Thus, while he went off to deliver Jerusalem, Bohemund, who had not even taken part in the march on the Holy City, profited from his absence to attack a place which he, Saint-Gilles, had solemnly handed over to the Byzantines! Raymond summoned Bohemund to raise the siege. Bohemund prepared to resist, but the Pisans, unwilling to start their crusade with a battle between Latins, abandoned him. Archbishop Daimbert, learning of the approach of these southern crusaders who had played such a great part in the delivery of the Holy Sepulcher, hastened to meet them. The chronicle shows him "throwing his arms around the Toulousains, big and little, shedding tears of joy." There followed a very eloquent speech: "I salute you, sons and friends of the living God, who, after leaving your families and your possessions, have not hesitated to risk your lives so far from home, in the midst of so many barbarous peoples, for the glory of the Lord! No Christian army has ever done such deeds!" These fine words met with a chilly reception. "If your sentiments are so Christian," riposted Saint-Gilles, "how does it happen that you are associated with the siege of a Christian city?" The next day, while Bohemund was withdrawing to Antioch, Saint-Gilles made his entry into Latakia, where the oriflamme of Toulouse floated proudly beside the banners of Byzantium.

And yet, in spite of Daimbert's defection, his agreement with Bohemund persisted. After the check to their designs on Latakia, the two allies made the pilgrimage to Jerusalem together. On December 21, 1099, they were received by Godfrey of Bouillon in the Holy City. And immediately, on the initiative of Daimbert, the question of the patriarchate arose.

On the morrow of the capture of Jerusalem, the duke of Normandy's chaplain, Arnulf Malecorne, had been more or less regularly elected patriarch. He was a highly intelligent cleric, with remarkable natural eloquence, but a political intriguer whose private life lacked sanctity. Daimbert had no difficulty in proving the defects of such an election. He had Arnulf deposed and himself named to the patriarchal see in his place. In reality, in both cases it was profoundly regrettable that the choice for such an important post was imposed by local politics, instead of being left to the wisdom of the papacy. For Daimbert, too, was far from faultless. A man of action rather than a churchman, he had a strong personality but lacked moderation. More energetic than need be, even more ambitious than Arnulf, authoritarian and overbearing, he was accused of having, during a mission in Spain, diverted to his own profit part of the sums intended for the Roman court. Hardly had he been named patriarch when he invited Godfrey to surrender Jerusalem to him and go and live, a king without a kingdom, in some other place to be conquered from the Turks. Godfrey, no doubt somewhat taken aback, finally yielded, at any rate in principle; for, exhausted by so many difficulties, he died in Jerusalem on July 18, 1100, without having had the time to fulfill his undertaking.

Daimbert thought the time had come finally to constitute Judaea as a patriarchal patrimony. He knew that for this purpose he could count upon his friend Bohemund of Antioch and wrote to him accordingly. But lo and behold, instead of the ally whom he expected, he was to see the arrival of a singularly inopportune visitor, Godfrey of Bouillon's own brother, Baldwin of Boulogne, count of Edessa, who claimed possession of Jerusalem as of right.

4

THE FOUNDER OF THE KINGDOM OF JERUSALEM
Baldwin of Boulogne

BALDWIN of Boulogne, brother of Godfrey, was a fine type of baron. He was taller than his brother, and men applied to him the words of the Book of Samuel in speaking of Saul: "From his shoulders and upward he was higher than any of the people." With his brown hair and beard, but very white complexion, with his aquiline nose, his energetic and masculine appearance, he commanded attention. His expression, his language, his demeanor all breathed a deliberate gravity. Thus, he was never seen without a mantle on his shoulders, so that, as the chronicler tells us, at first sight you would have taken him for a bishop rather than a knight. In fact, like many younger sons, in his youth he had been destined for the Church. "He learned enough letters as befits a young cleric and was enrolled in the chapters of Reims, of Cambrai, and of Liège." But this clerical apprenticeship did not last long. He gave up, in good time, a career for which he was not fitted and returned to the secular world. And yet, from his sojourn in the Church, he was always to retain certain habits of mind, dignity, the spirit of moderation, diplomatic tact. Much given to women, he is praised by the chronicler for having at least avoided scandal, so that even his familiars were usually ignorant of his adventures.

Baldwin, as we shall see, was one day to be the main beneficiary of the crusade, the first king of Jerusalem. But at the outset, he had cared little about the crusade, at any rate from the spiritual point of view, and he had been the first to quit the march on Jerusalem for more lucrative operations. As early as September 1097, during the crossing of Asia Minor, he had left the crusading army, in company with Tancred, to attempt the personal conquest of Cilicia. His misunderstanding with Tancred had meant the failure of the venture; but Baldwin, without even taking part in the siege of Antioch, had almost immediately abandoned the crusade again to seek his fortune in the direction of Edessa.

The city of Edessa, the modern Urfa, east of the Euphrates, at that time constituted a little Armenian principality, an island washed on all sides by waves of Turks. Thoros, the Armenian chief who had succeeded, almost by a miracle, in maintaining this Christian bastion in Moslem country, was beginning to despair. He was aging; and the Turkish invasion seemed inevitable, when the news of the Frankish victories reached him. At that very moment, one of the crusader chiefs, our Baldwin, had just made a successful attack on the neighboring Turkish stronghold, Tel-Basheir, or as the crusaders called it, Turbessel. Thoros joyfully looked upon this as providential aid. He invited Baldwin to Edessa and welcomed him as a savior. Evidently, the Armenian prince counted upon taking the Frankish chief into his pay as a mercenary, and richly paid at that. But Baldwin had quite different ideas. Once within the city, he stated his terms: he would share the power with Thoros or quit Edessa forthwith, leaving it to the Turkish attacks. Thoros had no alternative but to yield. He recognized Baldwin as his adopted son and heir. In accordance with the ceremony of the time, the old Armenian passed his "son," stripped to the waist, between his shirt and his breast, embraced him, and sealed their mutual undertaking with a kiss.

There follows a very tangled story which shows us Baldwin in a somewhat unfavorable light, although displaying consummate political skill. All these Christian communities in the East were bedeviled by rivalries between sects and by family jealousies. Thoros had bitter enemies, not only among the Syrian Christians, but also among his own Armenian fellow-believers. They parleyed with Baldwin, offering to make him sole master of Edessa, if he would let them get rid of Thoros. At their instigation, on March 7, 1098, a riot broke out against the old Armenian prince. The populace, clamoring for his death and hailing

Baldwin, besieged him in his castle. Baldwin, with great dignity, affected to try to calm them down, to assume the defense of his adoptive father, to act as mediator. In fact he went to Thoros and suggested that the insurgents should be appeased by an opportune distribution of largesse. Thoros, trembling, handed over the keys of his treasures, asking only for permission to retire safe and sound. Baldwin swore it on the holy relics "calling to witness archangels, angels, and prophets." But on the morrow, as the old man, trusting to the pledged word, was tranquilly preparing to quit Edessa, the populace, armed with sticks and pikes, fell upon him and massacred him. "Tying a rope to his feet, they dragged his body through the streets" and it was thus, concludes the chronicler dryly, that Baldwin of Boulogne remained sole master of Edessa.

Baldwin sought to legitimize his elevation in the eyes of the local population. First, he married an Armenian princess, Arda, the daughter of a lord of Taurus. Then he liberated from the Turks, the neighboring strongholds, especially Saruj and Samosata. The "county of Edessa" thus became a princely domain, extending from the frontiers of the principality of Antioch to the verge of Kurdistan.

But these campaigns cost dear. The mailed fist of the Frankish chief fell on the shoulders of the wealthy Armenian burgesses, demanding gold, always more gold. Many, regretting their conduct toward the unfortunate Thoros, began to hate the terrible protector they had given themselves. Twelve of the most notable formed a plot to get rid of him, even with the help of the Turks if need be. But he had his spies everywhere. Warned by a loyal Armenian, he struck hard and fast. The main culprits had their eyes put out, in the Byzantine fashion; the rank and file merely had their noses, hands, or feet cut off and were then expelled.

These were the last rebellions. The Armenians understood that they had met their master. How could they stand up against this extraordinary Frank, more cunning than a Levantine and equally unscrupulous, more subtle than an Arab and equally secretive, more brutal and quicker on the riposte than a Turk, surpassing the valor of the Turks in dash and military skill? For the rest, the benefits of his strict administration began to be felt: order, safety, wealth, daily victories over the Turks, wealth and victories from which the Armenian element greatly benefited. Moreover, the Armenians who had formerly suffered so much from the scorn and religious persecutions of the Byzantines, found a quite different attitude among the rough Frankish knights. Between the Franks and the Armenians there was no race prejudice, no religious hostility. Marriages between Frankish barons and Armenian noblewomen, between Armenian lords and Frankish chatelaines began to multiply. Baldwin himself had given the first example, as Alexander the Great had set the example for unions between Macedonians and Iranians.

On this narrow stage of the county of Edessa, Baldwin I thus showed himself as an unscrupulous adventurer, but also an adventurer of genius and already by that time the outstanding statesman whom later events will teach us to know better. He seemed destined to lead the Frankish expansion in the direction of Diyarbekir and Mesopotamia, when on September 12, 1100, he received unexpected news: his brother, Godfrey of Bouillon, had just died and a delegation of Palestinian knights was offering him the throne of Jerusalem. But in the meanwhile, the patriarch Daimbert, with the aid of the Normans, was in the course of seizing power. Baldwin had not a minute to lose if he was not to be faced with an accomplished fact.

His attitude on receiving this message depicts the man. With a brevity worthy of Tacitus, his chaplain, Fulcher of Chartres, shows him "fittingly sad at his brother's death but even happier with the expected inheritance." His mind was made up at once. So far he had lived only for his county of Edessa, in favor of which he had deserted the crusade. But as soon as he glimpsed the crown of Jerusalem, he did not hesitate. Godfrey had not known what to do with this crown of David, had not even placed it on his head. Baldwin would soon show what he would make of it! Immediately he entrusted the county of Edessa to his cousin, Baldwin of Le Bourg and, at the head of 400 knights and 1,000 foot soldiers, set off for Jerusalem on October 2, 1100.

The journey from Edessa to Jerusalem with such a small force was a hazardous enterprise. From Jerusalem, Daimbert had written to Bohemund to stop Baldwin from passing when he crossed the principality of Antioch. And if he surmounted this first obstacle, the Turks of Damascus were waiting for him in the defiles of the Lebanon to crush him beneath the mere weight of numbers. But fortune favored the bold Baldwin. At the very moment of Godfrey's death, Bohemund, who was campaigning in the direction of Melitene, had just been captured by the Turks; at the moment when he was called upon to intervene in the succession of Jerusalem, he was biting his nails in the depths of some fortress in Asia Minor. Baldwin, far from being received as an enemy at Antioch, was therefore welcomed as a brother. He left it after three days and, by way of Latakia and the Alaouite coast, took the Lebanon coast road. There his companions were seized with fright; at every bend in the road the Turkish army might rise up. Half of them quit. His firm front daunted the others: "If any man be afeared, let him return home!" But when they reached Jabala they were no more than 160 knights and 500 foot soldiers.

The uneasiness which reigned in the little troop was justified. The Turkish king of Damascus, reinforced by the Arab Emir of Homs, was lying in wait for Baldwin between Tripoli and Beirut, at the most dangerous point on the road, where it passes through the gorges of Nahr el-Kelb near the deeply embanked mouth of the river. The ambush was so well prepared that Baldwin should have succumbed. By an unhoped-for chance, he was warned in time by the Arab cadi of Tripoli who, embroiled in a mortal quarrel with the Damascenes, betrayed the Moslem cause in his own favor. The situation of the Franks on arriving at the pass of Nahr el-Kelb was nonetheless desperate, especially as, assailed in front by the army of Damascus, they found themselves harassed on their right flank by an Arab flotilla sailing from Beirut. In the dramatic words of a chronicler: "Out to sea, the enemy ships; on the other flank, the sheer mountain; in front, the whole Turkish army." Night fell, a night of anguish during which the bivouac was constantly harassed by the Moslem archers. The feelings of Baldwin's entourage are frankly confessed by his chaplain, the good Fulcher of Chartres: "Oh, how I wished I were back in Chartres, or Orleans! And I was not the only one . . ."

Next morning, at first dawn, Baldwin, realizing that a breakthrough was impossible, feigned to beat a retreat. The Turks flung themselves after him, in hot pursuit; but in their precipitation, and owing to the narrowness of the Lebanese coast road, they thrust forward a squadron of 500 horsemen in the van, followed at a distance by the infantry. This was exactly what Baldwin was counting on. When he had lured this vanguard far enough, he wheeled about and charged. The narrowness of the pass prevented the Moslems from taking advantage of their superior numbers to deploy. As they came up in dispersed order, breathless from the chase, they were crushed by the concerted, massive Frankish counterattack. Fleeing in disorder through the narrow corridor, they spread panic throughout the mass of the Damascene army, which scattered into the mountains, the malik of Damascus leading the rout.

The way was open. Baldwin pressed forward and made for Jerusalem by way of Carmel and Jaffa. As he neared the Holy City, he was met by a joyous procession of the whole Christian population, with the prelates of each rite, chanting hymns and canticles, come to greet the brother and heir of Godfrey of Bouillon "as their lord and their king." Spontaneously and enthusiastically, they all rallied around him, not only in memory of the good duke who had governed them so paternally, but because this little Christian colony, lost in the midst of the Moslem world, felt the instinctive need to gather round a strong man. It was the voice of the masses. Daimbert, seeing his projects wither away, was forced to comply, whether he would or no. At one moment, even, in fear of reprisals, he took refuge in the Church of Mount Sion where, as William of Tyre prettily says, "he busied himself in prayer and read privily in his books." But Baldwin was too shrewd to compromise himself by taking vengeance before he was firmly established on his throne. Affecting to overlook his own causes of complaint, he immediately undertook a great expedition at the head of the Christian army across the massif of Judaea to the south of the Dead Sea. He even made a southward thrust as far as "Le Vaux Moise," the modern Wadi Musa, in the heart of the desert of Arabia Petraea.

This expedition finally established Baldwin's authority. On his return, the Patriarch Daimbert resigned himself to crowning him king of Jerusalem, and the ceremony took place in the Church of the Holy Virgin at Bethlehem, on Christmas Day 1100.

Baldwin, of set purpose, was to take this royalty very seriously, deliberately surrounding it with all the pomp of the East and investing it with an almost Biblical majesty. He would sit enthroned, robed in a burnous of gold brocade, his beard as long as that of a Byzantine *basileus*, and with a great gilded buckler borne before him. Like a sultan, he would let himself be "adored" by the Moslem embassies and would take his meals in their presence, sitting cross-legged on a carpet.

Not because he was vain, or taken in by all this pomp, but because, in the new environment in which he was summoned to live, he discerned in it a means of government.

The last opposition came from Tancred, who, recently invested with the principality of Galilee by Godfrey, could not resign himself to becoming a vassal of Baldwin, with whom he had been on bad terms since 1097. Very fortunately, the people of Antioch, who had been without a chief since the capture of Bohemund by the Turks, at this juncture offered Tancred the regency of their principality. The great Frankish city of the north gained a valiant defender, and Baldwin remained sole master in his kingdom of the south.

The new king of Jerusalem set to work at once. At the time of his accession, his authority scarcely extended beyond the precincts of the walled cities and the countryside remained at the mercy of the raiding Arabs. Baldwin turned their own tactics against them, personally organizing and leading counterraids which fell upon their camping-grounds out of the blue. Some of the pages of his biography read exactly like the accounts of the movements of a modern mobile column during the French campaigns in Algeria or Morocco, others of similar raids on the "smalah," the treasures of the Arab camps. One day Baldwin learned from his spies that a great encampment of Arabs, with their tents, their wives, their children, their horses, their camels, and their donkeys, had established itself in Transjordan. Rallying all the forces he could find, he set off on the instant, crossed the Jordan without giving the alarm, filed up the dry bed of a wadi within reach of the enemy, and waited for nightfall. At dead of night he fell upon the sleeping camp and in the first surprise captured the whole of this nomad city. Only a few chiefs among the Arabs had time to mount their horses and flee. But, among the crowd of prisoners, the king of Jerusalem was told of a high-born young woman, the wife of a powerful sheik, who was expecting a child. He hastened up, brought her down from the camel's back, had a tent arranged for her with the richest pillows that could be found; and in a great chivalrous gesture, doffing his royal mantle, he covered the young Bedouin with it, and took leave of her, leaving her with water, provisions, maidservants, and two she-camels to feed the coming child. As soon as the Franks had departed, the sheik, in mortal anguish, came seeking his wife; he found her on the spot, in the sumptuous apparel which Baldwin had left her.

From that day forth, he swore eternal gratitude to the Frankish prince. We shall see that he soon had occasion to give practical proof of it.

At the same time as cleaning up the Palestine hinterland, the main concern of Baldwin I was to conquer the ports, which were still mainly in the hands of the Egyptian garrisons. One after the other he gathered in Arsuf, which capitulated, and Caesarea, which was taken by assault (April–May 1101). The Cairo government, however, unable to resign itself to the loss of these strongholds, concentrated a powerful army before Ascalon in August, estimated at some thirty thousand men. Baldwin called upon all the Frankish garrisons of the country, but when, on September 7, he took up his position before Ramleh, all he could muster against the Arab masses were 260 horsemen and 900 foot soldiers. To make his little army more mobile, he divided it into five echelons. The first three were routed, and it was Baldwin himself who, with the two others, had to reinstate the battle. The True Cross, borne before him by Bishop Gerard, helped to revive men's courage. Before charging, he made a short speech to his men, the gist of which has been preserved for us by Fulcher of Chartres: "Should you be slain, you win a martyr's crown; should you be victors, you win glory immortal. As for flight, it is useless: France is too far!" In a gesture like that of Philip Augustus at Bouvines, the king prostrated himself at the foot of the True Cross and publicly confessed his sins to Bishop Gerard. Then mounting his steed, an Arabian called Gazelle, because of its fleetness, he charged at the head of his troops. The True Cross, borne by Gerard, advanced behind him. One of the Egyptian emirs broke through to try to capture it; he was killed in the attempt. Another who drove at Baldwin was cut down at the same time as his horse, at a single stroke, by the king. Before these men of iron, Egyptians and Sudanese gave way. The whole Moslem army took flight toward Ascalon. Within a few minutes the Egyptian camp and everything in it had fallen into the hands of the Franks. Baldwin forbade his folk, on pain of death, to halt the pursuit for the sake of pillage. The "chase" was ended only with nightfall, within sight of Ascalon. Baldwin then sounded the rally and led back his soldiers to share with them the riches of the Egyptian camp.

It was only a brief respite. In May 1102, a new army of 20,000 Arabs and Sudanese issued from Egypt and again advanced along the Jerusalem road as far as Ramleh. This time Baldwin, intoxicated by his earlier successes, lacked prudence. Without waiting to mobilize the garrisons of Galilee, he set off to meet the invaders with the knights of Jerusalem alone. It was only on debouching onto the plain of Ramleh on May 17, when he discovered the size of the enemy army, that he realized the abyss into which his rashness had led him. But it was too late to draw back. "Seeking no more than to sell their lives dearly," the little troop charged. So rude was the clash that for an instant the Egyptians "stood amazed," thinking that the king's suite was no more than a vanguard. But Baldwin and his men soon found themselves overwhelmed by numbers. Most of his companions were killed. With a last handful of faithful, he took refuge in the village of Ramleh, which was at once besieged by the whole Egyptian army. Only nightfall stopped the victors from carrying this feeble defense, but it was evident that on the morrow all would be over with the king of Jerusalem.

It was then, according to William of Tyre, that a romantic intervention occurred which brought salvation. Toward the middle of the night an Arab chief appeared before the walls and demanded to speak to the king personally. The mysterious visitor was introduced: it was the sheik whose young wife Baldwin had saved and freed the year before on the occasion of the raid in Transjordan. The chivalrous Arab had come to warn the king that he must make his escape before dawn, while there was still time. Baldwin, at the urgent prayer of his people, tried this last chance. Mounting Gazelle, he set off cross-country at dead of night, through the enemy bivouacs. His flight was at once reported, and a throng of Arab horsemen dashed after him. Almost all his servitors were killed or captured. Only the speed of Gazelle saved her rider, who disappeared in the mountain gorges.

The following morning, the Egyptian scouts appeared before Jaffa brandishing the severed head of Gerbod of Winthinc, who was Baldwin's double. Baldwin's wife, Queen Arda, who was in the town, believed with all the inhabitants that the king had perished; but on May 20, to the general amazement, a barque appeared in the offing with Baldwin's personal oriflamme streaming in the wind.

After wandering two days on the mountain, Baldwin had in fact succeeded in reaching Arsuf, where a hardy English corsair named Goderic had agreed to carry him by sea to Jaffa. The Egyptian fleet was cruising off the coasts. To reassure the defenders of Jaffa when they sighted the ship at a distance, Baldwin broke out the royal standard at the masthead; but at this sight the enemy squadron gave chase in the hopes of capturing him. Happily, the sea rose and the wind veered to the north, favoring Goderic and stopping the Egyptian sail, so that the royal barque, riding the storm, came safe to port, without mishap.

The arrival of the "resurrected" Baldwin seemed to the defenders of Jaffa to smack of the miraculous. "It was like the morning star which heralds the approach of day." At the same time, the Frankish chivalry of Galilee arrived overland under its chief, Hugh of Saint Omer, lord of Tiberias. Finally, a Christian squadron of two hundred ships providentially landed a great pilgrimage at Jaffa, including many English, French, and German knights. The reconstituted Frankish army soon found itself in a state to resume the offensive. On May 27, Baldwin made a surprise attack on the Egyptian army between Jaffa and Ascalon and this time won an outright victory.

The Frankish superiority over the Egyptian forces was decisively re-established. In 1104, Baldwin took advantage of a voyage by a Genoese squadron to seize from the Egyptians the coast town of Saint-Jean-d'Acre, destined to become the greatest Christian port in the Levant (May 26, 1104). The following year the Cairo government made a last effort. Its army advanced as far as Ramleh, reinforced by Damascene contingents. Battle was joined before Ramleh on August 27, 1105. "The Franks shouted their war-cry: *Christus vincit, Christus regnat, Christus imperat!*" At the outset, the Turkish cavalry of Damascus wrought great havoc among them, riddling them with arrows, according to their custom. The exasperated Baldwin, grasping his white standard from the hands of his squire and holding it at arm's length, charged the Turks at a furious gallop and scattered them. He then turned back against the Egyptian ranks. The infantry, consisting of fellahin and Sudanese, courageously allowed themselves to be massacred where they stood; only the Arab cavalry was able to get away. . . .

The occupation of the Palestine littoral by the Franks caused enormous disturbance to the internal trade of the Moslem world. Caravans between Cairo and Damascus or Baghdad were obliged to go around by the desert tracks, through the valley of Idumea, to round the Dead Sea on the south, and then go up again by the valley of the Jordan on the Transjordan side. The chronicles of the time show us one of these caravans from Egypt halting near Jordan "in the darkness and silence of the night." But King Baldwin was warned by his scouts. With sixty knights he went down to the river in pitch darkness and took the caravan by surprise. The "bag": "eleven camels loaded with sugar, four camels loaded with pepper, seventeen loaded with oil and honey." A little later, a much more important windfall: an enormous caravan of four thousand camels, returning from Arabia to Transjordan, captured by the Anglo-Norman crusader, William-Cliton, grandson of William the Conqueror. It is true that the Moslems matched raid for raid. The lord of Tiberias, Gervase of Bazoches, thus fell into an ambush and was taken prisoner to Damascus. The Turkish captain who governed Damascus, the brutal Toghtekin, offered Baldwin to liberate his vassal against the cession of Tiberias and Acre. Baldwin, statesmanship personified, was unshakable: "Money as much as you will, more than a hundred thousand bezants if need be! But even if you reduce my whole family to captivity, with all the other Frankish chiefs, I will never yield the smallest of our towns for their ransom!" On this refusal, Gervase was shot to death with arrows in the great square of Damascus; his scalp, with its white locks, was borne before the emir on a pole, but the Frankish conquests remained intact.

Whenever a Christian squadron cast anchor in Levantine waters, Baldwin seized the occasion to capture with its aid the coast towns still in Egyptian power. We have just seen that in 1104 a Genoese fleet had enabled him to take Acre. On May 13, 1110, the presence of Genoese and Pisan ships likewise enabled him to capture Beirut; and on December 4 following, thanks to the support of a Scandinavian fleet, led by King Sigurd of Norway, he forced Sidon to capitulate. At this date the whole of the Palestine littoral, except Tyre in the north and Ascalon in the south, had therefore been snatched from Egypt and solidly annexed to the Frankish kingdom.

While in the south, in Palestine, Baldwin was founding the kingdom of Jerusalem within its historic limits, in the north of Syria his old rival Tancred, summoned to the regency of the principality of Antioch during Bohemund's captivity (1100–1103), "also did manful work." He consolidated the Norman principality in the east by victorious expeditions against the Turkish kingdom of Aleppo, and in the west succeeded in giving it its seafront by capturing the great port of Latakia from the Byzantines (end of 1102). As for Raymond of Saint-Gilles, count of Toulouse, after his disappointment at seeing Antioch and Jerusalem assigned to others, he had set off for Constantinople to concert with the Emperor Alexius Comnenus. Alexius appointed him to lead across Asia Minor the new crusades which were now arriving from France, Germany, and Italy.

The first of these new "crusades of reinforcement" or of "exploitation," which had been organized in the West on the news of the liberation of Jerusalem, consisted of pilgrims from Lombardy. Reaching Byzantine territory by the Danube route, the Lombards encamped near Constantinople. Their expedition, which included a host of noncombatants, resembled in many respects the People's Crusades of 1096, whose troublesome exploits it was to repeat. In spite of the objurgations of their chiefs, the Lombard pilgrims set about pillaging Byzantine territory, stealing cattle and crops and even going so far as to plunder churches. When the Byzantine police intervened, the most headstrong had no hesitation in assailing the imperial palace of Blachernae. The archbishop of Milan, their titular chief, succeeded in appeasing them. The Lombards were joined by another reinforcement crusade, French this time, and all accepted the leadership of Raymond of Saint-Gilles, who crossed over into Asia at their head (April–May 1101).

No question seemed to arise about the route to be chosen to cross Asia Minor: the only course open was to follow the tracks of the First Crusade, through Nicaea, Dorylaeum, and Iconium, where the staging posts and water points were well known, and go down to Antioch, as in 1097. But a sudden passion, such as often arises among mobs, seized the Lombard pilgrims; before going down to Syria, they must go and free Bohemund. But Bohemund was a prisoner of the Turks in the fortress of Niksar, in the northeast of Asia Minor, at the other extremity of the peninsula, toward the Caucasus. To reach him (assuming that the Turks did not move him even farther away) they therefore had to turn their backs on Syria, completely disregard the objective of the crusade, and commit the whole expedition to a march without a term and without an issue. This was the objection of the barons, starting with Raymond of Saint-Gilles. But there is no arguing with mob psychology. Being their chief, Raymond had to follow them.

And the crazy anabasis started. After Ankara, which they reached on June 23, they found themselves in the mountain solitudes, without towns or crops, where the Turkoman cavalry harassed the crusaders dying of fatigue and hunger. They found themselves riddled with arrows at long range, without being able to join battle hand to hand. Their bravado changed to despondency, and soon to panic. A little before Amasya, the Turks, deeming the Frankish column sufficiently demoralized, barred the road. The Lombards took flight. Raymond of Toulouse, with the French and the Germans, stood his ground until nightfall, and then lost heart like the rest and fled toward the Black Sea with his Byzantine guides. Riding hell bent for leather he reached the first port on the coast, where he took ship for Constantinople. When his flight was known in the crusading army, there was a general stampede. Of at least 150,000 crusaders numbered in the expedition only a few thousand managed to reach Sinop. All the rest were massacred or taken captive by the Turks (July–August 1101).

The first result of this disaster was to rob the Franks of the moral benefit of the victories of Godfrey of Bouillon in Asia Minor. The Turks, who since 1097 had been defeatists, again felt themselves to be *ghazi*, victors. This was immediately visible in this same summer of 1101 when Count William of Nevers with 15,000 crusaders tried to follow the same route as Godfrey of Bouillon, through Phrygia and Lycaonia. On his arrival at Eregli, east of Konya, he was encircled by the Turkish cavalry and his troops, riddled with arrows, were almost all massacred on the spot. A similar fate was waiting for a last pilgrimage of 60,000 souls, led by William IV of Poitiers and Welf IV of Bavaria. They too reached Konya but were unable to revictual themselves, since the Turks had laid everything waste before them. On their arrival at the Eregli river, as the wretches, tortured by thirst, flung themselves in disorder on the river banks, the Turkish bowmen emerged on the other bank and then on every hillside, surrounding this lamentable troop, where every arrow found its mark. It was a nameless massacre (September 5, 1101). Only a few knights escaped. The beautiful Margravine Ida of Austria, who rode with the Bavarian army, vanished without a trace: slain, or captive in some remote harem.

The disaster of Anatolia had very serious consequences for the future of the Latin East. The throngs who rushed to be massacred there constituted the second wave, after the conquest of Jerusalem, the "wave of exploitation," designed to consolidate the success and convert the Frankish principalities of Syria into genuine colonies.

Frankish Syria was never again to find this reinforcement of 200,000 men, this immigration of a whole people. From now on they must labor more modestly, on a narrow plane, limited to the possibilities of the moment. The count of Toulouse—one of those responsible for the disaster, since he had been unable to stand up against the follies of the Lombard mob—was the first to realize it. After the disaster of 1101 he ceased to be the turbulent, proud, and somewhat overbearing prince we have seen. This universal candidate for all the thrones of the East was to found a modest Provençal county on the Lebanese coast. It is true that this labor was no doubt to be more reasonable and sounder than his first dreams of a paladin.

It is also true that, before resigning himself to this end, Saint-Gilles was to suffer one last disillusionment. After the disaster of Anatolia, he still thought of disputing Antioch with Tancred; and with this end in view, he had just landed at the mouth of the Orontes when he was taken prisoner by an adventurer and handed over to his rival for cash. Tancred, moreover, proved himself a good prince and set the count free easily enough, but only after obtaining from him an express waiver of all claims over Antioch. It was then that Raymond bethought himself again of the fair lands of Tortosa and Tripoli which he had formerly traversed in the course of the First Crusade. Between the kingdom of Jerusalem, finally fallen to Baldwin of Boulogne, and the principality of Antioch, finally in the hands of Bohemund and Tancred, there lay a favored Riviera, which must have reminded him of the scenes of his native south. At that very moment a Genoese fleet was cruising off the coast. Raymond gained the support of the Genoese captains and with their aid attacked the town of Tortosa, in the Arab Emirate of Tripoli. On April 21, 1102, he gained possession of the stronghold, where he established his residence until such time as he could make himself master of the metropolis of the region, which was now his goal, Tripoli itself.

The emirate of Tripoli belonged to a family of Arab cadis, more or less theoretically subject to Egypt, the Banu Ammar, very astute politicians, intellectual and cultivated minds (they possessed one of the finest libraries in Islam), far from fanatical, who had so far maintained courteous relations with the Franks. The Banu Ammar thus hoped to ride out the storm and keep their independence; it was enough for them to supply the Christian convoys traveling between Antioch and Jerusalem and passing by their peninsular Tripoli of el-Mina, that almost impregnable "Lebanese Gibraltar."

The situation changed when a Frankish prince set up his home in the country, with the firm resolution of making himself its master and ending his days there. It is true that Raymond of Saint-Gilles had very few companions, four hundred men on the most generous estimate; but in spite of the current insignificance of his resources, far from confining himself to his new possession of Tortosa, he thrust his attacks right up to the walls of Tripoli. In the picturesque words of Radulph of Caen, "he ventured to besiege this populous city singlehanded." It should be added that the Maronite Christians of the mountains gave him invaluable support. With their assistance, and that of a Genoese squadron, he captured from the folk of Tripoli, on April 23, 1104, the town of Jebail, the ancient Byblos, the Gibelet of the chroniclers. With Tortosa in the north and Gibelet in the south, the outline of the future county of Tripoli was already traced. In the center its natural capital was missing, Tripoli itself. As we have already said, the Arab Tripoli of the eleventh century, locked in its rocky peninsula of el-Mina, protected by a fairly narrow isthmus, was singularly difficult to take. Benefiting from all the advantages of an island, supplied by sea by the Egyptian fleet and thus communicating with the rest of the Moslem world, the Banu Ammar waited for their enemy to become discouraged. But Saint-Gilles, to mark his inflexible determination and insure the permanent blockade of the town, installed himself before it and, on the rocky spur which overhangs the gorge of the Qadicha, built a fortress which he called Mount Pilgrim and which the Moslems called after him the Castle of Saint-Gilles, Qalat Sanjil, on the site occupied by the present citadel of Tripoli (1103).

It was at Mount Pilgrim that Saint-Gilles died on February 28, 1105. It was a melancholy destiny for this high baron, who, after being the first to give his support to the crusade, after being the first confidant of Urban II, had seen all the advantages he might have expected from it slip away from him one by one. Others had taken his place at the head of the great pilgrimage. Neither of the great conquered cities, Antioch or Jerusalem, had fallen to his lot. The reinforcement crusade which he had led across Anatolia in 1101 had failed lamentably. After the shipwreck of these vast hopes, he had been compelled, in the twilight of his life, to settle for a corner of the Lebanese coast, and there again he disappeared from the scene without tasting the joy of entering the Promised Land of Tripoli. But after many errors, and many shortcomings too, he had the supreme consolation of being able to say that he died at his task, faithful to his duty, refusing to quit that Holy Land where he had found so much bitterness. Nor must we forget his humanity to the Moslem prisoners on the capture of Jerusalem.

Raymond's Lebanese heritage fell to his cousin, William-Jordan, count of Cerdagne (1105-1109). From Mount Pilgrim, William continued the investiture of Tripoli with the same obstinacy. In despair, the chief of the Banu Ammar came to implore the aid of the Turkish atabeg of Damascus, and then of the caliph of Baghdad, offering them all kinds of valuable presents (1108). Alas, his listeners took his presents but gave him nothing in return except fair words. And when the emir returned, disillusioned, to Syria, he found that the people of Tripoli, tired of waiting, had handed themselves over to the caliph of Egypt. As for William-Jordan, while he was no more able than his predecessor to take the impregnable Tripoli, he nevertheless captured, in April 1109, in spite of the intervention of the Damascenes, the important stronghold of Arqa, and even added to it the castles of Jebel Akkar.

While, away from the mainstream of history, on their corner of the Lebanese coast, Raymond of Saint-Gilles, and then William-Jordan, were patiently constituting the future county of Tripoli, the principality of Antioch in the north was experiencing a succession of highly dramatic events.

We have seen that, since 1100, the prince of Antioch, the Norman chief Bohemund, had been a prisoner of the Turks in Asia Minor, while his nephew Tancred governed his "princedom" in his stead. He was despairing of ever regaining his liberty when, at the beginning of 1103, the Turkish chiefs began to quarrel among themselves about his prospective ransom. This ransom his jailor, Gümüshtekin, emir of Sivas, intended to keep for himself. The Seljuk sultan of Konya, Gümüshtekin's suzerain, wanted his share and turned to threats. Some echo of the dispute certainly reached the astute Norman in his prison. He contrived to make known the liking which he felt for Gümüshtekin, to such good purpose that one day Gümüshtekin descended into his dungeon to consult that inventive spirit on the best way of resisting the Seljuks. Agreement was soon reached. Bohemund promised not only to pay the emir alone the full price of his redemption but also to be his loyal ally and help him to conquer Seljuk Anatolia. Upon which, he was at last restored to freedom (May 1103).

Bohemund therefore returned to Antioch, where Tancred, who had governed so well in his absence, handed over the power to him. The next year, the two Norman chiefs, at the request of their neighbor, Baldwin of Le Bourg, count of Edessa, organized a great expedition with him into the Moslem Al Jazira. Their first objective was the stronghold of Haran, southeast of Edessa. But a thrust of this kind in the direction of Baghdad could not fail to stir up the Turkish emirs in the neighborhood. Several of them, the atabeg of Mosul and the Ortoqids of Diyarbekir, joined forces and hastened to the relief of Haran. The clash came on the banks of the Balikh on May 7, 1104. The Turkish squadrons fronting the count of Edessa feigned flight at the first onset. In this way they enticed the chivalry of Edessa away from that of Antioch, right into an ambush, where, behind a fold in the ground, another corps of 10,000 Turks was waiting. In an instant Baldwin of Le Bourg and his folk were surrounded. Baldwin was taken prisoner, while most of his companions were massacred. On the other wing, the Normans at first had the advantage; but left dangerously in the air after the disaster of their allies, they could do no more than break off the engagement in time by a precipitate retreat.

The Turks, after this somewhat unhoped-for victory, moved to besiege Edessa, almost devoid of defenders. Tancred shut himself up in the stronghold, while Baldwin hastened to bring relief from Antioch. Pending the arrival of these reinforcements, Tancred had only a handful of men with him, while the plain was covered far and wide with Turkish encampments. He put a bold face on it, admirably seconded, moreover, by the Armenian population, which was determined at all costs not to fall back again under the Turkish yoke. Nevertheless, while he affected the most tranquil confidence, to keep up the morale of the population, he sent secret message after secret message to Antioch to warn his uncle Bohemund that the town was at the end of its tether. Bohemund, in spite of the risks he ran himself (the Aleppo Turks had just invaded his principality of Antioch), rallied 300 knights and some 400 foot soldiers and set off for Edessa. But for all his haste he could not reach it before the seventh day, and during that time the daily assaults of the Turks against the town became more and more violent. Tancred, despairing of the arrival of relief, and expecting every day to see the enemy reach the ramparts, took an extreme course, in agreement with the Armenian population. Preferring to die fighting, rather than to be sold on the slave markets of Islam, the besieged decided on a general sortie. Only this sortie, under Tancred's inspiration, was prepared with all the care of a pitched battle. Before dawn, every man in Edessa capable of wielding a weapon massed in silence behind the gates. The Turkish camp was sleeping, some soldiers exhausted by yesterday's attacks, others heavy with drink. In a flash, the gates opened and in a sudden pandemonium of clashing bucklers, war cries, and trumpet calls, all fell upon the enemy. The surprise was total; the Turkish camp was overwhelmed and taken. Groups of half-awakened sleepers were slaughtered before they could take up their arms. The rest, panic-stricken, took flight, at the very moment when Bohemund and the knights of Antioch finally arrived to finish off the victory.

Edessa was saved, but the disaster of Haran nevertheless had grave consequences. It marked the halt of Frankish conquests toward Mesopotamia, just as the disaster of Crassus, at this same site, then called Carrhae, had once marked the halt of the Roman conquest. The Aleppo Turks deprived Bohemund of most of his possessions east of the Orontes, and the Byzantines themselves took advantage of it to recover from him the port of Latakia. Beneath this twofold counterattack, Bohemund saw his work crumbling. To restore it from the foundations, he resolved to go and seek help in the West. Radulph of Caen gives us the gist of the speech he made to his faithful friends in the basilica of Saint Peter of Antioch: "Such a tempest rages against us that, unless we react, all is over with us. We are encircled. On the east, from the interior, the Turkish invasion; on the west, by sea, the Greek landings. We are no more than a handful of men, growing constantly fewer. We must have large reinforcements from France. Our salvation will come from there or from nowhere. I go to seek those reinforcements." He handed over the government of Antioch to Tancred and in the closing months of 1104 set sail for Italy.

Bohemund set off with rage in his heart against the Byzantines. It was the Byzantine attack which, taking him in the rear on the side of Latakia, had paralyzed him against the Turks. Decidedly, Byzantium was the worst enemy! And all his ancient rancors, all his youthful memories, from the time when he accompanied his father, Robert Guiscard, on the conquest of Macedonia, rose up in him again; it was a crusade against Byzantium that he was going to preach in Italy. From Italy he went on, with the same design, to France, where he was solemnly received by King Philip I (September 1105). Their amity was sealed by family alliances. A daughter of the king of France, the Princess Constance, was given in marriage to the Norman prince; and another, Cecilia, was sent to Tancred, "who wedded her with mighty great joy." Strong in this moral and material support, Bohemund landed in Epirus on October 9, 1107, and immediately laid siege to Durazzo, the great Byzantine fortress on the Adriatic; but this time he failed to recover the fortune of his youth. He was soon besieged himself by the Byzantine army, infinitely superior in numbers, and in September 1108 compelled to accept the conditions of the victors: he must bind himself closely as vassal of the Emperor Alexius Comnenus for the principality of Antioch, as well as for any other conquests he might make in the East.

This treaty, which would have marked the Byzantine solution of the crusades, was never executed, because Bohemund, after such a massive blow to his pride, had no heart to reappear in the East. Shattered by defeat, he languished a little longer in Italy and died there in obscurity around March 1111.

It was Tancred who restored the principality of Antioch (1104–1112). Bohemund, for his ill-fated Balkan enterprise, had emptied the treasury. Tancred refilled it after a brief but persuasive discourse to the country's hundred richest Greek or Armenian merchants. Then, having reconstituted his army, he met the Aleppo Turks in a great battle joined at Tizin, east of Arta, on April 20, 1105. Between the Norman army and the Turkish army, there stretched a rocky plain, unsuitable for cavalry maneuvers. Tancred, having observed it, halted shortly before reaching it. "Motionless, as though he were asleep," he allowed the Turks to commit themselves to the rocky zone and cross it in tranquillity; but as soon as they had passed it, "as though waking with a start," he charged. The tactics of the Turkish light cavalry were always the same: not to wait for a hand-to-hand encounter with the heavy Frankish chivalry, but to flee before it, riddling it with arrows, and then when the ironclad horses were as exhausted as their riders, to turn about suddenly and fall upon the dispersed and breathless pursuers and massacre them by weight of numbers. But on the terrain chosen by Tancred this game would not work. In withdrawing, the Turkish cavalry fell upon the rocky ground where galloping was almost impossible. Disconcerted by this obstacle, the Turks dismounted or dispersed. The Frankish knights forced a great part of them up against the rocks and butchered them. This victory restored to the principality of Antioch its territories beyond the Orontes, including Arta and Sermin. The following year, Tancred took advantage of the quarrels which divided the Arab chiefs of the Apamea region on the upper Orontes, to seize this important stronghold with the aid of a party among them (September 14, 1106). Further south, he entered into friendly relations with the chivalrous emirs of Shaizar, of the illustrious Arab house of Banu Munqid. The Munquidhite emir Usama, who has left us the recital of these events, shows us his kinsmen and Tancred competing in courtesy, exchanging highbred coursers, and taking pleasure, emirs and knights alike, in caracoling side by side. As for the Byzantines, nothing had been lost by the delay. In the middle of 1108, Tancred finally recovered the port of Latakia from them.

At the same time that he was governing Antioch on behalf of Bohemund, who was still in Italy, Tancred, as we have seen, was administering Edessa on behalf of Baldwin of Le Bourg, who was still a prisoner of the Turks. In truth he could have set Baldwin of Le Bourg free without too much difficulty by paying his ransom but, happy to receive the revenues of the fine county of Edessa, he was in no great hurry to provoke the event. It was the principal vassal of Baldwin of Le Bourg, Joscelin of Courtenay, lord of Turbessel (Tel-Basheir), who, a prisoner of the Turks like him, was the first to work for the deliverance of his suzerain after being redeemed himself. Baldwin of Le Bourg did the rest by concluding a pact of close alliance with his jailor, the Turkish chief, Jawali, who set him free in return for the promise of military aid in taking Aleppo or Mosul from the other Turks. But Baldwin was then to receive the most disagreeable surprise: Tancred, summoned to restore Edessa, turned a deaf ear. It was only with very bad grace that he finally complied (September 1108). The reconciliation was apparent only. A few months later, Jawali, at war with his countrymen, the Aleppo Turks, called upon Baldwin of Le Bourg and Joscelin of Courtenay, who, faithful to their pact, went to his aid. On his side, the Seljuk Ridwan of Aleppo called for help from Tancred, who complied. The strange spectacle thus ensued of one Turko-Frankish alliance fighting another. There was even a battle on the banks of the Euphrates, near Turbessel, between Tancred and the Aleppo Turks on one side and Baldwin of Le Bourg and the Turks of Jawali on the other, in which Tancred's men were the victors. Such a state of affairs, ten years after the First Crusade, while it could not fail to shock the pious souls, at least demonstrated that between Frankish feudalism and Moslem feudalism religious or racial hatred had lost much of its violence.

While the regent of Antioch and the count of Edessa were squabbling in North Syria, the Toulousain county of the Lebanon was equally troubled by other competitions between the barons.

William-Jordan had been reigning for four years over this state in the process of formation, in the firm hope of crowning his success by the imminent capture of Tortosa, when in February or March 1109 he found an unexpected competitor landing at Tortosa, his cousin Bertrand, the eldest son of Raymond of Saint-Gilles, come to claim his father's heritage. William naturally refused to hand over lands which he had defended and enlarged. The two adversaries looked for outside support. William turned toward Antioch, where Tancred promised him aid and protection. Bertrand, on his side, appealed to King Baldwin I of Jerusalem. Laying the whole case before the royal tribunal, he claimed the intervention of Baldwin to enable him to enter upon his heritage and, for the rest, declared himself vassal, for that heritage, to the crown of Jerusalem.

Baldwin, whose whole policy was to convert his Judaean kingdom, hitherto so restricted, into a Syrian-Palestinian kingdom embracing all the Frankish lands, was not the man to let such an opportunity slip. He immediately told Tancred and William-Jordan that, Bertrand being under his protection, he forbade them to undertake anything against him. Then, adopting the tone of a suzerain, which brooks no reply, and speaking "in the name of the whole Church of Jerusalem," he summoned them both to a royal assize before Tripoli, at the same time seizing the opportunity to reprimand Tancred for his bad behavior to the count of Edessa. And constituting himself arbiter of all these Frankish quarrels, the king announced his firm determination to restore concord between the barons, without which the conquests of the crusade could not be preserved.

Fitting the deed to the word, Baldwin proceeded before Tripoli in person. The exasperated William-Jordan was ready to appeal to arms; but Tancred, a shrewder politician, who knew what kind of a man Baldwin was, calmed his ally. Obedient to the royal reprimand, they both went down to Tripoli, where they were joined for their part by Baldwin of Le Bourg, count of Edessa, and his vassal, Joscelin of Courtenay, lord of Turbessel. There was therefore a full muster of the high barons of Syria before Tripoli when the king opened, probably at Mount Pilgrim, a solemn assize. The adversaries were summoned to plead their causes in public. The king then compelled a reconciliation, first between Tancred and Baldwin of Le Bourg and then between William-Jordan and Bertrand, and then gave judgment between the last two. The heritage of Raymond of Saint-Gilles was divided. It was decided that William-Jordan should keep Tortosa and Arqa, but that Bertrand should have Gibelet, Mount Pilgrim, and, as soon as it had capitulated, Tripoli.

Once agreement was established on these bases, advantage was taken of the concentration of Frankish forces, as well as of the presence of a powerful Genoese squadron of sixty-six ships, to put an end to the resistance of Tripoli. The relief squadron dispatched from Egypt failed to arrive in time. The Tripoli Arabs, left to themselves, exhausted by a siege which had lasted some six years, offered to capitulate, on condition of being allowed either to emigrate freely or to remain as subjects of the Franks on payment of an annual tribute. On July 12, 1109, the Franks entered the fortress. The capitulation was scrupulously honored by the king and by Count Bertrand. Only the Genoese sailors indulged in pillage and massacre in their sector. In spite of these excesses, since their support had been decisive, Bertrand granted them extensive trading privileges as well as granting the little town of Gibelet (Jebail) to the Genoese family of Embriaco in fee.

Thus was the Toulousain county of Tripoli finally established, extending along the Lebanon coast between the principality of Antioch and the kingdom of Jerusalem. According to the arbitration of Baldwin I, this county was to be shared between Bertrand at Tripoli and William-Jordan at Tortosa. This was obviously a source of complications for the future. An "accident," which seems too opportune not to have been provoked, put an end to this delicate situation. One evening a brawl broke out between the retainers of the two houses; William-Jordan hastened to separate them and at that moment was shot in the ribs by an arrow and fell dead. "Some say that it was Bertrand who treacherously contrived this foul deed, but no man could ever know the truth or discover the assassin. The fact remains," adds the chronicle cautiously, "that William's share reverted to Bertrand." And Fulcher of Chartres, for his part, philosophically concludes: "Some lamented, others were well content. Bertrand remained sole master of the county, he who had sworn himself the king's liege-man."

It was high time for the Frankish princes to reunite under the energetic drive of Baldwin I. For the first time since the capture of Jerusalem, the Turkish world was now stirring with a view to a counter-crusade. In 1110 the Seljuk Sultan of Persia organized a great expedition for this purpose, at the head of which he placed his lieutenant, Mawdud, emir of Mosul. In April or May 1110, Mawdud, with a powerful army, laid siege to Edessa.

On the approach of the Turks, the count of Edessa, Baldwin of Le Bourg, hastily dispatched Joscelin of Courtenay to Palestine to demand help from King Baldwin I. The situation was all the more serious since Prince Tancred of Antioch, who, being nearer, could have furnished more rapid aid, again gave proof of ill will. Baldwin I set off at once, rallying all the available contingents on his route. In a few weeks he had thus mobilized 15,000 men, with whom he appeared in the plain of Edessa. The chronicle joyously describes the arrival of this reinforcing army, "banners and helms gleaming under the rays of the summer sun, the trumpets sounding bravely, all the tumult of a great army." The Turks had not waited for it. They had beat a retreat toward Haran.

Edessa was saved, but the king of Jerusalem felt the need to put an end to these dissensions between the Franks. In the event of a fresh Turkish attack on Edessa, they must be able to count upon the aid of the chivalry of Antioch. The king therefore summoned Tancred to explain his defection and, if need be, to state his complaints before his peers. So bitter was the animosity of the Norman prince that he hesitated to obey. He finally agreed to comply, under pressure from his entourage and because, in the presence of the Turkish menace, any longer absence would have been equivalent to treason. Correctly, on his arrival, he came to salute the king, by whom he was cordially welcomed. When Baldwin then asked him the reasons for his attitude, he replied by claiming the suzerainty over Edessa, "the town having at all times been a fee of Antioch."

Albert of Aix gives us the gist of the reply of Baldwin I, a veritable royal pronouncement, full of force and majesty: "My brother Tancred, what you ask is unjust. You argue from the status of the country under Moslem domination, but you must remember that, when we set off for the Holy War, it was agreed that each of us should keep whatever he took from the infidels. For the rest, you have constituted a king, that he might serve you as chief, safeguard, and guide in the preservation and in the extension of our conquests. That is why I have the right, in the name of all Christendom, here represented, to demand your sincere reconciliation with Baldwin of Le Bourg. Otherwise, if you prefer to intrigue with the Turks, you cannot remain one of us, and we shall fight you without mercy." This time Tancred finally acquiesced.

Unfortunately, in the face of the Turkish reaction which was beginning to take shape, the Frankish chiefs had to resign themselves to a painful sacrifice. While naturally retaining all their fortified towns, they evacuated all the native Christians—Armenian, "Greek," or Syrian—from the open towns and countryside of the county of Edessa lying on the eastern bank of the Euphrates. This exodus, enforced by military necessity and decided in the interests of the populations themselves, was disturbed by the incursion of the Turkish cavalry, which, at the moment of the crossing of the Euphrates, fell upon the columns of emigrants and massacred multitudes with showers of arrows under the eyes of the powerless Franks who wept with rage. Tancred, exasperated by these scenes of horror, took immediate vengeance on his nearest neighbors, the Aleppo Turks. In the course of a punitive expedition he seized two strongholds of the kingdom of Aleppo, Athareb and Zerdana, and forced the Turkish king of Aleppo and the

Arab Emirs of Shaizar and Hama to recognize themselves as his tributaries (end of 1100).

And yet a second counter-crusade was in preparation. In the souks of Aleppo indignation arose against the audacity of the Frankish raiders who were intercepting trade between the coast and the interior and condemning the rich caravaning city to waste away. Unable to stir their Turkish King to energetic action, a number of Aleppo burgesses went to Baghdad to rouse a clamor in the great mosque one Friday, the Moslem day of prayer, demanding the intervention of the caliph and the sultan against the accursed Franks. The demonstrators aroused the populace, interrupted the prayers, broke up the *minbar*, and intimidated the caliph and the sultan to such purpose that they promised to send a relieving army to Syria. Once again, it was the atabeg of Mosul, Mawdud, who was given command of the Turkish forces.

In the spring of 1111, the Turkish army, in full muster, sounded the walls of Edessa. Reinforced the year before by the king of Jerusalem, the city was impregnable. Mawdud made for Aleppo, which he meant to make the hinge of his campaign against the principality of Antioch. But there a surprise awaited him. The king of Aleppo, Ridwan the Turk, seeing such a formidable army come to his aid, was the first to take fright. The Franks seemed to him much less redoubtable than all these compatriots and co-religionists come from all the corners of the Seljuk Empire to defend him. And refusing to break the truce which he had concluded with Tancred, he shut the gates of Aleppo before the stupefied Mawdud, who was forced to change his plan of campaign by warring against the Franks in the direction of the upper Orontes, where at least the other local Turkish chief, Toghtekin, atabeg of Damascus, joined up with him.

Meanwhile, the Franks had completed their concentration. Baldwin of Le Bourg, count of Edessa, King Baldwin I of Jerusalem, and Count Bertrand of Tripoli, with a grand total of 16,000 knights, mounted sergeants, and infantry had hastened to the side of Prince Tancred of Antioch, directly threatened. The Christian army moved into position near Apamea on the middle Orontes, a central point to keep watch on Syria, Lebanon, and Palestine at the same time. The Turkish army lay a little farther south, at Shaizar. For several weeks the two adversaries observed each other, marching and countermarching, but not venturing to join battle. A limited action on September 29, 1111,

yielded no result. Finally, faced with the close-knit phalanx of Frank-
ish forces, as well as the lack of zeal on the part of the Syrian Moslems,
Mawdud lost heart. The Turkish Grand Army crossed back over the
Euphrates without having scored any success. . . .

It must be recognized that this result was the doing of Baldwin I
himself. Frankish Syria, built up of shreds and patches, at the hazard
of individual initiatives, still had no overall existence, no coherence, at
the time of Godfrey of Bouillon's death. It was Baldwin I, who by
assuming first the royal title and then the royal functions, with all the
obligations involved in title and functions, by unceasingly rendering his
potential vassals the services of a feudal suzerain, by forcing them to
unite in face of the enemy, really created a Frankish Syria. The
campaign of 1111 clearly showed him in this role of uncontested chief,
federator of the Frankish energies. Henceforth until 1186, Frankish
Syria was to form, in spite of its feudal partition, a united whole. The
monarchic institutions founded by the genius of the first Baldwin were
to ensure the country ninety-six years of stability. Frankish Syria had
found its Capetians.

Not the least merit of Baldwin I was his success, by dint of firmness
and good grace, in silencing Tancred's opposition and rallying his old
personal adversary to the royal policy. Tancred had become a determined partisan of Frankish concord when he died in Antioch on
December 12, 1112.

Tancred was certainly the real founder of the principality of Antioch. It is true that the first idea of the Norman establishment went
back to his uncle, Bohemund. It was Bohemund who had first set his
sights on the valley of the Lower Orontes. But his adventurous spirit
had constantly launched him on distant enterprises, to which he had
finally succumbed. For this grandson of the Vikings, his Syrian duchy
was visibly only an episode, a phase, a stepping-stone. His dream was
nothing less than Constantinople, the Empire of the East. Tancred, on
the contrary, devoted himself singly to Syria. In Bohemund there was
still the restlessness of the great Norman adventurers of the eleventh
century, men like Roussel of Bailleul, today the possessors of immense
provinces, tomorrow captive and despoiled of everything. Tancred,
for his part, was already settled on his territory. Patiently, jealously,
from Latakia to Athareb, he enlarged his domain. The bad grace, the

bad faith, which he showed when he had to restore the county of Edessa to Baldwin of Le Bourg attest in this Norman to a land hunger, a spirit of enclosures, and a sense of deep roots which are highly characteristic. Like Baldwin I in Palestine, he laid the foundations in North Syria for a lasting dynastic tradition, already adapted to its environment.

Tancred's coinage is the symbol of his work. The legends are in the Greek language; the Norman chief is represented in a costume partly Byzantine, partly Moslem, wearing on his head the ample *kaffleh* wound in a turban. On one of his coins, moreover, we read the unexpected title of "Grand Emir Tankridos." There is no doubt that this aspect of a Christian emir represented the image which the Norman conqueror wanted to create in the minds of his Eastern subjects.

King Baldwin's policy of reconciliation had been so fruitful that, toward the end of his life, Tancred had been charged with teaching the art of arms to the young Pons, son of his old enemy, Count Bertrand of Tripoli. Did the page show a secret admiration for Tancred's very young wife, the Capetian Princess Cecilia of France? And did Tancred perceive it? If so, he never showed it; but on his deathbed he entrusted Cecilia to Pons, asking him to marry her when he should be no more. In accordance with his last wishes, Cecilia therefore married Pons as her second husband and reigned with him over the county of Tripoli. She seems to have brought the young count as part of her dowry the famous fortress afterward known as the Krak des Chevaliers, which Tancred had taken from the Arabs in June 1110 and which then became part of the Toulousain county.

The dying Tancred left the principality of Antioch to one of his cousins, the Norman-Italian Prince Roger of Salerno. The chroniclers have been rather hard on this young man, who had married the sister of Baldwin of Le Bourg but whose ardent temperament recked little of the laws of marriage. Even in Sicily, all these Norman princes had allowed themselves to be greatly influenced by Arab polygamy, and it was naturally much worse in a Levantine climate and among the habits of the Levant. Roger was a true Norman also in his "love of gain," but even the chronicler who assigns him all these defects is bound to admit that "in all truth he was a knight and a valiant one." In fact, no more magnificent paladin ever governed Frankish Syria. His short reign (1112–1119) is one epic course from victory to victory until the day when his reckless daring earned him a hero's death.

He was soon to have an opportunity to prove his valor by coming to the aid of King Baldwin I.

The atabeg or Turkish governor of Mosul, Mawdud, whom the Seljuk Sultan of Persia and the caliph of Baghdad had placed in command of the counter-crusade, had not forgotten his mission. Having failed in 1110 and 1111 through the fault of the Syrian Moslems, he returned to the attack in 1113 when circumstances were more favorable. In May of that year, he crossed the Euphrates and joined forces on the upper Orontes with the atabeg of Damascus, Toghtekin. The two Turkish chiefs then invaded the kingdom of Jerusalem through Galilee, which they ravaged cruelly. Then, before the approach of the Frankish army, they took up their position at the southern end of the Sea of Galilee, behind the mouth of the Jordan.

At news of the invasion, King Baldwin I called urgently upon the other Frankish princes, especially Roger of Antioch and Pons of Tripoli. Unfortunately, the ravages of the Turks had exasperated him. Repeating the rash act which had cost him so dear in 1102, he would not wait for the arrival of Roger and Pons. With the contingents of the kingdom of Jerusalem alone—700 knights and 4,000 foot soldiers —he hastened to meet the Turks and took up his position quite close to them at Sennabra near the southwest shore of the Sea of Galilee (June 20, 1113). The Turks, seeing his confidence, lured him into a trap. From the east bank of the Jordan they dispatched to the other side, in the direction of Sennabra, 2,000 picked horsemen. Fifteen hundred lay in ambush behind the bridge over the Jordan; the remaining 500 went to provoke Baldwin at Sennabra. Foolishly, Baldwin fell upon them and fell right into the ambush. He was already in a very bad way, when the main body of the Turkish army arrived in a whirlwind over the Jordan bridge and crushed him by weight of numbers. The king, banner in hand, tried to rally his men but found himself so hard pressed that, once again, he owed his safety solely to the speed of his horse. The whole camp, including the royal tent, fell into the hands of the Turks. Many fugitives were drowned in the waters of the Sea of Galilee. Most of the knights, however, were able to find refuge in the town of Tiberias (June 28, 1113).

As in the days of Ramleh, Baldwin could see the abyss into which his impetuosity had cast him. The misadventure was all the more bitter since it would have been sufficient to wait two or three days to receive the reinforcements from Antioch and Tripoli. Roger and Pons in fact arrived with the flower of their chivalry. Baldwin frankly avowed his error and they took counsel together. Reconstituted, and now at full strength, the Frankish army again represented a respectable force. But as the Turks were still superior in numbers, they lay in wait on the heights west of the Sea of Galilee while enemy raiders ravaged the plain. The worst thing was that the Arab fellahin joined the invader in sacking the open towns. Baldwin, made cautious by experience, had the will power to submit to these provocations impassively for a whole month. Moreover, August was approaching, the moment when the Italian squadrons landed the annual pilgrimage in the Holy Land. This year there were 16,000 pilgrims, a substantial reinforcement which was to reverse the proportions of the two armies. In addition, the Turkish army was exhausted by the heat and short of supplies. Mawdud realized that the campaign had been a failure. He dismissed the greater part of his troops and retired to Damascus in company with his ally, the Atabeg Toghtekin (August 30, 1113).

It was at this point that a somewhat mysterious drama occurred, whose consequences completed the disunion of the Moslem forces, to the advantage of the Franks. On Friday, October 2, 1113, as Mawdud was attending public prayers in the great mosque at Damascus, an assassin fell upon him and mortally wounded him with repeated dagger strokes. Who had armed the killer? Public opinion accused Toghtekin. It is certain that the atabeg of Damascus, accustomed to play the sovereign, cannot have relished the installation at his side of the supreme representative of the sultan. In any event, the Moslem world laid the crime at his door, and Toghtekin was soon reduced to allying himself with the Franks.

In 1115 the sultan of Persia sent a new Turkish army to Syria, under the command of the Emir Bursuq, with orders both to pursue the counter-crusade with success and to restore the Moslems of Aleppo and Damascus to obedience. Toghtekin and the other threatened emirs measured the whole extent of the peril. The sultan's authority over Moslem Syria could be restored only at the cost of their own eviction. Against the menace of the Turkish central authorities they had no hesitation in declaring their solidarity with the Franks. The spectacle was therefore seen of the chiefs of Moslem Syria and the Frankish princes joining forces to bar the road to the sultan's army.

The allies joined up in the summer of 1115 in the region of Apamea on the Middle Orontes, a central point well chosen to protect both Aleppo and Antioch, Damascus and the kingdom of Jerusalem. King Baldwin I, Prince Roger of Antioch, Count Pons of Tripoli, the emirs of Aleppo and Toghtekin, atabeg of Damascus, were all there. The chronicle takes delight in showing us the Turk Toghtekin and Roger riding out side by side, "like good and loyal companions in arms."

Bursuq realized that he could not break this front. He made a feint of renouncing his undertaking and beat his retreat toward Al Jazira. The allies, unsuspecting, dispersed to their own homes. Immediately, he came back to Syria and invaded the part of the principality of Antioch lying east of the middle Orontes.

Roger of Antioch leaped to arms. There was no time now to call upon the king of Jerusalem or the atabeg of Damascus. Roger contented himself with calling on the aid of the count of Edessa, Baldwin of Le Bourg and, crossing the Orontes with him at Jisr-esh-Shugur, advanced to meet the Turks under the shelter of the wooded massif of Feilun, which concealed their march. He sent one of his best knights, Theodore of Barneville, to reconnoiter and had just halted when Barneville came galloping back, hell bent for leather, to say that the Turks were close at hand, on the other side of the wood, pitching their tents with the greatest security at the foot of the hill of Tel-Danith. The recital of Walter the Chancellor reflects the epic joy of the Norman army at the news of the surprise in store. Roger lost no time in sounding boot-and-saddle: "In the name of our God, to arms, knights!" The relic of the True Cross was displayed before the squadrons which deployed toward Tel-Danith. It was dawn on September 14. Roger galloped in the center, Baldwin of Le Bourg, on the left wing, on the right the native cavalry of the Turkopoles, the Arab scouts of Frankish Syria.

When all this cavalry fell upon them, the Turks were moving toward Danith in the utmost disorder. "The baggage train and beasts of burden were in the van of the army, and the troops marched behind the baggage, hand in hand; all were lulled into the greatest security, not thinking that anyone would attack them; the troops had not yet reached the camp, prepared a march ahead; the tents, already pitched, were still unoccupied except by the army sutlers." The Frankish cavalry, like a raging storm, fell first upon the camp, almost void of defenders, and took it in an instant, and then upon the Turkish divisions, which came up in successive detachments, in dispersed order, and were taken completely by surprise, one after another. Bursuq,, with 800 horsemen, tried to rally his men on the hill of Tel-Danith; but the hill was taken by assault by Baldwin of Le Bourg, and the Turkish chief had to resign himself to flight. He was to die of chagrin on his return to Hamadan.

This brilliant victory won the prince of Antioch an unrivaled prestige in the Moslem world. Under the name of Sirojal (Sir Roger) he was, like Richard the Lionhearted at a later date, to be immortalized in legend. Without a fight, by the mere fact of military pressure, the Turkish Arab kingdom of Aleppo came under his protection.

Meanwhile, in Palestine, King Baldwin I was successfully completing a task which lay close to his heart, the occupation of Arabia Petraea. As early as November and December 1100, as we have seen, he had sent out a first reconnaissance as far as Petra. In 1116, "always eager to blaze new trails," he pushed farther into the depression of the Wadi el-Araba, which from the south of the Dead Sea runs in a long narrow valley to the Gulf of Akaba on the Red Sea. At Shobak, on a hill to the north of the ancient Petra, he had just built the fortified castle of Montreal, designed to dominate the whole valley. Plunging beyond Montreal, he thrust as far as Aila on the Red Sea. For half a century the Franks were to be able to intercept at will the caravan trade between Egypt and Moslem Asia and even to control the pilgrim road to Mecca. In March 1118, Baldwin I sent out a reconnaissance expedition along the coast of Philistia toward the Nile Delta, in the direction of the Pelusiac Branch and the town of Farama, which was found undefended. Just as the chroniclers formerly showed us the Franks amusing themselves by bathing and fishing in the Red Sea, they now paint the pride and wonderment of Baldwin on contemplating "the great Egyptian river." But it was in this exploration of the neighborhood of the delta that the king contracted the illness which was to lay him low.

Before closing the reign of Baldwin I, a brief word remains to be said about what may be called his internal policy. For this prodigious warrior was also one of the most lucid organizers of his time.

One of the questions which concerned him most was peopling Palestine with Christians. He had been very struck by the fact that, at the time of the Turkish invasion of 1113, some of the fellahin or Moslem peasants who were subjects of the Franks had made common cause with the enemy. Moreover, the Arab population of the towns had been exterminated or expelled at the time of the conquest and the cities of Palestine had remained almost empty. It was unfortunately impossible to stimulate adequate Latin immigration, the "population crusades" having wasted away in the deserts of Asia Minor in 1101. It was then that Baldwin I summoned to Palestine all the communities of native Christians, both Greek and Syrian, scattered throughout Moslem Syria and Transjordan. He settled them in the towns and villages, granting them the franchise of all the houses and lands abandoned by the Moslems. Thus an Arab-speaking Christian population was created in the towns as well as in the countryside to support the Frankish political and military leaders. To gain a solid foothold in the country, the new kingdom had in fact to be based on a close association between Franks and Syrians. It was the great merit of Baldwin I that he understood this in spite of all the rivalries between rites which disturbed (and still disturb today) the peace of the Holy Places.

At the same time, moreover, those Frankish conquerors and pilgrims who stayed on in Syria adapted themselves from day to day and gave birth to a new people, and even to a colonial spirit, whose appearance was expressly welcomed by the chronicler Fulcher of Chartres, chaplain to Baldwin I: "Westerners, we have been transformed into dwellers in the East. Yesterday's Italian or Frenchman, transplanted, has become a Galilean or a Palestinian. The man of Rheims or of Chartres has been transformed into a Tyrian or a citizen of Antioch. Already, we have forgotten our origins. Here one man now holds his house and home with as much assurance as though it were by immemorial right of inheritance in the country. Another has already married a Syrian, an Armenian, sometimes even a baptized Saracen, and lives with a whole fine native family. We speak all the diverse languages of the country in turn. The settler has become a native; the immigrant cannot be distinguished from the old resident. Every day relations and friends come from the West to join us. They do not hesitate to leave all their possessions there behind them. Indeed, the man who was poor at home attains opulence here; he who had no more than a few deniers, finds himself master of a fortune. The man who did not possess even a village in Europe finds himself in the East lord of a whole city. Why should we return to the West when the East gives us all our hearts' desires?"

We have seen how, by a generally very skillful policy toward the native population, Baldwin I succeeded in firmly establishing the kingdom of Jerusalem in Eastern lands. It remains to recall how he likewise succeeded in establishing Frankish royalty within Latin society.

At the outset, as we have said, Baldwin had to combat the Patriarch Daimbert. He had succeeded in being crowned king by Daimbert. But, apart from Baldwin's own grudge, the sovereign was stirred up against Daimbert by the deposed former patriarch, Arnulf Malecorne. Baldwin, at Arnulf's instigation, appealed to Pope Paschal II, accusing Daimbert of having formerly fomented civil strife between the Franks in the presence of the enemy, an accusation which was unfortunately justified, since a council held at Jerusalem under the presidency of a papal legate prohibited Daimbert from officiating at the Good Friday ceremonies on the Mount of Olives. And yet the council and the king were in favor of indulgence when shortly afterward, at the height of the war against Egypt, Baldwin begged the patriarch for a loan to equip his troops and Daimbert swore that he had no more than 200 silver marks laid by. The king was inclined to believe him, when Archdeacon Arnulf Malecorne and other clerics demonstrated that the patriarch was hiding enormous sums. Furious, Baldwin burst into the patriarch's palace. That very night a great banquet was in progress; the dishes were particularly choice and the wine was flowing freely. On a sudden Baldwin I broke in among the guests. His shattering indictment, the substance of which is preserved for us by Albert of Aix, pilloried the avarice of the faithless prelate: "You spend your time in banqueting while night and day we risk our lives for the defense of the Church. Careless of our soldiers' suffering you devour the offerings of the faithful among yourselves. But I swear to you that unless you pay the troops their wages this very instant, you will not long fill your bellies with the tributes of Christendom!" To which Daimbert apparently answered that the priest was entitled to live from the altar and it was not for the Church to be the serf of royalty. But the king continued, in a paroxysm of rage, "Let those who serve the altar live from the altar, you say? So be it! In that case my soldiers shall be the first to live from it, for it is they who best serve the Church, since they defend her against the Saracens day after day! And it is not only the alms of the Church that I will have to pay my troops, but all the gold of the Holy Sepulcher which I will take to equip the army, for the Saracens are at our gates! When they have been repulsed, when the Holy Land is out of danger, I will return to the Church a hundredfold that which I borrow from it!" No doubt, as Albert of Aix points out, Baldwin's former ecclesiastical studies, his knowledge of the canon law and of sacred eloquence were not without value to him in this vehement diatribe.

An even greater scandal came to the king's service. Prince Roger of Apulia had sent the patriarchate a thousand bezants to be shared among the canons of the Holy Sepulcher, the Hospital, and the pay of the knights. Daimbert, in his senile avarice, kept it all for himself. On learning of this, the king made the scandal public and Daimbert was declared deprived of his see. But the obstinate old man still would not desist. He retired to Antioch, among his old Norman friends, whom he succeeded in convincing that he was in the right. In the autumn of 1102, when Baldwin, threatened by an Egyptian invasion, could not do without the aid of the Normans, Daimbert succeeded in getting their backing and, under pressure from them, was reinstated in his patriarchal see. Always the politician, Baldwin yielded, concealing his anger. But as soon as the Egyptian danger was averted, he asked for the case to be referred to the papal legate, Cardinal Robert of Paris. Daimbert, finally convicted of simony and the misappropriation of church funds, was again condemned by the cardinal-legate and the synod. He left Palestine for the last time, for the greater good of the Church and of the crown.

A holy man, Evremar of Thérouanne, was elected patriarch in his place and in 1105 was to prove himself also of stout heart when he bore the True Cross in the midst of the melee at the battle of Ramleh. There is no need to recount here how Evremar subsequently fell victim to the intrigues of the ambitious Archdeacon Arnulf Malecorne, who, formerly dismissed from the patriarchal see for unworthiness, was always plotting how to get back. For the moment, deeming that the time was not yet ripe, Arnulf contented himself with securing the election of the archbishop of Arles, Gibelin of Sabran, who, apart from his great sanctity, had the additional merit of being very old (1108). On Gibelin's death, Arnulf finally succeeded in being restored to the patriarchate (1112). Archbishop William of Tyre, who pursues "Malecorne" with his spite, applies to him the most uncomplimentary verses of the Book of Job: "It is because of the sins of the people that God allows the triumph of the hypocrite." Indeed, while Arnulf merits praise for his devotion to the interests of the king and the kingdom, and for his undeniable Frankish patriotism, we are bound to admit that, in his desire to please Baldwin I, he sometimes carried complaisance to the extent of complicity. An example was the affair of the king's marriages.

While he was still only count of Edessa, Baldwin, it will be remembered, had married Princess Arda, the daughter of an Armenian chief of the Taurus, a political marriage if ever there was one, which won him the support of the predominant Armenian element in Edessa. But after his coronation in Jerusalem, where the Armenians counted for nothing, this union was a burden to him. In the same cavalier fashion in which he had deposed the patriarch, he placed his wife in a convent. "Of his own authority, he entered her into religion and made her become a nun in the Church of Our Lady Saint Anne." It is true, adds the chronicle, that he took it to heart to enrich the convent. On the precise motives for his decision, the good William of Tyre loses himself in conjectures. "Some men said that he left her for a richer bride, since she was dowerless, others that he had perceived her to be very flighty." The queen, in any case, seemed at first highly delighted to enter into religion and led a most edifying life in the convent, after which she modestly prayed the king to let her go to Constantinople to see her parents and beg an endowment for her nunnery. Once out of the kingdom, she joyfully cast aside her nun's habit and gave herself up entirely to pleasure, "delivering her body to striplings and to other folk." As for King Baldwin, it is said that he took no less pleasure in the return to a bachelor life. But the bachelor life brought him no money, and it was then that he cast his eyes on Adelaide of Sicily.

Adelaide was the widow of the Norman Count Roger I of Sicily, who had died in 1101. Despite her ripe age, she was one of the finest matches of the century. Baldwin set his sights on her. He was impecunious in the extreme and the pay of his knights was a constant problem to him. He asked for the dowager's hand in marriage. She was flattered at being chosen again by a knight of such prestige, moved at the thought of wearing with him the sacred crown of Jerusalem. The marriage treaty was concluded; and early in August 1113, Adelaide landed at Acre.

Albert of Aix depicts for us with all the wealth of a tapestry the arrival of the Sicilian squadron escorting the royal bride. There were two triremes, each manned by five hundred picked warriors, and seven other vessels loaded with gold, silver, purple, precious stones, rich fabrics, and shining armor. In the vessel which carried the princess, a gilded mast gleamed in the sunlight, and the two prows, encrusted with gold and silver, were no less marvelous to behold. In another ship, the Arab bowmen of the Sicilian Guard displayed their burnouses of a dazzling whiteness. Baldwin, for his part, came to greet his bride in his great ceremonial royal robes, with all his dignitaries and all his pages in their finest array, their horses and mules caparisoned in purple and gold, to the fanfare of trumpets and joyful music. The streets of Acre were covered with many-colored carpets, purple banners waved from the balconies, and the joy was universal.

But once the festival was over, the irregular situation, to say the least of it, had to be faced. Baldwin's former wife was still alive. The king was therefore a bigamist. Adelaide, it appears, was very distressed to learn of it officially, though it seems somewhat strange that she had not known of it earlier. . . . Baldwin, moreover, had transferred to his own coffers, with inelegant haste the riches brought him by his new bride. As for her scruples, he calmed them with the aid of the Patriarch Arnulf Malecorne, who made no bones about such a trifle.

Rome was nevertheless disturbed, both by the king's bigamy and by Malecorne's complaisance. The courtly patriarch was summoned by Pope Paschal II, who bade him end the scandal. On his return to Jerusalem, Arnulf therefore broached the subject with the king. For a time Baldwin turned a deaf ear; then, following a serious illness in March 1117, he yielded. Adelaide was dismissed. The unfortunate princess wept copiously and complained bitterly that she had been tricked. The king had indeed waited to make peace with his conscience until he had completely devoured the rich dowry brought from Sicily. . . . But when he died soon after, on his return from the Egyptian frontier on April 2, 1118, the scandalous situation nevertheless existed of the king of Jerusalem's dying excommunicated.

Baldwin of Boulogne, the first Frankish King of liberated Jerusalem, was therefore certainly not a saint, as was his brother Godfrey of Bouillon; but from the political point of view, he had undoubtedly been the man of the hour, cut to the measure of the epic, or rather dominating it, since he alone among all these paladins fully understood how to make this epic a reality, to his own advantage. In him the unscrupulous adventurer had quite naturally and quite continuously given place to the statesman. Violence and patience, fire and caution, hypocrisy or cynicism, loyalty, brutality, or perfidy, crimes as well as virtues—but crimes committed for the public safety, virtues of a chief —all these elements in a closely woven personality were controlled and dominated in him by reasons of state, ordered with an eye to reasons of state. The ancient Greeks, in the manner of empire builders, would have surnamed him Baldwin the Founder. This Frankish state of Jerusalem, born of surprise, was to find itself, once established by him, so firmly founded overnight that no one after him ventured to challenge it. It is in this fact that the formidable adventurer transcends the adventure. He made this far borderland of Christendom what it must be if it was to remain viable, a solid military monarchy. The patriarchate, in the hands of his friend Arnulf Malecorne, became the faithful partner of this policy. However free his morals, moreover, it must not be forgotten that before girding on the sword, Baldwin had been a son of the Church, always physically retaining the dignified bearing of the former canon of Cambrai and intellectually the ordered Roman mind. He created majesty. He even created a legitimacy by divine law—and the most sacred in the Christian world—by linking himself with the royalty of David and of Solomon. In the eighteen years of his reign he even succeeded in laying the foundations of a monarchical tradition, equal, because founded on the rock of Sion, to that of the Capetien kings of France, the Norman kings of England, or the Germanic Roman Emperor.

And the whole subsequent history of the kingdom of Jerusalem remains his work.

5

THE CONSOLIDATION
OF THE CONQUEST
Baldwin II

FATE willed it that, at the moment of the death of Baldwin I, his cousin, Baldwin of Le Bourg, count of Edessa, had just set out to perform his devotions at Jerusalem. He arrived in the Holy City on the very day of the king's funeral and was immediately proposed for the vacant throne by the leading direct vassal of the crown in Palestine, Joscelin of Courtenay, lord of Tiberias. Joscelin had formerly possessed the lands of Turbessel (Tel-Basheir) in the county of Edessa, which he held in fee from Baldwin of Le Bourg; but having quarreled with Baldwin, he was stripped of these possessions and had taken refuge with the king, who had invested him with the fee of Tiberias (1113). To the general surprise, instead of seizing the opportunity to show his resentment, he constituted himself, on the death of Baldwin I, the grand elector of Baldwin of Le Bourg. The other barons, greatly edified by such moral virtue, seconded him. Baldwin of Le Bourg was proclaimed king (1118). In reality, Joscelin had no doubt counted on the new king, owing him his throne, to show his gratitude. And so it was. The count of Edessa, on ascending the throne of Jerusalem, ceded Edessa to Joscelin.

Baldwin of Le Bourg, henceforth to be called Baldwin II, was the son of the count of Rethel in the Ardennes. Tall, good-looking, high-colored, with fair but scanty hair, soon to turn white, his beard also scanty but worn very long, in the fashion of the day, he was, like his predecessor, an accomplished knight. His character, however, was very different. Rather than the harshness and rough violence of which Baldwin I had so often given proof, the new sovereign preferred, if not, as has been said, dissimulation and ruse, at least malicious subtlety and ingenious calculations. In a comic scene worthy of the best fables, William of Tyre gives us a glimpse of this side of his character.

At the time of the story, Baldwin II, who was still only count of Edessa, was in serious financial straits, the pay of his knights being beyond his means. Now, he had married the Princess Morphia, daughter of the lord of Melitene, the Armenian Gabriel, and Gabriel was very rich. To get out of his difficulties, after conniving with his knights, he went, escorted by them, to visit his father-in-law. The good old man, delighted to see him (for, unlike Baldwin I, Baldwin II was an ideal husband), greeted him affectionately; "he embraced him, made great cheer, and installed him as best he could. Baldwin stayed at Melitene I know not how long. Father-in-law and son-in-law were the best friends in the world." One fine day, as they were talking affectionately in the palace, up came Baldwin's knights in a body to the door and their spokesman (who had naturally concerted the whole thing with Baldwin in advance) firmly demanded their pay or else the surrender of the promised pledge. In answer to Gabriel's anxious questions, Baldwin confessed with embarrassment that he had promised his knights, if he could not pay them, to let his beard be cut off. On hearing these words, the excellent Gabriel almost fell over backwards, "for the Armenians, like the Greeks, are accustomed to wearing their beards as full as possible and consider it a dishonor to have even a single hair plucked from them." Baldwin begged his knights for more time. Firm refusal on their part: pay on the nail or off with the beard! The scene had been so well played that the worthy Armenian himself offered to pay the 30,000 bezants or so which were necessary, but not without making his son-in-law swear never, never again to pledge his beard—"which Baldwin very willingly swore," concludes the chronicler drily.

Another story, still of the time when Baldwin II was no more than count of Edessa, shows him in the same light, though this time the scene ends with a touch worthy of Corneille himself. The lands of Edessa, which had just been cruelly ravaged by the Turks, were suffering from a veritable famine and once again Baldwin found himself in dire financial difficulties. His vassal, on the other hand, Joscelin of Courtenay, whose fief of Turbessel, protected by the course of the Euphrates, had escaped invasion, was swimming in wealth. Drunk with prosperity, Joscelin was tactless enough to utter imprudent words; he, Joscelin, could buy up the whole land of Edessa from his impecunious suzerain, who would do much better, if he could not keep up his rank, to go back and live in France. Learning of these discourtesies, Baldwin pretended to be seriously ill and summoned Joscelin to his bedside. Joscelin, convinced that he was being called to enter into an inheritance, obeyed with alacrity. On being ushered in, he found Baldwin in bed and asked solicitously after his health. "Much better than you would wish!" replied Baldwin, and throwing off the mask, he rounded violently on Joscelin, recalling all his benefits, like Augustus and Cinna: "Joscelin, have you anything here except what I have given you?"—"Nothing, sire!"—"Then how can you reproach me with my present poverty as a shame?" And after overwhelming him with invective, he cast him into a narrow dungeon and only released him on depriving him of his fief. . . . We have seen, moreover, how the two men, equally astute, took advantage of the events of 1118 to become reconciled, to their greater mutual advantage of.

Still other characteristics, enumerated by the chroniclers, demonstrate that flexible tenacity which was the whole basis of Baldwin II's temperament. It must be added at once that, with him, ruse never degenerated into treason, or energy into brutality, as with his predecessor. His firmness was always tempered with moderation and, in the end, with clemency. The fact is that Baldwin II, like Godfrey of Bouillon before him, was profoundly Christian. Baldwin I had lived on the fringe of the Church; he had imposed an openly simoniac patriarch on the faithful and, almost right up to his death, had remained in a state of bigamy. Baldwin II, on the contrary, was extremely pious; the chronicle describes his knees all callused from his frequent devotions. The influence of religion was clearly visible in his high sense of duty and the admirable way in which he was to exercise the craft of kingship as a Christian king.

In the exercise of power, we see Baldwin II as a diligent and punctilious administrator (he was nicknamed "the Goad"), a conscientious and methodical captain (the way he was to save and restore the principality of Antioch after the disaster of 1119 is above all praise), a prudent head of state, without the fiery temperament of Baldwin I but without his gambler's tricks either.

His private life, unlike that of Baldwin I, was irreproachable. He was always faithful to his Armenian wife, the Princess Morphia, and gave her four daughters, Melisende, Alice, Hodierna, and Joveta (or Yvette). Sober and simply dressed, "without arrogance and without pride," he differed in that too from his predecessor, who had always shown himself fond of luxury and pomp. Economical, and even a little parsimonious in the ordinary way of life, he nevertheless knew how to spend, and to spend magnificently. To sum up, he proved himself at Jerusalem, on a wider stage, what he had already been at Edessa: "He ruled well and vigorously and made himself beloved by his subjects and feared by the enemy."

Four years after his accession, Baldwin II had to defend the royal authority against a somewhat unexpected revolt. "The devil, who has never loved peace, sowed discord in the land." In 1122, Count Pons of Tripoli refused homage and feudal service. It was the whole monarchical organization of Frankish Syria, as triumphantly established by the late king, which was challenged. Baldwin II, furious with rage, called the ban for a march on Tripoli. The monarchic sentiment was already so strong that barons and knights shared the king's indignation. When the royal army, leaving Acre, was nearing the Lebanon, the knights of Tripoli themselves approached Pons and convinced him of his folly. They led him repentant to the king, who pardoned him.

Under the reign of Baldwin II, the force of Frankish Syria was considerably strengthened by the creation of the Order of Knights Templar and the conversion of the Order of Hospitalers into a military order.

The Hospitalers derived their name from a charitable establishment, both hostelry and hospital, founded around 1070 for poor pilgrims. The establishment was converted at the time of the First Crusade by a holy man called Gerard, who came from the town of Martigues in Provence and must be regarded as the true founder of the Order of Hospitalers. Gerard died about 1120 and was succeeded as grand master of the order by Raymond of Le Puy, who profoundly changed its character by turning the charitable community into a militia of knightly monks vowed to the defense of the Holy Sepulcher. The Order of Templars, on the other hand, had a military character from the outset. Founded in 1118 by Hugh of Payens, a knight from Champagne, who installed it in Solomon's Temple (the modern Mosque of al-Aqsa), it took from that the name of the Order of Templars. The two orders gave the kingdom of Jerusalem what it most needed, a standing army to which the feudal array afforded no equivalent. By their incomparable bravery, their spirit of sacrifice, and their knowledge of Moslem warfare, Knights Hospitaler and Knights Templar rendered inestimable service to the Frankish cause. It was only later that made proud by their valor and their wealth, they developed a tendency, especially the Templars, to follow a troublesome particularist policy and too often gave proof of insubordination to the kingdom as well as to the Church.

Baldwin II had to give of his full measure following the dramatic events which overwhelmed the principality of Antioch in 1119.

At the beginning of 1119, Prince Roger of Antioch was on the point of taking the great Arab town of Aleppo. The people of Aleppo called on the aid of a Turkish chief of Diyarbekir, Ilghazi, of the Ortoqid clan, emir of Mardin. At the beginning of June, Ilghazi, coming down from Diyarbekir with a powerful army, invaded the principality of Antioch from the direction of Roudj, east of the Orontes between Jisr-esh-Shugur and Maarat al-Numan.

At this news, Roger of Antioch called upon King Baldwin II and Count Pons of Tripoli for help. Baldwin and Pons made their preparations at once, urging Roger to wait for them before starting operations. But the castellans of the lands beyond the Orontes, whose crops were being devastated by the Turkoman bands, begged Roger to come without delay. To satisfy them, without waiting for help from Jerusalem and Tripoli, he faced the Turks with his own unaided forces. Obsessed by gloomy forebodings, the patriarch of Antioch, the aged and holy Bernard of Valence, in a pathetic scene, tried in vain to make Roger see reason. He remained unshakable in his senseless resolution. He thanked the patriarch and gave him his last will and testament. Bernard, after blessing the army, took the road toward Antioch with tears in his eyes. And Roger set out to meet his fate.

After crossing the Orontes at the Iron Bridge, Roger took up his position with his army, on June 20, halfway to Aleppo in the plain known as the Field of Blood, where the modern village of Dana now stands.   On the evening of the twenty-seventh, he learned that the Turks had attacked the small neighboring stronghold of Athareb.   The night of June 27–28 was an anxious one.   As the enemy drew nearer, the army began to realize more clearly the magnitude of the folly which had been committed.   Walter the Chancellor, an anguished witness, tells the strange story of a sleepwalker who, that very night, wandered through the camp foretelling disaster.   Roger was so upset that he sent his chamberlain back to Arta to put the precious vessels which had followed the camp in a place of safety.

The next morning, Saturday, June 28, at dawn, the archbishop of Apamea called the whole army together and preached a moving sermon, speaking as a priest and a soldier, then celebrated the holy office, heard the public confession of the warriors, and gave them the general absolution.   Then he confessed Roger in private in his tent (the life of that fiery paladin was far from being exemplary).   After putting his conscience in order with God and distributing alms to the poor of the army, the prince of Antioch summoned his squires, whistled up his hounds, called for his falcons, mounted and, careless of the impending drama, set off hunting.   But as he rode out he met a scout returning hell bent for leather; enormous Turkoman masses were arriving, not only by the Athareb road, where they might have been expected, but also, after a detour behind the hills, from the other three corners of the horizon.   The Field of Blood was surrounded!

Roger at once gave his last orders to his troops.   Hardly had he done so when a second scout, the squire Aubry, rode up, his face streaming with blood, the sole survivor of a massacred patrol.   And at the same moment innumerable squadrons of Turkomans crowned all the heights. Roger, after throwing himself for the last time at the foot of the Cross, uttered his war cry, "In the Name of Our Lord Jesus Christ, as befits true knights, for the defense of the faith, forward!"   But against more than 40,000 Turks there were only 700 knights and 3,000 foot soldiers. . . .

In spite of this overwhelming superiority of numbers, the valor of the Normans almost drove the enemy back at the first encounter, but this advantage did not last.   The Frankish army was soon completely surrounded.   The Turkish cavalry returned to the attack again and again, riddling the Franks with javelins and arrows. The Turkopole contingent, which formed the Frankish left, gave ground. To crown their misfortunes, at that very moment a violent cyclone blew in from the north, raising a sandstorm which for some instants blinded the knights.

The Frankish army, shaken by the flight of the Turkopoles, crushed by the sheer weight of numbers, was almost entirely destroyed. Roger of Antioch remained alone with a handful of faithful companions. Having refused to wait for the king and the count of Tripoli, he realized that he was personally responsible for the disaster. He knew how to die like a knight. "He willed not to flee nor to look behind him" but hurled himself into the thick of the Turkish squadrons. He met his death from a sword stroke across the eyes and fell at the foot of the Cross. Out of so many heroes, only 140 men were able to win safety.

Ilghazi installed himself in Roger's tent to preside over the partition of the booty. As for the prisoners, the Turkomans gave vent to all their native savagery on them. They were dragged naked under the lash, roped together in files of two or three hundred, to the vineyards of Sarmeda. In the torrid June heat they were dying of thirst. Ilghazi had water jars placed within their reach. Those who approached them were massacred. All would have perished on the spot had he not wished to display the spectacle of his triumph before the populace of Aleppo. The Arab mob joined the Turkoman mercenaries and some of the captives were tortured to death.

The Turkish vanguard advanced as far as Antioch, and for a moment it looked as though the city would be taken. But the Patriarch Bernard of Valence saved the situation. He grouped the Latins together, formed them into a militia, and disarmed the native Christians, especially the Greeks, who had a tendency to turn traitor. Night and day, the heroic old man inspected the ramparts and kept up the courage of those around him. Finally, King Baldwin II arrived.

As soon as Baldwin had received the appeal of the prince of Antioch he had marched out, accompanied by Evremar, archbishop of Caesarea, bearing the True Cross. On the way, he had been joined by Count Pons of Tripoli. On nearing Latakia they encountered Turkoman scouts, whose presence announced only too clearly the disaster which had befallen the prince of Antioch.

Baldwin II was welcomed at Antioch as a savior, not only by his sister, Princess Hodierna, Roger's widow, and the Patriarch Bernard of Valence, but by the whole population. Immediately named regent of the principality, he rapidly reconstituted the political and military authorities and then, with Pons of Tripoli and Joscelin of Courtenay, set out to meet the Turks. The clash came at Tel-Danith, beyond the Orontes, on August 14. The Turks were commanded by the Emir Ilghazi, now supported by Toghtekin, atabeg of Damascus; the Franks by Baldwin II and Pons of Tripoli. The action started badly for the Franks, but Baldwin restored the situation by charging at the head of his chivalry. "He called upon Our Lord to save His people, pricked spurs and flung himself into the thickest of the fray." This time, it was the Turks who beat the retreat. The king was unwounded, although his horse had been hit. Even more surprising was the case of Archbishop Evremar of Caesarea who, without breastplate, clad in his episcopal vestments and bearing the True Cross, also returned without a scratch from the front of the battle line, where he furiously anathematized the infidels.

The Turks avenged their defeat by massacring the last prisoners who still survived. Among them, Robert, lord of the castle of Saône, counted on redeeming himself on the ground of previous courteous relations with the atabeg Toghtekin. But when the atabeg saw him arrive, "he rose, tucked the hem of his robe into his belt, brandished his sword and smote off the head of the Frank." The other prisoners, tied to a stake, served as target practice for the drunken Turkomans. Ilghazi, finally dead drunk like his men, summoned the whole Aleppo mob to witness the massacre of the last forty captives. Their throats were cut before the doors of his palace, which were splashed with blood. Useless atrocities. The king of Jerusalem had repaired the consequences of the disaster; and when he returned to Palestine, the principality of Antioch was finally saved.

Baldwin II was still obliged to return several times from Jerusalem to Antioch to defend the northern principality against fresh Turkish inroads. In 1120 and 1122 we thus find him again scouring the lands beyond the Orontes, his army moving in close column, without allowing itself to be alarmed by the whirlwind tactics of the Turkoman squadrons or lured into a dangerous pursuit by their feigned flights.

His prudence and firmness finally wore out the adversary, who, without further combat, evacuated the lands beyond the Orontes.

At this juncture a new burden fell upon Baldwin. In September 1122, Joscelin of Courtenay, count of Edessa, was taken prisoner by the Turkish chief Balak, who shut him up in the citadel of Kharput in the heart of the Kurdistan mountains. The king of Jerusalem thus found himself obliged to assume the regency of Edessa at the same time as that of Antioch. As he came to put the county of Edessa in a state of defense, a similar misfortune befell him. On April 18, 1123, as he was hunting with the falcon in the valley of the upper Euphrates, ignorant of the proximity of the Turks, Balak, who had been keeping watch from behind the mountains, fell upon him and took him prisoner. Baldwin went to join Joscelin in the dungeons of Kharput.

The captivity of Baldwin II placed Frankish Syria in a singularly disturbing position. The kingdom of Jerusalem, the principality of Antioch, and the county of Edessa found themselves simultaneously deprived of their chiefs. Only one of the four Frankish princes, Count Pons of Tripoli, was still at the head of his states. Such a situation, had it arisen a few years earlier, would no doubt have led to disaster, but the Frankish dominion was now firmly enough established to withstand a shock. The barons of Jerusalem entrusted the regency to the constable, Eustace Garnier. When the Egyptians sought to turn the situation to account by seizing Jaffa, Eustace Garnier inflicted a resounding defeat on them at Ibelin (Yebna) on May 29, 1123. At the same time, at Antioch, the old patriarch, Bernard of Valence, had resumed the direction of affairs and the principality set about preparing to repel invasion. Balak had indeed just broken into the territory across the Orontes, where he took the town of Albara. But there he was met with the most incredible news. Baldwin II and Joscelin, whom he had left in the oubliettes of Kharput, had made themselves masters of the fortress!

The episode is one of the most romantic in the whole story. From the depths of their dungeon, the two captives had found ways and means of contacting the Armenians of the country. Through them, Joscelin was able to pass a message to his Armenian subjects of Edessa, bidding them come and free him. Now, since he had become count of Edessa, the lord of Courtenay had been skillful enough to form a very

close attachment between the Armenian element and himself. Fifty of
these brave people, men of high heart and deep cunning, conceived an
incredibly bold plan to save him. They disguised themselves, some as
beggars, others as monks, and with arms concealed under their clothing
set out for Kurdistan. At Kharput, the Turkish authorities, taking
them for Armenian subjects of the emir, allowed them to enter without
demur. Once on the spot they acted out the concerted scenario with
prodigious coolness. After contacting their Armenian fellow-country-
men, they penetrated to the prison at dead of night, butchered the
Turkish sentinels, reached the tower where Baldwin II and Joscelin
were imprisoned and freed them. At the same moment, the Armenian
population of Kharput, springing to arms, liquidated the Turkish garrison and occupied the citadel.

By an unexpected stroke of luck the king of Jerusalem, the day
before still a captive in the citadel of Kharput, now found himself
master of that fortress, his enemy's capital. It now remained either to
hold it or to make a sortie, both equally difficult, since the Turks, now
recovered from their surprise, were closely investing the stronghold,
and they were in the heart of the Armenian Taurus and the wild
mountains of Kurdistan, beyond Diyarbekir, in the depths of the
remote valley of the Muradsu. It was agreed that Baldwin II, with the
Armenians, would hold the fortress, while Joscelin, at his own risk and
peril, would try to seek help from Syria.

The odyssey of Joscelin of Courtenay from Kharput into Syria is
one of the most astonishing pages of this history. He sallied out by
night with only three companions, three Armenians familiar with the
country, and was fortunate enough to traverse the Turkish encampment without being taken, sent back one of the Armenians to Kharput,
as agreed, to let Baldwin know that he had crossed the danger zone,
and with the two others plunged by moonlight into the gorges of
Mezre. The three of them had taken nothing with them but two small
wineskins and a little dried meat. Hiding by day in woods and caves
and marching by night, they headed for the Euphrates. There, of
course, there were no boats, and Joscelin could not swim. He inflated
his two wineskins, fixed them to his belt, and pushed by the two
Armenians, excellent swimmers, reached the west bank; but he was
exhausted, dying of fatigue and hunger, his feet a mass of blood. He
collapsed at the foot of a nut tree, hidden by the bushes, and fell asleep.

He had meanwhile sent in search of bread one of his companions, who was fortunate enough to fall in with a peasant, Armenian like himself, whom he brought to Joscelin with a handful of figs and grapes. But the peasant recognized his count and flung himself at his feet, calling him by name. Joscelin begged him for help in reaching Turbessel, promising him the greatest rewards. Fulcher of Chartres has preserved the picturesque dialogue for us. "Tell me, what is your fortune, that I may multiply it tenfold." "I ask nothing for saving you," replied the peasant, "for I remember you once gave me alms. I will repay your kindness. But, if you would know, lord, I have a wife, a young baby, a she-ass, and two oxen, as well as a pig. With my family and my beasts, I will lead you where you will. But I will kill the pig and cook it for you." "Do not kill your pig, brother, you will attract the attention of the neighbors. But let us set off at once!" The little troop immediately started off, the count riding the ass and, as a stratagem, bearing the crying and struggling infant in his arms.

The picturesque procession ultimately reached Turbessel. Joscelin was saved. There he found his wife, who had believed him dead, weeping for joy and his knights and was able to reward the good Armenian peasant, his guide. But it was no moment for sentiment. He hastened forthwith to Antioch and thence, hell bent for leather, to Jerusalem. After climbing Calvary and dedicating a fragment of his Kharput prison chains as an ex-voto, he assembled the chivalry of Jerusalem, Tripoli, and Antioch and at their head, the True Cross by his side, set out again by forced marches for Kharput. But on reaching Turbessel, he learned that his efforts were in vain: the Turks had recaptured the stronghold.

What had happened was this: on learning that Kharput had been surprised and that the Frankish chiefs, only the day before still his captives, now commanded as masters in his own castle, his family home, Balak almost choked with rage. "Swift as an eagle," he raced back from Aleppo to Kurdistan. Arriving before Kharput he offered Baldwin II safe-conduct back to Syria against the immediate surrender of the fortress. Baldwin, mistrusting the word of the Turks and hoping to be relieved in time by Joscelin, refused. But the fortress was built on a particularly soft chalky rock where Balak's engineers dug such deep saps that one of the towers collapsed. Baldwin had no alternative but to yield (September 16, 1123). The Turkish chief spared his life and that of his nephew, Waleran of Le Puiset, but had the rest of the prisoners dashed from the ramparts. The unfortunate Armenians who had allied themselves with the Frankish escapade were flayed alive, or lashed to pikes to serve as targets for the soldiery.

Not only did the Franks not allow themselves to be abashed by their king's new captivity, but it was during this captivity that they achieved a conquest of the utmost importance, the taking of Tyre.

In May 1123, there arrived in Levantine waters a powerful Venetian squadron, captained by the Doge Domenico Michiel: 300 vessels, 15,000 seamen, the finest armada which the great Italian republic had sent to sea for many years past. At that very moment the Egyptian fleet was anchored off Ascalon. On hearing this, the doge divided his ships into two squadrons. The first, by far the largest, under his own command, sailed down the coast in the direction of Jaffa, slowly enough at first and careful not to give the alarm. The second, only eighteen vessels strong, put out to sea and then set course for Ascalon, in the guise of a simple pilgrim convoy seeking to land. The eighteen ships arrived off Ascalon in the last hours of night. At first dawn, the Egyptian admirals, sighting this false convoy, put out to sea, gleeful at the thought of capturing it. Continuing their stratagem, the eighteen ships feigned to refuse battle and gave way without taking flight, occupying the enemy long enough to allow the doge with the grand fleet, which now came up at full speed, all sails set and all oars plying, to take a hand in the game. The Egyptian admirals, caught between the two Venetian squadrons, were thus compelled to accept an unequal combat and lost nearly all their vessels (May 30, 1123).

The destruction of the Egyptian navy ensured the Venetians of the absolute mastery of the sea. The Franks took advantage of this to lay siege, in concert with the doge, to the great fortified seaport of Tyre, which had, up to then, remained in the power of the Moslems. The task was eased by quarrels between the Egyptian party and the Damascene party who disputed the town. The Cairo government and the atabeg of Damascus were finally reconciled and joined forces to defend Tyre, but the hour was late; the Franks were already at the gates.

The Frankish army was commanded by the Constable William of Bures, lord of Tiberias, who had just been named regent of Jerusalem on the death of Eustace Garnier, and by the Patriarch Gormond of

Picquigny. It invested the city from landward, while the Venetians blockaded by sea (February 1124). The siege was particularly difficult. Tyre, on its rocky peninsula, already constituted a very strong position, and Toghtekin had been able to introduce in time a strong garrison of Turkish bowmen. Count Pons of Tripoli brought the besiegers valuable reinforcements. The Egyptians attempted a diversion by sending a detachment from Ascalon to threaten Jerusalem. In the absence of the chivalry, every man of whom was at the siege of Tyre, the burgesses of Jerusalem rushed to the gates and put up such a bold showing that the invaders retired. William of Tyre is justly proud of the bearing of these "simple folk," worthy of the commoners of Bouvines. The atabeg of Damascus, Toghtekin, tried one last maneuver to relieve Tyre at the head of the Turkish cavalry. He could not get through to the town, whose defenders resigned themselves to capitulation. On July 7, 1124, the royal banner was raised above the walls and the Frankish army made its entry. Under the terms of the capitulation, the inhabitants were left entirely free to withdraw with all their wealth or to remain under Frankish dominion. The chronicle even shows us the emigrants fraternizing with their victors and curiously visiting their camp and inspecting their siege engines.

Such a relaxed spirit on the conclusion of such a tough siege indicates the progress made in religious pacification after twenty-five years of coexistence between Franks and Arabs. A modus vivendi tended to become established, even under conditions of almost constant hostilities. Relations were becoming more courteous. Even in war, Franks and Moslems were learning to esteem each other.

It is impossible to overestimate the importance to the Franks of the capture of Tyre. It finally made them masters of the whole seacoast and gave them possession of a redoubt easily defensible because of its almost insular character. In the hour of disaster, in 1187, when Jerusalem had succumbed, Tyre was to be the bulwark of Frankish resistance, and the starting point of reconquest. As for the Venetians, to whom the success was largely due, they were given very considerable trading and political privileges in Tyre, with one third of the city and the right to set up a virtually autonomous trading commune there.

While the Constable William of Bures and the Patriarch Gormond of Picquigny were conquering Tyre in his name, King Baldwin II

finally regained his freedom. His jailor, the Emir Balak of Aleppo, had
been killed in a war between Moslems. On August 29, 1124, the Emir
Timurtash, Balak's successor, freed his captive against a ransom of
80,000 dinars, 20,000 of which were payable in advance, and the return
of certain territories beyond the Orontes. "Freed of his fetters, Baldwin was led to be received by Timurtash. After eating and drinking
with the emir, he received the gift of a royal tunic, a golden cap, and
ornamented buskins. He was even given back the valuable horse he
had been riding on the day he was taken prisoner."

Free at last, Baldwin went first to Antioch, since it was the affairs of
the principality which were at stake. Had he not promised to yield
back to the Turks some of the fortresses beyond the Orontes? But
there was a legal issue. The only legitimate proprietor of the principality of Antioch was the young Bohemund II, son of the great
Bohemund, who was still a boy and who was being brought up in Italy
by his mother, Constance of France. Did Baldwin, who was merely
regent of Antioch, possess the right to alienate a patrimony which did
not belong to him? The Patriarch Bernard of Valence denied his legal
right to do so and Baldwin II, being the man we know, obviously had
no compunction in allowing himself to be convinced. He apologized
most politely to the Turks: the patriarch forbade him to cede the cities
beyond the Orontes, and Baldwin was most distressed but of course he
could not disobey his religious authorities. Basically, it was on a
similar pretext that Francis I, once free of Charles V's prisons, was to
refuse to perform the clauses of the Treaty of Madrid relating to the
cession of Burgundy. What was more impudent was the way in
which Baldwin II thought of raising the 60,000 dinars' ransom which
he still had to pay to the emir of Aleppo. "Nothing simpler," said the
good folk of Antioch. "Go and besiege Aleppo, exact 60,000 dinars as
a tribute of war, and hand them over correctly to the emir!"
Evidently, as the Arab historians point out, the Turks had made a
pretty bad bargain in liberating this "sly old fox."

But Baldwin II showed so much good grace and comradeship in his
relations with the Moslem chiefs that they do not seem to have borne
him a great grudge. He was the best friend of the Arab sheik Dubais,
chief of one of the principal Bedouin tribes of Al Jazira. This desert
king dreamed of capturing back Aleppo from the Turks. At the end
of 1124, Baldwin laid siege to the town with him. It was saved only at

"On November 27, 1095, the tenth day of the Council of Clermont, Pope Urban II summoned the whole of Christendom to arms." (*Les passages d'Outre-Mer*, by Sébastien Mamerot, from a fifteenth-century ms.)

The arrival of Pope Urban II in France. (*Roman de Godefroi de Bouillon,* from a fourteenth-century ms.)

The objective of the crusade: to reconquer the Holy Sepulcher. (*Chronique de la conquête de Jérusalem,* from a fourteenth-century ms.)

Constantinople was reached on August 1, 1096. (*Les voyages d'Outre-Mer*, by Bertrandon de la Brocquière, from a fifteenth-century ms.)

"The superior wisdom of Godfrey of Bouillon early made itself felt on the journey across Hungary." Godfrey of Bouillon and the king of Hungary. (*Chronique de la conquête de Jérusalem*, by William of Tyre, from a fifteenth-century ms.)

"At Antioch, the crusaders had to convert this desultory siege into an effective blockade." The capture of Antioch. (*Chronique de la conquête de Jérusalem*, by William of Tyre, from a fourteenth-century ms.)

"What did the Byzantines want? Diplomatic guarantees...oaths of fidelity?" Ambassadors before the emperor of Constantinople in the time of Godfrey of Bouillon. (*Conquête de la Terre d'Outre-Mer*, by William of Tyre, from a fourteenth-century ms.)

"The heavy Frankish cavalry." Comrades of Godfrey of Bouillon. (*Chronique de la conquête de Jérusalem*, by William of Tyre, from fourteenth-century ms.)

"Baldwin of Boulogne, brother of Godfrey, was a fine type of baron." Godfrey of Bouillon and his brother, Baldwin of Boulogne. (*Roman de Godefroi de Bouillon*, from a fourteenth-century ms.)

"The Egyptian garrison had the terrible Greek fire." Godfrey (on the top of a mobile tower, crown on his head) before Jerusalem. On the left, Peter the Hermit, who had rejoined the army of Godfrey of Bouillon. (*Roman de Godefroi de Bouillon*, from a fourteenth-century ms.)

The Moslem army. (*Roman de Godefroi de Bouillon*, from a fourteenth-century ms.)

"The Patriarch Daimbert resigned himself to crowning Baldwin king of Jerusalem on Christmas Day 1100." Coronation of Baldwin of Boulogne. (*Chronique de la conquête de Jérusalem,* by William of Tyre, from a fourteenth-century ms.)

"For his eldest daughter Melisende, Baldwin II finally chose Count Fulk of Anjou to be her husband." The marriage of Fulk and Melisende. (*Chronique de la conquête de Jérusalem,* by William of Tyre, from a fourteenth-century ms.)

the last minute by the arrival of Turkish reinforcements led by the atabeg of Mosul, Il-Bursuqi, the White Falcon.

The union of Aleppo and Mosul in the hands of the same Turkish chief forced the Franks to take the defensive. Baldwin II had scarcely returned to Jerusalem when an invasion of Antioch territory by Il-Bursuqi called him back to the Orontes. After two years of captivity, followed by a fresh war against the Turks in the north, the king had been able to allow himself only two months' rest in his capital; and now he must once again mount horse to save Antioch, set out again for these wars across the Orontes where his brother-in-law Roger had ended by meeting his death. We know that this time he could not help feeling that the voice of duty was stern indeed. He nevertheless obeyed it and, in company with Pons of Tripoli, reached the principality of Antioch. The Turks, under the command of the two atabegs of Aleppo-Mosul and Damascus, were besieging the fortress of Azaz, in the northeast of the principality. Baldwin thrust as far as Azaz, feigned a retreat, and then, when the Turks launched themselves in pursuit, borrowed their tactics, suddenly wheeled about, formed a battle front, and charged. The Turks, conversely renouncing their usual method, had abandoned the bow and the scattered whirlwind to accept hand-to-hand combat, the fray of sword and lance. In this game, the heavy Frankish chivalry regained all its advantages. The Turks were crushed, with heavy losses and took flight "so shamefully that not one looked behind him." Baldwin II, "joyful and honored," made a triumphal re-entry into Jerusalem. To crown his joy, his youngest daughter, the little Joveta, who was then five and had been kept as a hostage, was returned to him through the chivalrous loyalty of the Arab Emirs of Shaizar.

At the beginning of 1126, the tireless Baldwin II led a great expedition against Damascus. On January 13, in fine weather, the army crossed the Jordan south of the mouth of the Yarmuk and penetrated the Hauran. "Before dawn," writes Fulcher of Chartres, "the trumpets sounded the advance. Men folded their tents and made haste. The donkeys brayed, the camels uttered their characteristic cry, the horses neighed. Then, led by its guides, the column thrust into enemy country." The army, after going back up the south bank of the Yarmuk, struck north, straight for Damascus, as far as Tel el-Saqhab, twenty-two miles from the great city, where it met the Damascene forces, led by the Atabeg Toghtekin in person. It was one of the hardest fought battles of the epoch. Baldwin II, as was his wont, rode in the thickest of the fray, "calling the good knights by name and summoning them to do their best." The Turks took the Frankish baggage train by surprise and carried off the royal chapel; and then the whole Damascus army charged, and the Franks were beginning to give ground when Baldwin II, rallying them, led a sudden counterattack. At that moment, Toghtekin was unhorsed, which started the rout among his forces. The Franks pursued the enemy as far as the meadows of Coffar, near Kiswe, on the southern outskirts of Damascus. Baldwin II, after this excursion into the heart of enemy country, returned triumphant to Jerusalem. He had little respite: Count Pons of Tripoli called for his help in taking the fortress of Rafaniya in the Alaouite mountains north of the Krak des Chevaliers. On March 31, 1126, the stronghold capitulated.

Baldwin II, in the words of the chronicler, "was assuredly not idle." Ceaselessly racing from the confines of Diyarbekir to the Egyptian frontier, ruling both his Palestine kingdom and the regency of Antioch, he was nevertheless anxious to be able to hand that city over to the legitimate heir of the principality, the Norman Prince Bohemund II, son of the great Bohemund, who was still in Italy. At last, in October 1126, Bohemund II landed at the mouth of the Orontes. He was then eighteen and already an accomplished knight. Immediately, he conquered all hearts by his youthful good looks, his nobility, and his grace. "He was tall, very straight and very handsome, with fair hair, good features, gentle and kind. Among a thousand, he stood out as the prince." "He was very young," confirms the Armenian chronicle, "and his chin was still beardless, but he had already proved himself in combat. He was tall in stature, lion-faced, with very fair hair." A good Christian, well behaved, eloquent and well informed, as became a Norman, as soon as he spoke he won over all who heard him. "His ascendancy was irresistible," says Matthew of Edessa. Generous as well, and magnificent in the manner of the great Bohemund, his father, this Prince Charming seemed destined to bring happiness to Frankish Syria. King Baldwin II, who came to meet him, gave him his second daughter, Alice, in marriage.

For his eldest daughter, Melisende, Baldwin II had long been looking for a match throughout France, since her future husband would reign over the kingdom of Jerusalem after him. His choice finally fell upon Count Fulk of Anjou, who landed at Acre in the spring of 1129 and married Melisende on June 2.

Soon after this marriage, which ensured the succession of his dynasty, Baldwin II resumed his project of conquering Damascus. The Turkish Toghtekin, who had governed the great Syrian city since 1103, had just died (1128). Against his son Buri ("the Wolf") the terrible sect of the Ismailis or Assassins, the anarchists of Islam, was fomenting a dangerous religious and social agitation. Sworn enemies of Moslem orthodoxy and society, the Assassins had no compunction in reaching an understanding with Baldwin II and proposing to hand over Damascus to him. So great was the hatred of these mystical and fanatical revolutionaries for their fellow-citizens that they preferred to deliver their country over to the Franks and see Islam crumble rather than renounce their millennial dreams. With all his practical sense, Baldwin II was careful not to repel their advances. Unfortunately, the Damascus authorities got wind of the plot and executed the Assassin chiefs before they had time to act. The sectaries at least had the time to deliver to the Franks the important frontier post of Paneas (Baniyas), which guards the pass between Galilee and Damascus (September 1129). Baldwin II again tried to take Damascus. In November of that year he laid siege to the great city with the support of three other Frankish princes, Joscelin of Edessa, Bohemund II of Antioch, and Pons of Tripoli, but the elimination of the Assassins, by depriving him of the intelligence on which he was counting, thwarted the expedition.

At the same time, there appeared in the north the Turkish chief who was to begin the concentration of the Moslem forces: the Atabeg Zengi, already governor of Mosul, was also appointed by the sultan as governor of Aleppo and took possession of the city on June 18, 1129. We shall see what a menace the arrival of Zengi was to constitute for the Latin East. Shortly after, an unexpected misfortune struck the Franks. In February 1130, the young Prince Bohemund II of Antioch, the hope of Frankish Syria, was killed by the Turks in the course of an inroad into Cilicia.

The death of Bohemund II was a catastrophe for the principality of Antioch which, at the moment when the Turkish peril again became a menace, once again found itself without a defender, in the same position as after the tragic death of Roger. Once again, the folk of

Antioch turned to Baldwin II, already qualified, moreover, to intervene as father of Princess Alice, widow of Bohemund II. But it was precisely from this side that the most unexpected of obstacles arose.

Alice had had a daughter by Bohemund II, Constance, who, under feudal law, was the heiress of the principality but whose minority ensured the young widow of a long regency, or at least of a large share in the regency. But the willfull young woman was determined to remain sovereign mistress of the country, even if she married again. A bad mother, a rebellious daughter, a faithless Frank, she had no hesita tion, with a view to firmly establishing her usurpation and eliminating her own daughter, in claiming the protection of the Turks, and specifically of Zengi, the atabeg of Aleppo. Exercising her personal charms on the Turkish chief, she sent him the gift of a richly caparisoned courser of great price, "a palfrey whiter than snow, shod with silver, with reins and breastplate of chiseled silver, the saddle covered with silver brocade." But the messenger was arrested on the way. Led before the king, he confessed everything.

Baldwin II, dumbfounded, and furious at such treason coming from his own daughter, set out immediately for Antioch. Alice, dropping the mask, shut the gates of the city in his face. By the lavish distribution of gold, she had tried to create her own party; but in the face of such felony the notables revolted and, in spite of her orders, opened the gates to the king. Alice, terrified, barricaded herself in the tower, and then, on the intervention of the notables, came down from her refuge and threw herself at her father's feet. In spite of his violent rage, Baldwin listened to the voice of fatherly love. Or rather, in his great wisdom, he acted like a king and a father. He deprived Alice of the city of Antioch and all rights over the regency. He proclaimed himself sole regent in the name of his granddaughter Constance, making everyone take the oath of fidelity to her and taking every precaution against "the malice of her mother." Then he enfeoffed Alice with the two seaports of Latakia and Jabala.

It was Baldwin II's last political act. Falling ill in Jerusalem, he had himself borne to the patriarch's palace, in order to be nearer the Holy Sepulcher. He sent for his eldest daughter, Melisende, and his son-in-law, Fulk of Anjou, and their child, the future Baldwin III, who was then three. He abdicated in their favor and, after blessing them, assumed the monastic habit so as "to die in poverty." It was in this garb that he passed away, on August 21, 1131, in the presence of the patriarch.

Of all that had been placed in his trust thirteen years before, nothing, spiritual or temporal, had been lost. All had been maintained, enlarged, consolidated. He was a true knight, a wise statesman, and a good king.

6

EQUILIBRIUM BETWEEN FRANKS AND MOSLEMS

Fulk of Anjou and Zengi

FULK of Anjou, the new king of Jerusalem, was not, like his two predecessors, the younger son of a great house, for whom a throne in the East was an unexpected stroke of luck. He was one of the greatest barons of France, possessor of that county of Anjou which he had enlarged out of the Maine and which he had made into "the most highly centralized and solidly established state of Capetian France." In 1128 he had crowned his Angevin work by a master stroke, by obtaining for his son, Geoffrey Plantagenet, the hand of the Princess Matilda, heiress of the Norman kingdom of England. In this way, he had laid the foundations, to the benefit of his house, of the Plantagenet empire, shortly destined to become one of the greatest powers in the West. He had been a widower for three years when, at the instance of King Louis VI of France, the king of Jerusalem had offered him, with the hand of Princess Melisende, the reversion of the kingdom of Jerusalem. Once arrived in Palestine and once married, the man who in France had victoriously stood up to the Anglo-Norman and the Capetian constrained himself, so long as Baldwin II lived, to be merely a faithful lieutenant or rather, as William of Tyre says, a real son. After burying Baldwin II beside his predecessors on Calvary, he was crowned king at the Church of the Holy Sepulcher with Melisende on September 14, 1131.

Fulk was then about forty. Redheaded, of fairly slight build, he was a man of great endurance, widely experienced in military matters, humane, genial, upright, very generous to the poor and to the Church. All his biographers praise his piety, his loyalty in his relations with his vassals, his propriety of behavior. At the beginning of this "new life" opened up to him by his accession to the throne of Palestine, he was still a doughty and alert knight. Finally, his achievements in Anjou were a guarantee of his mature sense of politics.

All these qualities were not too much at a moment when Syrian Islam, with the Atabeg Zengi, was setting about achieving its redoutable unity.

The accession of the Atabeg Zengi at Aleppo and his reign over the dual principality of Aleppo and Mosul (1129–1146) mark, from the Moslem point of view, the turning point in the history of the Crusades. In some respects, Zengi can be compared with Baldwin I, the founder of the Moslem monarchy with the founder of the Frankish monarchy. This energetic Turk was as devoted to the Holy War of Islam as Baldwin I ever was to the crusade, since his whole life was spent, like that of Baldwin I, in fighting the enemies of his faith. As devoted— but no more; for him, as for Baldwin I, the holy war, to which he devoted himself body and soul, which became the whole meaning of his existence, was also his stepping stone, the willful reason and means of his own rise. Like Baldwin I, he used and "realized" the holy war for the benefit of his own royalty. Thanks to the halo thus acquired, he was able to give his power a semblance of legitimacy which impressed his contemporaries. Just as Baldwin I had linked his titles with the old royalty of the Bible, so Zengi recalled that his father, the White Falcon, had been nominated prince of Aleppo by the Sultan Malik Shah. In spite of an interruption of some thirty-four years, he re-established dynastic continuity at Aleppo and founded it on the word of the last great Seljuk, the source of all legitimacy in the Turkish world.

Like Baldwin I too, Zengi was a soldier full of fire, a strict and intelligent administrator. As tough and unscrupulous as the first king of Jerusalem, with the unfortunate addition of a streak of cruelty, the first king of Moslem Syria, more feared than loved, was nevertheless able to win the unshrinking devotion of his soldiers, since their fortune was founded on his, every victory of the chief meaning booty and fiefs to be distributed among his officers.   And certainly without being in any way skeptical (the Moslem faith of this Turk was as absolute as the Christian faith of a Baldwin I), he was not the political dupe of the holy war.   Baldwin I, it will be remembered, had abandoned the crusade in cavalier fashion to lay personal hold over the county of Edessa.   Similarly, Zengi's real aim was perhaps not immediately to take the city of Antioch but to snatch Damascus away from the other Turko-Syrian dynasty.   His essential program (which in the long run was all the more dangerous for the Franks) remained the unification of Moslem Syria, a political result which, once achieved, would ensure the military superiority of the Moslems over the Christians.

It is to the honor of King Fulk that he realized this and did everything in his power to prevent it.

Hardly had King Fulk ascended the throne when a great void appeared among the Frankish princes in the north.   The count of Edessa, Joscelin of Courtenay, died.

The old baron had been seriously injured by the collapse of a tower during the siege of a Turkish fortress.   His death was imminent from day to day when the Turks laid siege to his castle of Kaisun in the Taurus.   At this news, Joscelin bade his son go to the relief of the fortress.   But this son, Joscelin II, a paltry warrior as subsequent events were to prove, excused himself on the plea of the numerical inferiority of the Christians.   The old hero had not a moment's hesitation. Unable to mount horse, he had himself borne in a litter in the midst of his knights and marched on the enemy.   His firm bearing intimidated the Turks, who immediately raised the siege.   The chronicle of *Eracles* here attributes to Joscelin a magnificent act of grace, worthy of some romance of chivalry.   The dying man, victor without a battle, such power did his mere name have over his enemies, learned of their precipitate flight.   He ordered his litter to be set down and, raising his hands to the sky, exclaimed: "Good Lord God, I return Thee thanks and grace with all my soul that Thou hast willed that, at the end of my days, before me, I who am half dead, I who am feeble and already almost a corpse, before me, the enemy should take such fright that they dared not stand their ground to await me but fled at my approach. Good Lord God, I gladly recognize that all this flows from Thy goodness and Thy courtesy." "And, having spoken, he recommended his soul to God and expired in the midst of his army."

This baron of the vanguard, pattern of the Frankish princes of the first generation, hewn to the very measure of the Epic, was succeeded by Joscelin II, the pusillanimous heir whose defection had darkened his last day. The son of a Levantine mother, the new count of Edessa, half Levantine himself, was small, dark, stout, and ugly, sensual and so given to lechery that he was a cause of scandal, even in a society that was easygoing enough. He abandoned residence in Edessa, which was too much of an exposed combat station, in favor of Turbessel, in the shelter of the Euphrates. Thirteen years later, this systematic desertion was to lead to disaster.

At Antioch, the situation was even more serious. The dowager Princess Alice, an intriguing Levantine, greedy of power and honors, again started her machinations to disinherit her young daughter and reign on her own. To get herself restored, she brought into the game her two neighbors, Joscelin II of Edessa and Pons of Tripoli. The barons of Antioch, feeling that the reign of this woman would be the ruin of the principality, appealed to her brother-in-law, King Fulk. Fulk set off at once; but at the entry to the county of Tripoli, Pons barred his way, an act which was all the more culpable since Pons had married Cecilia, the king's half-sister. The king then leaped into a bark with a single companion and, from Beirut, landed at the mouth of the Orontes. The barons of Antioch hastened to join him. At their head he marched against Pons, who with the army of Tripoli moved to dispute Antioch with him. He met the count at Rugia, joined battle and put him to flight. Fulk made his entry into Antioch with a host of captive knights of Tripoli in his train. It was a harsh lesson but essential to bring the princes back to obedience. Fulk, moreover, soon pardoned Pons and sent him back his knights. At Antioch, he put an end to the intrigues of his sister-in-law, assumed the regency himself, and entrusted the administration to the constable, Reynald Mazoir.

Shortly afterward, Count Pons of Tripoli, who had behaved so badly to the king, humbly appealed to him. He had been worsted by the Turkoman bands who had invaded his county and found himself besieged by them in the fortress of Montferrand or Baarin, some thirty miles east of Tortosa, in the heart of the Alaouite mountains. At the call of Pons, Fulk marched out. When he got as far as Tripoli, he was met by his sister, Cecilia, who begged him, in tears, "to save her lord." Faced with his sister's tears, Fulk, finally forgetting his ancient grievances and, moreover, mindful of his royal duty, set out again for Montferrand and relieved the besieged.

Everywhere, royalty was fulfilling its mission of protection. Hardly had he saved the county of Tripoli when Fulk went to the defense of the principality of Antioch against the Aleppo Turks. He defeated them in a surprise night attack near Qinnasrin. In sum, the Angevin monarch had the advantage over the Turks everywhere when he found himself paralyzed by the intrigues of a court romance, between Hugh of Le Puiset and Queen Melisende.

Hugh of Le Puiset, of a family of Orléanais origin, was a cousin of Baldwin II, who had taken him into his family at a very early age and given him the county of Jaffa. He is depicted as one of the noblest lords of his time, "wise and eloquent, tall and well made, fair-skinned but high-colored, a proud and hardy knight, the most courteous and generous of men." The protégé of Baldwin II, who treated him like a son, brought up with his daughters, he was the court favorite. Hugh was, above all, the familiar friend of Princess Melisende, since married to Fulk. The new queen's cousin and childhood friend, he continued to associate with her quite freely. This intimacy aroused a certain ill will. "Many people thought ill of it," and King Fulk first and foremost. Fulk, who was over forty, only showed himself more jealous of his young wife. He ended by hating the handsome knight in whom he suspected a rival. Hugh, sensing this, sought to protect himself against the royal vengeance by creating his own party among the barons. The nobility was soon split between the king and the count of Jaffa.

Hatred was boiling up on both sides when the drama exploded with a scandal. The instigator was Count Walter of Caesarea, a young and brilliant knight, like Hugh, but estranged from him by family quarrels. One day, in front of the whole court of Jerusalem, before all the lords and all the prelates, Walter (perhaps in secret agreement with the king) accused the count of Jaffa of treason: "Hear me, sweet lords! I affirm that the count here present is plotting the death of the king. And if he gainsay it, I challenge him to single combat." He flung down the gage; Hugh accepted the challenge, and, according to usage, the royal court summoned them both to trial by battle.

On the appointed day, Hugh defaulted. Constrained to take a false oath to save the queen's honor, did he fear divine punishment? No one knows. His defection, which seemed either an act of cowardice or an avowal, prevented even his best friends from coming to his defense and enabled the king's council to declare him, by default and according to custom, guilty of treason.

On the news of his condemnation, Hugh took fright. In desperation, thinking that all was lost, he fled to Ascalon and placed himself under the protection of the Egyptian garrison. This time the treason was authentic, especially as the Egyptian army, based on the county of Jaffa, began to make dangerous inroads on the royal domain. But the people of Jaffa, indignant, opened their gates to Fulk, and the fugitive had no alternative except to sue for pardon. The patriarch of Jerusalem, the excellent William of Messines, "a wise and peaceful man" who agreed with the Scriptures that "if a house be divided against itself, that house cannot stand," made an urgent plea to the king. Indeed, favored by the civil war, the Damascenes recovered Baniyas from the Franks (December 15, 1132). This harsh lesson hastened the conclusion of the agreement. To give the king's anger time to cool down, it was agreed that Hugh should exile himself for three years, after which the old quarrels would be forgotten.

But now a fresh drama broke out. Hugh of Le Puiset, waiting to take ship for Italy, returned to Jerusalem. His reappearance, after the murmurs about his relations with the queen, and above all after the indignation aroused by his treason with the Moslems, was, to say the least of it, premature. In fact, one evening when he was throwing dice in the Bazaar of the Furriers, a Breton knight set about him with his sword and left him on the ground for dead. The murderous attack caused a change in public opinion and nearly started a riot. The sentiments of the crowd swung around to the side of the gallant knight, brought up from early youth in Syrian lands, against the jealousy of the "foreign" king. From there it was only a step to accusing Fulk of having his rival assassinated by way of vengeance. But Fulk in fact had nothing to do with the assassination, the Breton knight having acted on his own initiative, a warped mind who wished to make Hugh expiate his treason with Egypt. But the king, recognizing the need to clear himself on the spot, summoned the court of barons and bade them judge the murderer. They condemned him to

death by having his limbs severed one by one. The king ordered that
the execution should be public and forbade the miscreant's tongue to
be cut off, so that he could speak to the end. The terrible trial ended
in the complete justification of the king, for to the very end the
wretched man avowed that he had had neither instigator nor accom-
plice. After these frightful scenes, Fulk regained his popularity. The
strangest thing was that Hugh recovered. As agreed, he went into
exile in Sicily, with a heavy heart. It was there that he died, by sheer
accident, at the very moment when he was about to return.

What were Melisende's reactions to all this? Whether she felt a
simple childhood friendship for Hugh, or whether they were united by
a deeper feeling, she never forgave the count's enemies, especially after
his death. With her Oriental violence, at one time she meditated
terrible vengeance. She was animated by passion, hopeless passion,
turned solely to hatred. The more indulgent said that she was exasperated by the suspicions cast upon her conduct. Others deemed her
inconsolable "because the count was dead in exile and for love of her."
To revenge her handsome knight she plotted heaven knows what
dramas of poison. The king's personal friends dared not go out except
armed and escorted, so much did they fear a dagger stroke. "The
queen seemed out of her wits." Fulk himself several times felt his life
was menaced.

But Melisende's wrath finally cooled off. The "wiseheads" intervened to reconcile husband and wife. The hardest task was to get the
queen to tolerate, at any rate in official ceremonies, Hugh's old enemies. As for Fulk, once rid of his rival, he had only one desire: to win
his young wife's forgiveness for the pain he had caused her. The
astute Melisende was quick to see the ascendancy which such a feeling
gave her over her husband. She made great use of it, the love of
power replacing her other passions. From now on, nothing was
decided in council except with the will of this imperious woman.

This was to become evident in the affairs of Antioch.

At Antioch, during the minority of the child-princess, Constance,
the regency was lawfully exercised by Fulk. But two restless, ambitious souls were seeking to profit on the spot from the remoteness of
the king, the Patriarch Radulph, and the dowager Princess Alice.

Radulph of Domfront had succeeded the venerable Bernard of Valence as patriarch of Antioch at his death in 1135. Archbishop William of Tyre has left us an unfavorable portrait of this prelate, worldly, ostentatious, and coarse, more like a knight than a cleric. "He was a big, handsome man, good-looking, though with a slight squint; with a smattering of letters, he possessed a natural eloquence, the art of speaking with grace and wit, and generous gestures; he pleased both knights and populace. But he was light-minded, forgot his promises, and meddled too much in the affairs of this world." The candidate of the Norman nobility, who regarded him as one of themselves, popular with the masses because of his ostentation, his glibness, and his promises, he was able to intimidate the chapter by the threat of riots, and "bulldozed" his way into the patriarchate.

And yet this cunning man made two grave mistakes. He neglected to seek consecration by the pope; and instead of conciliating the canons of his chapter, still sullenly hostile, he condemned them to prison or exile. Tyrannizing over his clergy, scornful of the authority of the holy see, mixing only with men-at-arms while he put his canons in irons, he was the very pattern of those feudal magnates strayed into the Church of whom the Middle Ages are so rich in examples. "He became," says the Archbishop of Tyre, "of such arrogance that he seemed the successor rather of Antiochus of old than of Saint Peter or Saint Ignatius."

Meanwhile, the dowager Alice was beginning to re-establish her affairs. Could she not count on the full support of her sister, Queen Melisende? The queen's influence over the king became more and more evident as Fulk grew older. At the prayer of his wife, Fulk soon allowed Alice to return to Antioch and there distribute offices to her devoted barons, to such effect that the ambitious dowager, in concert with the patriarch and by agreement with him, again became mistress of the principality.

Nevertheless, however great the compliance of the aging Fulk toward his sister-in-law Alice, he could not allow the interregnum of an unscrupulous woman and a simoniac prelate to continue indefinitely in Antioch. The atabeg of Aleppo, Zengi, had taken advantage of the situation to win back from the principality, in the spring of 1135, a number of strongholds across the Orontes, including Athareb, Zerdana, Maarat al-Numan, and Kafartab. Furthermore, Alice's daughter, the young Constance, the sole legitimate heiress, was approaching marriageable age. Some doughty warrior, capable of defending the country against the Turks, must be found as a husband for her. Most of the barons of Antioch were of like mind. In secret (since both Alice and Melisende must be kept in the dark), their representatives came to Jerusalem to consult the king on the choice of a betrothed. He named the younger son of the count of Poitiers, Raymond, then aged thirty and resident at the court of England.

Still in secret, concealing themselves from the queen and the princess dowager, the king and the Antioch barons sent a confidential agent to England, the Knight Hospitaler, Gerald Jebarre. Gerald sought out Raymond of Poitiers and clandestinely showed him Fulk's letters. Raymond accepted. But the secret had finally leaked out. On the voyage, King Roger II of Sicily, who had pretentions to Antioch, ordered Raymond's arrest. Raymond managed to avoid all the traps set for him, by disguising himself and his companions as poor pilgrims or wandering merchants. In this way he was able to take ship without hindrance and landed safe and sound at Antioch.

At Antioch, new dangers. The imperious Alice, mistress of the city, had no intention of allowing herself to be ousted. And, at her side, Radulph of Domfront also had to be counted with, a personage as intriguing as herself, no less ambitious and even more cunning. The whole key to the situation lay precisely there. Raymond realized that the first thing to do was to win over the patriarch. Radulph welcomed his approaches but stated his terms, negotiating with the future prince of Antioch as equal to equal and dictating to him a pact which divided the sovereignty of Antioch between the two of them, in return for which he promised to ensure Raymond's triumph over Alice. Whatever Raymond may have thought of such pretentions, he was careful not to reject them. The main thing for the moment was to get rid of the dowager and marry the young heiress. He was ready to swear anything he was asked.

Radulph of Domfront kept his word. He sought out Alice and told her the tale that the handsomest knight in France had come to marry her and not her daughter. Such news was too flattering to the pride and coquetry of the romantic dowager to be disbelieved "and she had great joy of it." Far from opposing Raymond she therefore gladly allowed him to take over Antioch. Completely hoodwinked, confident and delighted, she was waiting in her palace until he should come to lead her to the altar when she learned that at that very moment he was in the process of celebrating his marriage with the young Constance, the patriarch officiating, in the presence of all the barons, henceforth rallied to Raymond's side. Half dead with rage and frustration, she withdrew to hide her shame in her fief of Latakia, swearing an evil death on the unexpected son-in-law who had so brilliantly outwitted her (1136).

But the alliance between Raymond and the patriarch was not to last long. The new prince of Antioch could not tolerate the partition of power which Radulph had imposed on him. The oath extracted from him, not without veritable blackmail, became unbearable. He proceeded by stages. He started by reaching an understanding with the adversaries whom Radulph numbered among the clergy. They brought the issue of the patriarchate before the court of Rome, alleging that Radulph's election had been wholly irregular. But Radulph, far from allowing himself to be intimidated, set out for Italy and pleaded his cause with so much eloquence that, after first finding all doors closed at the Lateran, he finished by obtaining from the indulgence of the Roman court the remission of his faults in return for a promise of amendment. He therefore returned to Antioch with a triumphant air. Unfortunately, hardly had he been restored when he set about persecuting his chapter again. The pope then sent as legate the bishop of Ostia, Alberic of Beauvais, who, after an exhaustive inquiry, finally deposed him. It was touch and go whether Radulph, barricaded with his men-at-arms in his palace, would not raise a rebellion against the twofold papal and temporal authority. He had to be dislodged by force (1139).

In the person of Raymond of Poitiers, the principality of Antioch had at last found a chief. This scion of the dukes of Aquitaine was one of the finest knights of the time. "Tall, better built, and handsomer than any of his contemporaries, he excelled them all in the art of arms and the science of chivalry." His strength was prodigious. He could bend a stirrup iron with one hand. "One day, riding a fiery stallion, he passed under an archway in which there was a ring. He hung from it by his hands, gathered his horse between his legs, and, spurring it violently and giving it the rein, was strong enough to hold it in." Unlettered himself, he enjoyed learned company. Munificent and liberal, to the point of recklessness, he was at the same time frugal and sober and throughout his life displayed exemplary fidelity to his young wife Constance. In return, he was a gambler, and a bad gambler, so angry when he lost as to be "out of his wits." Moreover, in politics, he too often acted from impulse and was quick to forget his oaths, as Radulph of Domfront had learned only too well. Finally, he was dangerously vindictive, as he was to prove on the fall of Edessa. . . .

The county of Tripoli changed masters at the same time as the principality of Antioch. Count Pons was killed in the course of an incursion by the Damascenes at the end of March 1137. He was succeeded by his son, the young Raymond II.

While the Frankish courts were indulging in these quarrels, war was raging among the Moslems too, but there with much greater political effect. The atabeg of Aleppo and Mosul, the energetic Turkish captain, Zengi, was trying to achieve the unity of Moslem Syria for his own benefit, as an indispensable prelude to the expulsion of the Franks. To this end, it was necessary to absorb the kingdom of Damascus, which belonged, as we have seen, to the dynasty of the Buri, Turkish also themselves. In June 1137, he went to the attack of the city of Homs, part of the state of Damascus, but King Fulk, with astute political sense, constituted himself the protector of Damascene independence. On the approach of the Franks, Zengi withdrew from Homs.

Zengi then turned against the Franks, and specifically against the county of Tripoli, where he attacked the fortress of Montferrand or Baarin, northeast of the Krak des Chevaliers. The count of Tripoli, the young Raymond II, appealed to King Fulk, who was both his suzerain and his uncle. "The king, who was like a father to his country," in the magnificent words of the chronicle of *Eracles*, set out at once for Tripoli. The situation was all the more serious, since at the same moment Raymond of Poitiers informed him, as we shall see, that the Byzantines had suddenly invaded the principality of Antioch. He too called for the urgent aid of the king of Jerusalem. It was a tragic encounter. The old question of the Byzantine claims over Antioch sprang suddenly to life again at the precise moment when Moslem Syria was beginning its redoubtable movement toward unity, when the counter-crusade, so long unsubstantial, was beginning to take shape in the person of Zengi. Which way to turn? To Tripoli against the

Turks? To Antioch against the Byzantines? Fulk decided to rush to the most urgent danger spot and drive back the Turks, after which he would go to Antioch to negotiate with the Byzantines. Here again we recognize that sentiment of Christendom which constituted the political greatness of the twelfth and thirteenth centuries and which was nothing other than the consciousness of European solidarity—worn so thin in modern times!

Fulk and Raymond II therefore set out by forced marches for Montferrand-Baarin, whose garrison, closely besieged by Zengi, and short of food, could not hold out for long; but they were lost in the mountains by their guides and surprised by Zengi at the moment when they debouched from the Alaouite mountains into the plain of Baarin. Part of the Frankish army, with Raymond II, was taken prisoner, while Fulk, with the rest, succeeded in breaking through and reaching Montferrand. Zengi at once resumed the siege with renewed ardor. As Fulk and his companions had been unable to bring any supplies with them, their arrival created fresh difficulties for the defense. In this tragic situation, the king succeeded in passing a call for help to the patriarch of Jerusalem, to Joscelin II, count of Edessa, and to Raymond of Poitiers, prince of Antioch. All of them immediately marched out to relieve Montferrand. Raymond, in particular, merits special praise, for Antioch itself was about to be besieged by the Byzantines: "If he departed, he risked the loss of his city, but his honor obliged him to go to the rescue of the king." "In the end," writes William of Tyre magnificently, "he commended Antioch to God and, leaving the Byzantines to lay siege to it, set out with his knights to relieve Montferrand." A passage of capital importance, which indicates the extent to which the monarchy created by Baldwin I and Baldwin II had achieved the moral unity of the Frankish colonies, since at this date, forty years after the independent foundation of the Norman principality of Antioch, the prince of Antioch had no hesitation in risking the fate of his lands to save the king of Jerusalem.

Zengi, learning of the approach of the relieving army, redoubled his efforts against Montferrand; it was essential that the fortress should fall before the arrival of Raymond of Poitiers. To this end, he invested Montferrand so closely, and so thoroughly intercepted all communication between the besieged and the outside world, that they were unaware till the very end that the *arrière-ban,* the whole body of

Christian vassals, was moving to save them. The relieving army had already entered the county of Tripoli when Fulk, in despair of ever seeing its arrival, and realizing that the garrison of Montferrand was reduced to the last extremities by famine, exhaustion, and epidemics, resigned himself to yielding the fortress. Zengi, who desired at all costs to make an end before relief arrived, and who was, moreover, gravely disturbed by the threat to his city of Aleppo constituted by the arrival of the Byzantines on the northern scene, granted the besieged extremely easy terms. He was satisfied with the conquest of Montferrand, allowed Fulk and his garrison to withdraw freely with their arms and all the honors of war, and even freed Count Raymond II of Tripoli and the other Frankish prisoners (August 10–20, 1137). Fulk thus extricated himself from an anguishing situation with the minimum of damage. In reality, for him as well as for Zengi, the peril was shifting. The Byzantine intervention introduced a redoubtable unknown factor into Syrian affairs.

No man was less like the traditional portrait of a "Byzantine" of decadence than the Emperor John Comnenus, the son and successor of Alexius on the throne of Constantinople. This knightly *basileus*, who spent his life at the head of his troops, had formed the project of restoring the Asiatic frontiers of the old Byzantine Empire by driving back the Turks on the plateau of Asia Minor, taking Cilicia from the Armenians, and imposing his suzerainty on the Franks of Syria and especially of Antioch. His brilliant and glorious reign (1118–1143) was wholly devoted to this task. In Asia Minor he had won back from the Turks Paphlagonia, the ancient Phrygia, and the coast of Adalia, and in July 1137 he had recovered Cilicia by subduing the principality recently founded by the Armenians in that province. From Cilicia he moved down to Antioch, to which he laid siege on August 29. We have seen that the prince of Antioch, Raymond of Poitiers, had the heroism to "confide to God" his menaced capital and set out himself to the aid of King Fulk, besieged by the Turks in Montferrand. As soon as the Montferrand campaign had ended, Raymond returned, and by an astonishing stroke of daring, succeeded in forcing the blockade and making his way into Antioch, where his presence restored the courage of the defenders.

Nevertheless, whatever the racial and confessional antipathy be-

tween Franks and Byzantines, their war, under the very eyes of the
Moslems, was a scandal and a peril for Christendom. Raymond of
Poitiers took the first steps. Following the very sage counsel of King
Fulk, he consented to recognize the Byzantine suzerainty over Antioch. The king of Jerusalem, with a lofty judgment, rightly thought
that the support of the Byzantines and the formation of a united
Christian front against Islam were well worth the recognition of this
theoretical suzerainty. Raymond therefore went in person to the
imperial camp, and according to feudal rites, kneeling before the
Emperor, "did him liege homage between his hands." John Comnenus was, moreover, satisfied with this symbolic gesture and the sight
of his banner floating above the citadel of Antioch, without seeking to
make a personal entry into the city. In this way he sought to spare the
self-esteem of the Franks, whom he wanted to make his friends. It was
agreed that he would help them to capture from the Moslems Aleppo,
Shaizar, Hama, and Homs and that then, but only then, the Franks in
return would yield back Antioch to him.

It must be admitted that this pact, in spite of the sore point of the
ultimate return of Antioch, opened up the fairest prospects for the
future. United in a common front—the front of Christendom itself—
Franks and Byzantines seemed invincible. The crusaders had only
been able to secure the Syrian seaboard, leaving the whole hinterland to
the Moslems, a dangerous situation, since it was from this hinterland
that Zengi and his successors were to launch themselves on the reconquest of the coast. For the first time since 1099, and before it was too
late, the Christians thought seriously about putting an end to this
partition and conquering the whole of Syria. Would the Greco-Latin
Crusade finally accomplish the unfinished work of the Latin Crusade?

The campaign opened in April 1138. The Emperor John Comnenus, Raymond of Poitiers, and Count Joscelin II of Edessa invaded
the territory of Aleppo—Zengi's own kingdom—and took the towns
of Biza'a, Athareb, and Kafartab but made the mistake of not profiting
by their superiority to surprise Aleppo itself. From there the great
Frankish-Byzantine army laid siege to the town of Shaizar on the
middle Orontes. The masters of Shaizar, the Arab emirs of the Mun-
qidite tribe, defended themselves with their customary valor. On their
side, the Byzantines brought into action a whole artillery of catapults,
perriers, and mangonels. John Comnenus himself, "armed with a

halberd, his iron casque on his head," encouraged the crews and personally supervised the firing. Unfortunately, his two allies, Raymond of Poitiers and Joscelin II, were far from seconding his efforts. In his heart, Raymond had little desire to barter his fine city of Antioch against the Moslem towns of the interior. While the emperor risked his skin, the prince of Antioch and the count of Edessa "retired to their tents and, clad in silken raiment, threw dice or played chess, mocking the fools who hazarded their lives." Their deliberate inaction did not take long to paralyze the efforts of John Comnenus. Indignant, he suddenly raised the siege and set out for Antioch (May 23, 1138).

This time, the Byzantine monarch insisted on making a solemn entry into Antioch as sovereign, on horseback, Raymond of Poitiers and Joscelin II serving as his squires. "Through the streets draped with silken hanging and precious carpets, to the acclamations of the populace, to the sound of flute and drum, the triumphal procession mounted to the Cathedral of Saint Peter, and then to the prince's palace where John Comnenus settled down, as though in his own home." "I know not how many days he remained there, he and his courtiers, relaxing from the fatigue of war and taking pleasure in frequenting the baths and hammams after the custom of the country." For the rest, he showered magnificent presents on Raymond of Poitiers, Joscelin II, the knights and even the burgesses of Antioch. When his authority was thus well established, he summonded Raymond and sharply ordered him to hand over the citadel to the Byzantine army. Raymond of Poitiers and his barons were taken by surprise. While the Franks still held the citadel, the Byzantine army had been introduced in force into the city proper. Raymond realized that he was indeed the emperor's prisoner, and the situation was all the more delicate since the emperor could justly reproach him with his deliberate inaction at the siege of Shaizar, or in other words, the violation of the Frankish-Byzantine pact against Islam. . . .

It was the cunning and resourceful Count Joscelin II of Poitiers who saved the situation. He gained time, pleading that for such an important act as handing over the citadel, the assent of the prince was not enough but that of the barons and the burgesses was also necessary. To avoid trouble, it was essential to prepare people's minds. Joscelin offered to do it, and the emperor could count on his zeal! This crafty discourse convinced John Comnenus. He allowed Joscelin twenty-four hours to deliver up the keys of the citadel. Meanwhile, the Byzantine soldiers held Raymond of Poitiers prisoner in his own palace.

Hardly out of doors, Joscelin set about violently stirring up the Latin population of Antioch against the Greeks who wished to dispossess them. It was not very difficult in this matter to awaken confessional hatreds. In a few instants, a riot broke out. Everyone leaped to arms to drive out the Byzantine soldiers. As for Joscelin, continuing his play-acting he galloped toward the palace and, simulating the utmost terror, flung himself at the feet of John Comnenus and recounted that the population of Antioch was in revolt, that he had tried in vain to calm them but had almost been torn to pieces and escaped only thanks to the speed of his horse.

It is not certain that the emperor was duped by this comedy, but outside the popular rising was in full cry. The Byzantine soldiers, surprised by the suddenness of the revolt, assailed in the midst of a maze of narrow streets, unable to regroup, found themselves disarmed and defenseless. John Comnenus realized that his show of force had failed. Putting a good face on ill fortune, he invited the barons to calm the people, saying that there had been a misunderstanding and announcing his departure. Seeing he had been tricked, he was determined, as a good Byzantine, to save face. The little speech to Raymond of Poitiers which William of Tyre puts into his mouth has all the finesse of a fable. It is the story of Reynard caught in a trap, who wants to get out of it with dignity. The emperor treats Raymond as his best friend and "orders" him to hold the citadel, and indeed the rest of the city, as a loyal vassal of the empire. On their side, Raymond and Joscelin energetically disavow the "crazy mob," the irresponsible elements who have fomented this absurd uprising.

John Comnenus professed to be convinced of their good faith and on the very next day took the road again for Asia Minor after perfectly amicable farewells with the two Frankish princes.

But, if diplomatic appearances were saved, the moral rupture between Franks and Byzantines was an accomplished fact, to the greater misfortune of Byzantines as well as Franks, and to the sole profit of Islam.

No one was happier at the collapse of the Frankish-Byzantine alliance than the atabeg of Aleppo, Zengi. He immediately resumed his program of usurpation. True to his plan, before attacking the Franks again, and precisely in order to be able to attack them with greater chances of success, he tried to absorb the other Turkish-Syrian kingdom of Damascus. In May and June 1138, he obtained from the Damascenes the cession of the town of Homs. In October 1139, he captured Baalbek from them, though not without flaying the governor, who had resisted him and crucifying the soldiers of the garrison. These atrocities only increased the hostility of the Damascenes toward him. When Zengi laid siege to their city in December 1139, they put up an energetic resistance under the command of their vizier, an old Turkish captain called Unur or "Aynard," as the chronicle of *Eracles* calls him, curiously Frenchifying his name. To repel Zengi's invasion, Unur had no hesitation in appealing to the Franks. For this purpose he sent to King Fulk the most seductive of ambassadors, the Emir Usama, of the great Arab family of the princes of Shaizar.

Usama has left us his own recital of his interviews with Fulk. "Men tell me," said the king, "that you are a noble knight. I had not the least idea in the world that you were a knight." "Master," replied Usama, "I am a knight after the fashion of my race and of my family. What we most admire in a knight is to be lean and long." The emir made several visits to Fulk and had no difficulty in persuading him: if Zengi, who already possessed Mosul and Aleppo, laid hands on Damascus as well, Frankish Syria would soon be pushed back into the sea. As the price of Frankish intervention, the Damascus government, moreover, undertook to restore to Fulk the frontier fort of Paneas or Baniyas.

Fulk, who had summoned the Frankish army to go to the relief of Damascus, had no need to join battle. On the news of his approach, Zengi raised the siege and went back to Aleppo (May 4, 1140). There is no doubt that the intervention of the king of Jerusalem saved the independence of Damascus. In gratitude, and according to the pledged word, the head of the Damascus government, Unur, came to help Fulk regain Baniyas (June 1140). The alliance between the two courts then became very close. Unur, accompanied by the Emir Usama, even visited Fulk, who was then at Acre. In the course of this visit, they admired, like the connoisseurs they were, "a great falcon, with thirteen tail feathers," which a Genoese had trained to hunt cranes. Fulk immediately gave it to them. At Tiberias the old constable William of Bures staged a tournament in their honor. Relations between emirs and knights were so confident that a Frankish lord offered to take Usama's son "and bring him up in the science of chivalry." At Jerusalem, Usama made friends with the Templars. "When I visited Jerusalem," he tells us himself, "I went to the Mosque of al-Aqsa, which was occupied by the Templars, my friends. Alongside was a small mosque which the Franks had converted into a church. The Templars allotted me that little mosque for my prayers." One day, when a newly landed crusader tried to stop the emir from performing the Koranic invocations, the Templars fell upon the intolerant newcomer, expelled him, and apologized to Usama: "He is a foreigner. He does not know the country!" And Usama emphasizes how greatly co-existence with the Moslems had changed the attitude of the Franks of Syria. The emir, for his part, visiting the Church of Saint John the Baptist at Sebastea, was astounded at the fervor of the Latin monks whom he heard reciting the office.

King Fulk thus tasted the results of his wise Moslem policy. The friendship of the vizier of Damascus guaranteed him against any attack from the side of Aleppo. The great Arab city, saved by him, had become his best ally. At home too, after the storms and dramas of the early days, peace had descended. Queen Melisende had forgotten her memories of Hugh of Le Puiset to turn to devotion. It was then that the most stupid accident put an end to the reign. It was at the end of the autumn of 1143. The court was at Acre. One day—probably November 10—Melisende wanted to rest in the fair meadows of Acre, "near the fountains." Fulk decided to accompany her and go hunting; but as he was chasing a hare, his horse stumbled and fell on top of him, crushing his skull. The king remained in a comma and died on the evening of the third day.

7

THE SECOND CRUSADE

In the Days of Melisende and Eleanor

KING FULK left two young children, Baldwin III, aged thirteen, and Amalric, who was only seven. Baldwin III was proclaimed king under the regency of his mother, Melisende. The chroniclers describe him as already a gifted youth, precociously conscious of his responsibilities. As for Melisende, her stormy youth lay far behind her. She was now "the great lady," pious and alms-giving, very jealous of her authority to boot, and "more redoubtable to the barons than to the simple folk." But if she governed the kingdom well enough, the loss of Fulk made itself cruelly felt in the principalities of the north; it was then that the Franks lost Edessa.

We have already seen how far Count Joscelin II of Edessa proved himself to be a lesser man than the legendary hero whose name he bore. The son of the first Joscelin and of an Armenian princess, he seemed to disclaim both his mountain ancestry and his Frankish heredity. Substituting intrigue for valor, and feeling out of place among his knights he had quit Edessa, where the proximity of the enemy condemned the population to a purely military life, to live in Turbessel, his castle across the Euphrates, protected by the river, where he spent his time in pleasure, "in carousal and lewdness." If he had only maintained a sufficient garrison in Edessa, all might still have been well. But he ate into the pay of his troops, with the result that his best soldiers left him and only a skeleton force remained to defend Edessa.

The atabeg of Aleppo, Zengi, learning of the situation, appeared out of the blue to besiege Edessa with a formidable army, richly equipped with engines of "bombardment." The siege opened on November 28, 1144. In the absence of Joscelin II, the defense was directed by the Latin archbishop, Hugh. The whole Armenian population, women, old men, and youths included, gave proof of magnificent heroism. But only one man could save Edessa: its nearest neighbor, Raymond of Poitiers, prince of Antioch. But he had just quarreled with Joscelin II. To all Joscelin's supplications he replied with sarcasms. The misfortunes of the count of Edessa filled him with joy. In his folly he did not realize that the Turks were closing in and that, once Edessa had fallen, he would have to bear the full brunt of their attacks.

Edessa, left to itself, was bound to fall. The Turkish sappers brought down part of the ramparts. The entry of the Turks was accompanied by scenes of horror (December 23, 1144), but the massacre and the pillage were stopped by Zengi himself, who recognized the importance of maintaining the trading prosperity of the city. He wreaked vengeance on the Latins alone. In contrast, anxious to rally the native Christians to his side, he showed every consideration for the Syrian clergy and the Armenian clergy. The Syrian element rallied to him without hesitation; these Arabic-speaking Christians always adjusted themselves easily enough to Moslem domination which, in any event, granted them special privileges. The Armenians, on the contrary, regretted the Frankish regime with which they had been so closely associated.

Zengi was assassinated by his pages on September 14, 1146. His kingdom was divided between his two sons, Ghazi, who took Mosul, and Nur ed-Din, who took Aleppo. The Armenians of Edessa profited by the change of ruler to plot with Joscelin II. On the night of October 27 they opened the gates of the city to their former count and his knights; the small Turkish garrison was massacred and the Frankish rule restored. But the Turks had retained the citadel, and Nur ed-Din hastened up from Aleppo in full force. Joscelin soon found himself caught in Edessa between the atabeg's large army, besieging him closely, and the Turkish garrison which, from the height of the citadel, kept up a hail of arrows on the defenders. In this desperate situation he resolved to force his way through the besiegers. The Armenians, who had invited him in, knew the fate which awaited them at the

hands of the Turks and took the desperate course of following him.
On Sunday, November 3, at dawn, the gates opened and the attempt at
a breakthrough began. Joscelin II and his knights, charging furiously,
succeeded for the moment in forcing a passage, but pursued and soon
encircled by the mass of the Turkish cavalry, they lost three quarters
of their numbers. It was only with the utmost difficulty that Joscelin,
thanks to the speed of his horse, managed to escape his pursuers and get
back to Turbessel. As for the Armenian population which had tried to
follow him, they were massacred by the Turks in an unspeakable
butchery. The survivors were sold like cattle on the Aleppo market.
"They were stripped of their garments, and, naked, men and women
alike, they were beaten with sticks and forced to run before the horses.
Those who fell behind were stabbed in the stomach by the Turks and
the road was strewn with corpses." This was a foretaste of the
Armenian massacres, followed by the deportation of the
survivors. . . .

Joscelin II's surprise attack for the recovery of Edessa thus ended in
a worse disaster than the catastrophe of 1144. The prince of Antioch,
Raymond of Poitiers, who had refused to come to Joscelin's aid, was
not long in suffering the punishment of his defection. Nur ed-Din,
now free to turn against him, took the important stronghold of Arta or
Artesia, the bulwark of Antioch northeast of the Orontes. After three
quarters of the county of Edessa had disappeared, it was now the turn
of the principality of Antioch to be dismantled.

At Jerusalem, the regent, Queen Melisende, was hardly following
any better foreign policy. The main danger to the Franks came from
the Turkish dynasty of Aleppo; King Fulk's whole diplomacy had
therefore been to maintain against the atabeg of Aleppo the independence of the other Turkish kingdom of Syria, that of Damascus. The
late king's alliance with the head of the Damascus government, the sage
Unur, had at the same time been a barrier to the achievement of
Moslem unity and brought the Franks certain happy frontier adjust-
ments. But in June 1147, an emir of the Hauran, in revolt against the
folk of Damascus, came over to the Franks. The court of Jerusalem
could not resist the temptation. Breaking the precious alliance with
Damascus for a dubious profit, and against the advice of Fulk's old
companions, they mounted an expedition in the Hauran. A campaign
among the volcanic rocks of this region is always a hazardous under-

taking. The march of the army was made all the harder by the beginning of the hot season and the lack of water. The Turkish cavalry of Damascus, joining the Arabs, harassed the invaders night and day. After reaching Basra, they had to beat a retreat, an exhausting retreat which almost turned to disaster. The young King Baldwin III—he was then sixteen—had insisted on accompanying the expedition. The situation soon seemed so critical that the barons counseled him to take flight with the True Cross on the best steed in the army and make for Jerusalem, hell bent for leather, to escape the impending catastrophe. The young king refused with nobility; he was determined to share all the perils of his companions to the bitter end. His determination no doubt saved the army, which would have been completely demoralized by his departure, whereas his presence communicated his heroism to all around. Strict discipline was imposed on knights and foot soldiers alike. The Frankish column, drawn up in serried ranks, the wounded in the middle, advanced in a line of battle, repelling all assaults, without allowing itself to be diverted by adverse feints, unshakable. The Moslems tried to stop it by a bush fire; the fire turned against them. Men recounted afterward that a supernatural apparition, "a knight with a crimson banner, mounted on a white charger," had guided the Christian army to the frontiers of the kingdom, and then mysteriously disappeared.

In the West, however, the fall of Edessa had stimulated the preaching of a Second Crusade. The first idea of this new call to arms seems to be due to King Louis VII of France; but it was Saint Bernard, by his preaching at the assembly of Vézelay on March 31, 1146, who was the leading spirit, unleashing an enthusiasm which recalled that of 1095. It was he too who, at the Diet of Spier, on December 25 to 27 of the same year, persuaded the Emperor Conrad III of Germany to follow the example of Louis VII and take the cross.

Germans and French followed the old route of Godfrey of Bouillon by way of the Danube, Serbia, Thrace, and Constantinople, the Germans a few marches ahead, not without exchanges of barbed pleasantries between the German rearguard and the French vanguard. As for the Byzantines, their relations with the crusaders were even worse than in Godfrey's time. Brawl followed brawl, and at one moment, Conrad III, losing patience, thought of laying assault to

Constantinople. It is true that the Byzantine Emperor, Manuel Comnenus, was betraying Christendom. At war a few months before with the Turks of Asia Minor, he had hastened to make peace with them on the approach of the crusade and thereafter never ceased to stir them up secretly against the crusaders.

Once in Asia Minor, Conrad III continued to follow Godfrey of Bouillon's old route, intending to cross the peninsula diagonally from northeast to southwest. But on reaching Dorylaeum, on October 25, 1147, he was abandoned during the night by his Byzantine guides. The next day he found himself assailed by the whole Turkish army. The horses of the Germans were exhausted by the march and by thirst, the knights stifled under their heavy armor, while the Turkish light squadrons eddied around them, never coming to grips and riddling them with arrows at long range. Conrad III, discouraged, ordered a retreat, with the Turks hard on his heels as far as the Byzantine frontier, inflicting enormous losses upon him. When he got back to Nicaea, about November 2, only a quarter of his army was left.

Meanwhile, King Louis VII of France had arrived at Constantinople on October 4. Leaving Metz in June 1147, he had suffered the same affronts as Conrad in crossing the Byzantine Empire. Like Conrad, and in spite of the flattering welcome extended to him personally by the Byzantine Emperor, Manuel Comnenus, he thought, or rather his advisers thought, of trying a surprise attack on Constantinople. He was, however, wise enough to dismiss this suggestion and at the end of October crossed over into Asia with his army. It was there, near Nicaea, that he learned of the disaster of the German Crusade, whose remnants he gathered up before going any further. Profiting from this example, he dropped the project of crossing Phrygia and took the coast route through the Byzantine provinces of Ionia, Lydia, Pisidia, and Pamphylia. But his march was nonetheless harassed by Turkish bands, operating with the tacit complicity of the Byzantine authorities. To traverse the gorges of Pisidia, he gave his men the strictest marching orders, but the head of his vanguard lost touch; the Turks, lying in ambush on the neighboring heights, immediately threw themselves into the gap, and the army found itself cut in two. The French, obliged to give battle in exceptionally unfavorable conditions, in the midst of the gorges, or on the sheer mountain side, among the precipices, suffered very heavy losses. Louis VII, cut off for a moment from his escort and pursued by a party of Turks, succeeded, by holding on to the lower branches of a tree, in hoisting himself onto an overhanging rock, where he stood his ground against the enemy. The chronicle depicts him, his sword red with blood, cleaving off the heads and hands of his assailants until they lost courage and gave up the fight.

This mountain surprise, murderous as it was, inspired the Turks with a salutory respect for the bravery of the Capetian army, which was able to reach the port of Attalia without incident. There, Louis VII, abandoning the overland route to Syria, decided to take to the sea. But the Byzantines, who had promised him ships, failed to deliver enough of them. Still trusting their word, he embarked with his chivalry for the principality of Antioch, the infantry being to follow in the next convoy. But the ships in this second convoy were still too few. A great many pilgrims were therefore left behind at Attalia. There they were betrayed by the Byzantines, who allowed them to be attacked by the Turkish bands. Most of them perished miserably.

Nevertheless, Louis VII and his knights had landed on March 19, 1148, at Saint-Symeon, the port of Antioch. The prince of Antioch, Raymond of Poitiers, came to greet him, in the midst of general rejoicing. With Louis VII was his young wife, Eleanor of Aquitaine, Raymond's own niece. Everyone knew the king's passion for her. Raymond confidently relied upon it to recover, thanks to Louis VII, the lands across the Orontes from the atabeg of Aleppo, Nur ed-Din. This was, moreover, in the best interests of the Christians themselves, since Nur ed-Din remained their chief enemy and the crusade had, in reality, only been undertaken to halt, after the fall of Edessa, the progress of the redoubtable Turkish chief, or of his father Zengi. Raymond already saw himself, thanks to the aid of the king of France, on the eve of taking possession of Aleppo, when he learned that, from a somewhat strange religious scruple, Louis VII refused to give his support. The Capetian in fact thought that, having taken the Cross to defend the Holy Sepulcher, he would have failed in his vow by making war on the Turks in the direction of Aleppo. As though in this year of 1148 the defense of Jerusalem had lain on the Jordan and not on the Orontes! The chroniclers add, and we can well believe them, that Raymond was exasperated at such narrow-mindedness.

Can the attitude of Louis VII, hard to understand from the political point of view, be explained by reasons of a different order? The king had taken umbrage at the amity which his wife Eleanor displayed for Raymond of Poitiers.   The long talks between uncle and niece could certainly be explained by the efforts of the prince of Antioch to obtain from the court of France the promised expedition against Aleppo; but, rightly or wrongly, Louis was suspicious of the nature of these inter-views.   Eleanor was indeed flirtatious, flighty, and already tired of her husband.   Did she find her uncle, still young and invested with the glamour of the East, a suitor more to her taste?   In any event, when the king invited his wife to follow the army to Jerusalem, she announced her intention of staying at Antioch beside Raymond and of divorcing Louis.   He carried her off by force and set off for Jerusalem by night, by a snap decision, without taking leave of the prince of Antioch.

At Jerusalem, Louis VII had been preceded by the Emperor Conrad III and the wreckage of the German Crusade.   The two sovereigns, once reunited in the Holy City, found themselves solicited by the regent Melisende to lay siege to Damascus.   They consented.   Thus the Second Crusade, launched in Asia by Saint Bernard for the purpose of retaking Edessa and the cities of the principality of Antioch from the Turks of Aleppo, the most redoubtable enemies of the Latin East, refrained from attacking them but, on the contrary, carried the war against the Damascenes, King Fulk's old allies!

The Franco-German Crusade, reinforced by the army of Jerusalem, therefore marched on Damascus, and the siege opened on July 24, 1148, with an attack on the side of the gardens, in the southwest suburbs.   The Jerusalem knights successfully cleaned up this maze of orchards, intersected by quick-set hedges, walls, and irrigation canals. The Germans then cleared the neighborhood of the Barada, the river of Damascus, northeast of the city, after a furious onslaught in which Conrad III bravely risked his life.   The inhabitants were beginning to despair.   Meanwhile the count of Flanders, Thierry of Alsace, one of the leading crusader chiefs, was obtaining from Conrad III and Louis VII the promise of the future barony of Damascus when, on July 27, by an apparently inexplicable decision, the Christian army evacuated the gardens and the banks of the Barada to camp southeast of the town. Excellent positions were lightheartedly sacrificed for an unfavorable disposition; the move was tantamount to abandoning the siege.   The Palestinian barons, who had given this strange advice to the crusaders, certainly seem to have wished to bring the enterprise to naught, either because (not without reason) they thought the rupture of the Frank-ish-Damascene alliance was a mistake or because their jealousy was aroused by the fact that the lordship of Damascus had been promised not to one of themselves but to one of the crusader chiefs. The fact remains that on July 28, the Christian army, recognizing that the operation had missed fire, struck camp and returned to Jerusalem.

The Syrian Franks and the crusaders arrived back in Jerusalem very displeased with each other. The crusaders looked upon the native-born Franks—the *poulains,* as they were called—as traitors. The chronicle of *Eracles* almost makes the crusaders say "Better the Turks than the Levantines!" William of Newburgh goes one better and writes that all these *poulains* were half Moslem. As for the barons of Syria, they were not far from regarding the crusaders from the West as dangerous fanatics, who came "to kill Moslems" without distinction of friend or foe, to the greater detriment of Frankish policy. And it must be admitted that the conduct of the Second Crusade, in refusing to attack the redoubtable atabeg of Aleppo for the sake of setting upon the inoffensive Damascenes, lent some color to this view. It was in these circumstances that Louis VII left Syria after Easter 1149. He had shown himself to be the poor creature whom history was to know better after his divorce from Eleanor and the sad decline which was to follow for the kingdom of France. . . .

The failure of the Second Crusade resulted in a very serious loss of prestige for the Franks in the world of Islam. The king of France and the emperor of Germany, the two most puissant princes of Christen-dom, had come and gone without doing anything. The atabeg of Aleppo, Nur ed-Din, who had for a moment trembled before them, resumed the course of his conquests. On June 29, 1149, he conquered and killed the prince of Antioch, Raymond of Poitiers, at the Fountain of Murad. After this triumph he despoiled the principality of Antioch of the last important strongholds it still possessed east of the Orontes, such as Harenc and Apamea. Antioch itself was saved only by the energy of the Patriarch Aimery of Limoges and above all by the prompt arrival of the young King Baldwin III (who was still only eighteen), who hastened up from Jerusalem with his chivalry. As for the strongholds in the north, such as Aintab and Turbessel, too exposed

to be defensible, the Franks evacuated the Armenian population in a
memorable retreat during which Baldwin III won the general admiration not only by his bravery but by his qualities of leadership.
Whereas in 1146 the evacuation of the Armenians of Edessa had ended
in disaster, the discipline imposed this time on the Frankish column,
and the extraordinary cool-headedness of the young Baldwin enabled
the emigrants to be conducted safe and sound to Antioch, without
their convoy, closely flanked by knights, sustaining any damage
(1150).

8

THE VERY PATTERN
OF A FRANKISH KING
Baldwin III

BALDWIN III had just attained his majority. He was a tall young man ("above average in height"), outstanding among all the knights of his court by his distinguished bearing and handsome features. High-colored, with fairish beard and hair, he had won the reputation of a brilliant talker and a gay companion, celebrated for the liveliness and bite of his repartees. Sober in meat and drink, though somewhat addicted to gaming, at that game of dice which was the peccadillo of the twelfth century, he was also said to be somewhat too given to gallantry, to the extent of scandalizing the good Archbishop William of Tyre by seducing a number of married women. It must be added that, later, once married himself, he displayed exemplary fidelity to his young wife. The same chronicler, for the rest, praises his humanity, his charity, his noble sentiments, his unshakable piety. After so many rude soldiers, a prince with a taste for letters now acceded to the throne of Jerusalem. "He loved to read or listen to the tales of historians. He enjoyed the company of learned men."

Above all, in the eyes of the Franks of Syria, Baldwin III had one immense advantage: he was the first king of Jerusalem born in the country, a true child of the Holy Land where everything, places and people, was familiar to him. "Endowed with an excellent memory, he was the first to recognize his subjects, even the most humble, and greeted them at once by their own names." A detail no less important in this eminently feudal monarchy, he was so steeped in the charters, rights, and customs of each lordship that he was known as the best lawyer in his kingdom. All these characteristics go to show that, in the son of King Fulk and Queen Melisende, French blood and Eastern blood (Melisende was half Armenian) blended in the most happy equilibrium. Perfectly adapted to his environment, the new monarch preserved on the soil of Asia all the freshness of the Angevin temperament. He was to prove one of the most accomplished representatives of Frankish Outremer, the very pattern of a Frankish King of the twelfth century.

But before he could give of his full measure, this highly gifted prince had to liquidate the past, and specifically to rid himself of the regency of his mother, Melisende.

After her stormy love life, the dowager, become devout in her later years, now only wished to be "the great lady and alms-giving" vaunted to us by the Archibishop of Tyre. Nothwithstanding this almost deathbed conversion, she proved herself imperious, jealous of her power, and not at all inclined to share it with her son. She had adopted as her confidential adviser a cousin of hers, Manasses of Hierges, a native of the district of Liège, whom she had appointed constable and who exasperated the barons by his insolence. The two of them together ran the kingdom. Baldwin III, who had proved himself a soldier at Aintab, was impatient with this tutelage. He had just been solemnly crowned on his majority, at the Easter festival of 1152, but the queen mother still said nothing about handing over the power to him. Supported by the barons, he called upon her to retire. Relying, for her part, on the support of the clergy, she merely consented to transfer to her son the coast towns of Tyre and Acre, while keeping Jerusalem for herself. This half-baked solution could not last. Baldwin III, quite legitimately incensed, took to arms. He started by eliminating the Constable Manasses of Hierges, whom he forced to capitulate in the citadel of Mirabel, the modern Mejdel Yaba, near Jaffa, after which he turned against his mother, who had barricaded herself in the citadel of Jerusalem. The Patriarch Fulcher of Angoulême tried in vain to intervene. Baldwin, resolved to make an end of it, opened the siege of the citadel. Realizing that all was up, the obstinate dowager resigned herself to yielding. She was allowed to retire to her fief of Nablus, where she found consolation in busying herself with ecclesiastical patronage.

Baldwin III was king at last.

It was high time, for the need of a strong central power was making itself felt throughout Frankish Syria. At Tripoli, Count Raymond II had just been assassinated by the Ismailis. King Baldwin III immediately assumed the regency alongside the Countess Dowager Hodierna, and in the name of her son, the young Raymond III, then some twelve years old (1152). In the north, since the tragic death of Raymond of Poitiers, prince of Antioch, Baldwin III had also had to ensure the defense of the country on behalf of his twenty-year-old cousin, Constance, Raymond's young widow. In the interests of the country itself he would have liked to remarry the young woman to some baron capable of taking command in this sector. But it was all in vain that he proposed to Constance the most desirable matches: "The Princess," says the chronicle, "was too well weary of a husband's power and of the small liberty of ladies when they have a lord." She answered the king outright that she had no intention whatsoever of marrying again. She laughed in the faces of her aunts who undertook to lecture her, declaring that she enjoyed the pleasures of widowhood and showing all her suitors the door.

So things stood when there was a dramatic reversal of events. Where all political maneuvers had failed, love succeeded in an instant. Constance, after capriciously turning down the finest matches, fell for a newly landed young French knight, Reynald of Châtillon. He was no more than a penniless younger son, but very handsome, glamorous in appearance, full of fire and spirit. That was all that was needed for the young widow, without taking counsel of anyone, to enter into a secret betrothal with him. The consent of Baldwin III was nevertheless required. Fascinated though she was, Constance insisted on this. Reynald of Châtillon did not hesitate for a moment. From Antioch he rode at full gallop to the other end of the Holy Land, to the camp at Ascalon, to throw himself at the king's feet. It can well be imagined that the king was somewhat exasperated by the caprices of his cousin in Antioch. Despairing of marrying her off as he wished, he must have thought that the choice which she had made would at least ensure the principality of a valiant defender. He consented, though without any great enthusiasm.

The romantic marriage of 1153 gave the government of Antioch to a splendid warrior, of magnificent daring, a true epic hero, but also a dangerous adventurer. Devoid of all political sense, as well as of all scruple, careless of the most elementary international law as well as of the sanctity of treaties, he was to stake the fate, first of the principality of Antioch, and later of the kingdom of Jerusalem, on simple throws of the dice which were nothing more than strokes of banditry into the bargain. In this way he recalled, at the interval of half a century and more, the great conquistadores of the First Crusade, Bohemund and Tancred. But Bohemund and Tancred, unscrupulous adventurers though they were, had proved themselves highly skillful diplomats. Moreover, in 1097, in the face of a fragmented, crazed, and demoralized Islam, there was everything to gain and almost nothing to lose from this reckless game. In the Frankish Syria of 1153, on the contrary, a more mature society, settled and assimilated to its environment, conservative, devoting all its efforts to maintaining the *status quo* and equilibrium in the face of a reorganized Islam, Reynald of Châtillon was bound, in no long time, to become a mortal danger. This glamorous soldier, but born to command a free company or a raid rather than a lawful barony, was to drive Frankish Syria to suicide.

His brutality manifested itself immediately after his rise, in a savage drama in which the victim was the patriarch of Antioch, Aimery of Limoges.

So long as Constance's widowhood lasted, Aimery, from his very office, had played a large part in the government. He was naturally bound to look askance at the arrival of the handsome lordling placed on the throne by a woman's caprice; and, since he had a biting wit, his gibes went around the town. He did not know the new prince of Antioch. Reynald of Châtillon was subject to terrible fits of rage during which no feelings of humanity troubled him. He had the patriarch arrested and imprisoned and then, worthy and venerable prelate though he was, ordered him to be whipped till the blood came, after which his head and wounds were anointed with honey and he was exposed, bound and naked, to the flies and wasps, under the burning Syrian summer sun. On learning of this act of barbarism, King Baldwin III could not contain his wrath. He commanded Reynald to release his victim forthwith and replace him on the patriarchal throne. Reynald complied, but Aimery had no desire to live alongside a wild beast; immediately on his release from prison, he left Antioch to settle in Jerusalem, where the affection of the queen dowager, Melisende, consoled him for his misfortunes.[1]

Reynald of Châtillon had only begun his outrages. His ill-fated influence was now to be exerted in the field of foreign policy. Faced with the Moslem revenge which was now beginning to take shape on the side of the atabeg of Aleppo, Nur ed-Din, the interest of the Franks was to maintain the utmost good understanding with the other Christian powers in the Levant, namely the Armenian state of Cilicia and the Byzantine Empire. It was already troublesome enough that Armenians and Byzantines were constantly at loggerheads. But the first act of Reynald of Châtillon was to meddle thoughtlessly in their quarrel. He started in 1155 by making war on the Armenians in the direction of Alexandretta on behalf of the Byzantines. Then, reversing his alliances, at the height of peace, he directed a pillaging expedition against the Byzantine island of Cyprus. He behaved like a bandit chief, sacking everything, violating the women, cutting off the noses and ears of the Greek priests, after which he put back to sea and returned to Antioch with an enormous booty. This crime against Christianity met with no immediate punishment, since the Byzantine Emperor, Manuel Comnenus, was occupied in Europe, but Reynald had made a dangerous enemy there. . . .

While the new prince of Antioch was compromising the Frankish dominion in Syria, Baldwin III was consolidating it in Palestine. The Moslem possessions, as we have seen, were divided among three dominions of unequal size. In the northeast the redoubtable atabeg of Aleppo, Nur ed-Din, whose policy of conquest aimed at uniting Moslem Syria for his own profit and then driving the Franks back into the sea. In the east, the kingdom of Damascus, in the power of another Turkish dynasty, but long since decadent, and coveted by Nur ed-Din. Finally, in the southwest, the Arab caliphate of the Fatimids, master of Egypt, and still in possession of the stronghold of Ascalon on the

---

[1] After this voluntary exile, Aimery was to hold the see of Antioch for a long time to come. His patriarchate, according to the Abbé Chabot, lasted from 1142 to 1194. The Abbé Chabot has established, from Michael the Syrian, that Aimery's successor was a certain Arnulf or Radulph II (about 1194–1196), who was succeeded in turn (about 1196) by Peter of Angoulême (*C. R. de l'Académie des inscriptions*, 1938, p. 460).

Palestine littoral. Like the state of Damascus, Fatimid Egypt was falling apart. The dramas in the style of Suetonius which periodically ravaged the court of Cairo—poison and stiletto, refinement in the art of treason, the dead bodies of viziers on the steps of the throne—reduced this putrefying court to impotence. Baldwin III took advantage of the situation to seize Ascalon. The celebrated stronghold, which had resisted all the efforts of his predecessors for half a century, threw open its gates to him on August 19, 1153. The population and the Egyptian garrison were allowed to retire with their arms and baggage, conditions which were scrupulously observed. This important conquest set the crown on the work of the crusade; from Alexandretta to Gaza the whole coast of Syria and Palestine now belonged to the Franks.

In the northeast, Baldwin III, resuming the wise policy of his father, Fulk of Anjou, constituted himself the defender of Damascene independence against the annexationist aims of Nur ed-Din. On two occasions, his intervention on this side forced the atabeg of Aleppo to give up. By about 1153, Damascus, saved by the Christian armies, had become a veritable Frankish protectorate. This abnormal situation, however, could not last. The community of religion and language between Aleppo and Damascus, the strength of Pan-Islamic feeling were bound to prevail in the end over the fragile constructions of diplomacy. The *Anschluss* was inevitable. It came about in part through the tenacity of Nur ed-Din and in part through the fatalistic resignation of the Damascenes. On April 25, 1154, Nur ed-Din made his entry into Damascus, dispossessed the local dynasty, and annexed the country. From the Euphrates to the Hauran, Moslem Syria was united and in the hands of a strong man. The Frankish monarchy and the Moslem monarchy, crusade and counter-crusade, were on their feet, face to face. And Nur ed-Din, whom we shall now learn to know better, was an adversary worthy of Baldwin III.

In the Turkish-Arab chaos of the first half of the twelfth century, Zengi, Nur ed-Din's father, had restored order and the principle of a stable and lawful government. Aleppo, thanks to him, had become the pole of attraction, the nucleus of the unification of Moslem Syria. Nur ed-Din now carried on his father's work, but rather in the way that Louis IX was to carry on the work of Philip Augustus in France. The politician was succeeded by the saint. Not that Nur ed-Din in any way abandoned (any more than Louis IX, moreover) the military tradition of his ancestors. On the contrary, he spent his life in holy war. But precisely the holy war, as such, was his whole *raison d'être*. He devoted himself to it with the ardent zeal of a dervish. He too was the holy emir. Become sovereign of all Moslem Syria, he continued, in his palaces of Aleppo and Damascus, to lead an astonishingly simple life, which, in the hours of religious exaltation, became almost the life of an ascetic, mortified by fasting and burned up by prayer. Though he spent his life making war, he was really much less of a soldier than his father, Zengi, and most of his successes were won by his generals. Although he was sometimes severe as an administrator, though without Zengi's fits of ancient Turkish cruelty, his government was remarkably wise and benevolent. On all these grounds, he won the esteem of the Franks, just as Louis IX was to win the esteem of the Moslems. Of course, he had the defects of his qualities. While he protected the doctors of the law, the learned and the sages, religious exaltation sometimes plunged him into strange mystic trances. High-strung and sickly, moreover, constantly *in articulo mortis*, he was far from possessing his father's powerful physical personality. In these states of mind he so completely subordinated his personal interests to the religious motive that those who were cunning enough to deck out their ambition under the pretext of the holy war suceeded in duping him, as happened in the case of the young Saladin. Finally, Baldwin III, a magnificent soldier and a very shrewd politician, never missed an opportunity during his fits of nervous depression and his frequent bouts of fever to gain great advantage over him at the right moment.

The war between Nur ed-Din and Baldwin III began in May 1157 with an attack by Nur ed-Din against the Frankish fortress of Baniyas, in Upper Galilee, at the foot of the massif of the Hermon, in the region of the sources of the Jordan. The city was taken, but the constable, Humphrey of Toron, entrenched in the citadel or upper city of Subeibah, held out long enough to enable Baldwin III, arriving hell bent for leather, to raise the siege. After this bloodless victory, the king of Jerusalem returned by short stages. He was camping without misgiving near Lake Hule, thinking that Nur ed-Din had returned to Damascus, when Nur ed-Din himself, who had concealed his troops among the reeds, the papyrus, and the rose laurels on the banks of the lake, unexpectedly emerged near Jacob's Ford and routed the Franks. Nur ed-Din immediately turned back to lay siege to Baniyas. With the king in flight and the Frankish army scattered or captive, the Turkish prince counted on capturing the fortress, but this time it was Baldwin III's turn to spring a surprise. In a few days the active Frankish king had assembled a new army with which he reappeared before Baniyas and forced the stupefied Nur ed-Din to beat a second retreat.

In this first clash of arms, the advantage therefore lay with the valiant king of Jerusalem. Baldwin III resolved to follow up his success, especially as Nur ed-Din had just fallen seriously ill. Followed by all the contingents of Frankish Syria, as well as by a high baron recently arrived on a pilgrimage, Thierry of Alsace, count of Flanders, Baldwin laid siege to the Arab town of Shaizar which commanded the course of the Upper Orontes. The city was taken and the citadel was about to capitulate, when discord arose among the Christians. Baldwin III had reserved the lordship of Shaizar for the count of Flanders. Jealous of this choice, the prince of Antioch, the ill-fated Reynald of Châtillon, wrecked the operation and allowed the fortress to fall back into the hands of the Moslems. Baldwin III consoled himself by going in February 1158 to recapture from the Aleppo Turks the important stronghold of Harenc, commanding the course of the Orontes east of Antioch. As Nur ed-Din, finally restored to health, came back to invest a Frankish position in the region of the Yarmuk, the tireless Frankish king took him by surprise north of the Sea of Galilee and inflicted a complete disaster on him. "Nur ed-Din, whose army had almost all taken flight, held out a little longer with a handful of faithful on an isolated hill; on the point of being captured, he fled in turn before the banner of Jerusalem." A day of glory, due to the personal courage of Baldwin III and to the fine conduct of the Flemish knights: "They bore themselves well that day, the men of Flanders."

Thus the duel between Baldwin III and Nur ed-Din, after dramatic ups and downs, ended in Baldwin's favor. The young monarch realized, however, that in order to combat the new Moslem monarchy effectively, the reconciliation of all Christians was not overmuch. Now that Moslem Syria had constituted its redoubtable unity, it had become essential to face it with the close union of Frankish Syria and the Byzantine Empire. An idea of genius, which might change the course of history. To achieve this aim and put an end to the old hatreds and consummate the great Christian alliance, Baldwin III asked for the hand of a Byzantine princess.

His wish was granted. In September 1158, in a fairy tale retinue, the Princess Theodora, niece of the Emperor Manuel Comnenus, landed at Tyre. She was very young, not yet fifteen, but very tall and very beautiful, with a dazzling fair complexion, thick fair hair, very elegant, and already infinitely seductive. She brought with her a dowry from the *Arabian Nights*, coffers full of golden bezants, jewelry, and precious stones, an infinitude of precious stuffs, silk and gold brocade, carpets and tapestries of inestimable value, all the refined luxury of Byzantium. The marriage was celebrated by the Patriarch Aimery "to the great joy of all the world." Baldwin III, who was only twenty-seven, immediately fell head over heels in love with his child-wife. Once so fickle, he loved only her until his death.

Politically, the joyful welcome of the fair Theodora is equally understandable. The young queen indeed brought the Franks every assurance of the Byzantine alliance and the promise of early intervention by the empire against Nur ed-Din.

The Emperor Manuel Comnenus, Theodora's uncle, was one of the greatest sovereigns Byzantium ever had. With him, the old empire had again become the leading power in the Near East. In 1158 he had subdued the Armenian principality of Cilicia and his possessions therefore now marched with the Frankish states. This proximity was bound to disturb the prince of Antioch, Reynald of Châtillon, from whom Manuel Comnenus would rightly demand redress for the sack of the island of Cyprus. A Byzantine army under Manuel's orders was indeed assembled at Mamistra, in Cilicia, a few days' march from Antioch. Reynald, feeling powerless to resist, took the line of suing for pardon. He presented himself at the imperial camp of Mamistra, in the guise of a suppliant, "bareheaded, barefoot, his arms bare to the elbow, holding his sword by the point and presenting the pommel to the emperor." On reaching the emperor's tent he prostrated himself in the dust, waiting until Manuel deigned to permit him to rise. It was this unprecedented humiliation which was the fruit of the act of banditry committed some years before against Cyprus. Manuel Comnenus finally pardoned Reynald but expressly compelled him to recognize Byzantine suzerainty over Antioch.

At this juncture King Baldwin III of Jerusalem arrived in his turn at the camp of Mamistra. Manuel was charmed by the good graces of the young sovereign whom the hazards of politics had given him as nephew. "They spent ten days together, and each day the affection of the emperor grew for Baldwin, whose precocious wisdom and courtesy he greatly appreciated. From that moment he loved him like a son." The visit of Baldwin III to Manuel Comnenus at the camp of Mamistra, following his marriage with the niece of the puissant *basileus*, marks the diplomatic triumph of the king of Jerusalem. The close association, sealed by a family union, between the Frankish royalty and the Byzantine Empire was indeed the only combination capable of putting a halt to the Turkish counter-crusade. Baldwin III, whose whole activity during his stay at Mamistra reveals his worth, immediately rendered a signal service to Manuel Comnenus, as well indeed as to the Armenians, by reconciling them. The Armenian prince, Thoros II, driven out of the plain of Cilicia by the Byzantine army, was still keeping up the campaign in the gorges of the Taurus. Baldwin, acting as mediator, obtained from him complete submission to the empire, and from Manuel the pardon of the now repentant rebel. In this way, he achieved the prodigy of grouping together, in spite of old ethnic, cultural, and confessional hatreds, the Byzantine, Armenian, and Frankish forces.

This accord was manifested by the solemn entry of Manuel Comnenus into Antioch in April 1159, an entry which, from the Byzantine point of view, had every appearance of a triumph. "Wearing the *stemma*, with its pendants, on his head, clad in a great imperial mantle, so loaded with precious stones that he could hardly move, holding the imperial insignia in his hands, Manuel rode through the city," writes Chalandon. Reynald of Châtillon, on foot, held his bridle. Behind him rode Baldwin III. The procession was received by the people and the clergy of the different sects, headed by the Latin patriarch in full pontificals, the Gospel in his hand. "Then, to the sound of drums and trumpets, to the chant of hymns, the procession entered the town through the colorful crowd, where Syrian rubbed shoulders with Norman, through streets gay with carpets, hangings, foliage, and flowers to the cathedral, from which the emperor proceeded to the palace. Nothing happened to trouble the imperial apotheosis. For eight whole days feast followed feast. In hunting parties and tournaments Greeks and Latins matched their skill." The recital of the chroniclers reminds us of some marvelous tapestry on the theme of a *chanson de geste:* "On a steed whose breastpiece and crupper were encrusted with ornaments of gold," translated Chalandon, "the emperor, robed in the great imperial mantle, attached by a fibula on the right shoulder, to leave his arm free, rode before the spectators, lance in hand, while at the head of the opposing party, the prince of Antioch, on a white horse, advanced, an embroidered coat of arms over his mailed hauberk, a conical casque on his head." The good personal understanding between the *basileus*-knight and the Frankish princes was strengthened by an unforeseen incident. On a hunting party, Baldwin III was unhorsed and dislocated his shoulder. Manuel hastened up, knelt beside the injured man, and thanks to his medical knowledge, gave him effective care. During his convalescence, adds the chronicle of *Eracles,* "the emperor went to see the king every day, and when the surgeons changed the dressings, he aided them very gently, so that he could not have done more had it been his own son."

The rejoicings over, Manuel Comnenus, Baldwin III, and Reynald of Châtillon joined forces and set off to make war on the atabeg of Aleppo, Nur ed-Din. The Turkish prince could hardly resist such a coalition. The "Byzantine epic," reinforced by the crusade—nothing seemed beyond the power of such a historic conjunction. The hour seemed unique. Why did the campaign misfire? Instead of laying siege to Aleppo, Manuel Comnenus was content to compel Nur ed-Din to free all the Christian captives held in the Moslem prisons; and then, taking leave of the Frankish princes, he left Syria and returned to Constantinople. In reality, in spite of the personal affection of the *basileus* for the king of Jerusalem, Byzantine diplomacy had no desire to eliminate the Turks, for fear of increasing the power of the Franks. It was determined to base its hegemony on the maintenance of equilibrium between Turks and Franks. An overcunning policy and stratagems which were soon to rebound against their authors. Manuel Comnenus would then understand the fundamental solidarity of Byzantium and Latinity in the face of the Moslem peril, but too late, after Nur ed-Din had annexed Egypt. It is a curious thing that in considering such events (as in the case of Philip the Fair and Francis I) the historians praise the deliberate sacrifice of the interests of Christendom as a proof of political wisdom, "intellectual enlightenment," and modernism. It was this state of mind which finally led, not only to the loss of the Holy Land, but also to the fall of Constantinople, or in other words, the de-Europeanization of a quarter of Europe. . . .

The first victim of this state of affairs was Reynald of Châtillon, prince of Antioch. On November 25, 1160, as he was leading a *razzia* in the Marash region, he was taken prisoner by the Turks. Flung into the dungeons of Nur ed-Din at Aleppo, he was to spend sixteen long years there. It must, however, be confessed that his captivity was probably a blessing in disguise for Frankish Syria. It nevertheless left the principality of Antioch without a defender, the young Bohemund III, heir to the lands, being too young to govern. The young man's mother, Princess Constance, demoralized by the loss of her beloved Reynald, was ready to throw herself into the arms of the Byzantines. Once again, the king of Jerusalem saved the situation. He hastened to Antioch, placed the city in a state of defense, reassured the Latin element, and assumed all the duties of regent.

This was the last political act of Baldwin III. On January 10, 1162, he died at Beirut, at the age of barely thirty-three, no doubt poisoned by his doctor. William of Tyre, an eyewitness, describes the grief of the people at this news and during the transfer of the body from Beirut to Jerusalem. Not only the Franks, but the Christians of other confessions joined in the funeral procession. The mountain folk came down in crowds to salute the coffin for the last time; even the Arabs themselves bowed before the man who had always been a just master and a chivalrous adversary. When it was suggested to Nur ed-Din that he should profit from the circumstances by attacking the Franks, the great atabeg nobly replied that it would be against his scruples to trouble the mourning for such a valiant warrior.

This salute from a loyal enemy accompanies Baldwin III to his tomb. The fourth King of Jerusalem left this world in the flower of his age, without a political error, without any stain. As a soldier and a captain, as well as a statesman and diplomat, all his activity bears the imprint of an early intellectual maturity accompanied by the radiance of youth. He had, by the conclusion of the Byzantine alliance, laid the foundation of a foreign policy which was wisdom, truth, and salvation itself. He had driven back Nur ed-Din on all sides. He laid down his life in the joy of a love in its prime, mourned by the Moslems as by his own people. The destiny of a young hero of antiquity lingered on into the heart of the Middle Ages.

9

THE FIRST
EGYPTIAN EXPEDITION
Amalric I

ᴮALDWIN III died childless and was succeeded by his brother, Amalric I (1162). In order to secure the throne, the new king had to sacrifice his wife, Agnes of Courtenay, to the hostility of part of the court. The ease with which he separated from her, although she had already given him a son, the future Baldwin IV, and a daughter, Sibylla, indicates how far he was prepared to sacrifice every consideration to the interests of his policy. He was then twenty-seven. He was a big man, "so stout that you would have said he had the breasts of a woman," but also above average height, a noble countenance, fair skin, a great aquiline nose, fair hair thrown back, flashing eyes, a thick beard. When he indulged in gaiety "his bursts of laughter shook his whole body." In spite of his stoutness, he was not a big eater or drinker. Neither was he a gambler, like his brother, and he preferred the noble relaxation of falconry or hawking rather than dice; but he proved himself terribly lecherous, and William of Tyre bemoans the number of his adulteries.

We learn from the same chronicle that Amalric had a slight impediment in his speech. Perhaps it was this which made him somber, taciturn, and distant. In fact "he never spoke to anyone if he could avoid it." This apparent coldness and his severe demeanor were all the more striking since he succeeded a prince who had won all hearts by his courtesy, his graciousness, and his universal ease of manners. It is quite certain that Amalric could prove himself hard enough, at any rate when he thought that reasons of state were at issue. The archbishop of Tyre, who nevertheless thought highly of him, depicts him as greedy for money and not overscrupulous as to how he got it, even at the cost of church property. But, as he told this prelate himself, this harsh taxation had no purpose other than the defense of the realm, the necessities of the holy war. The proof of this is that no one spent more lavishly when the country's interest was at stake. For the rest, he trusted his agents and rarely called them to account. Neither resentful nor vindictive, he forgot or turned a deaf ear to reflections on his person. This politician, who has been reproached with being sour and harsh, nevertheless had great breadth of vision and a fundamental goodness of heart. In war he was a tough soldier, indifferent to danger, insensitive to heat or cold, privations, and fatigue, a cool-headed and resourceful chief in the most difficult straits.

He was highly intelligent, with an intelligence which was both reflective and penetrating. Endowed with a prodigious memory, he was thoroughly versed in the "customs of the realm" and laid down the law like the best lawyer of the time. In the words of William of Tyre, alluding to his slight stammer, "it was easier for him to give good counsel than to tell a tale." Without being as lettered as his brother Baldwin III, he had great intellectual curiosity, "loving to read in books, especially history books." We know that it was he who invited William to write his great chronicle, "the history of his predecessors and his own." The archbishop of Tyre was quite dumbfounded one day when the king questioned him about the proofs of the immortality of the soul. The prelate having recalled the proofs drawn from the Holy Scriptures, Amalric demanded others, capable of convincing even the infidels, and only declared himself satisfied when William of Tyre invoked the purely philosophical need for a sanction for our acts in the other world, earthly life too often showing virtue ill rewarded and vice unpunished. Finally, Amalric, born in Palestine, took a great interest in native questions. He had presented to him the travelers brought by the caravan tracks from the heart of the Orient to the Syrian ports and questioned them at length on their own country.

While he was thus avidly interrogating the caravaners come from Aleppo, from Damascus or Cairo, while he was thus surveying the horizon of that Moslem world which pressed so closely on three sides of his narrow Christian kingdom, what thoughts passed through the mind of the taciturn Amalric? On the northeast and the east, the constitution of Nur ed-Din's great Turkish-Arab kingdom henceforth barred the way to all possible expansion of the Franks. In the presence of the new Moslem monarchy, obeyed at Aleppo and Hama, at Homs and Baalbek, at Damascus and in the Hauran, the kingdom of Jerusalem could do no more than stand on the defensive. On the other hand, however, all the news from Cairo showed that the decadence of the Fatimid dynasty and regime was now beyond repair. The tale was of nothing but seraglio tragedies, palace conspiracies, and barrack revolutions, among the intrigues of a court which was perhaps the most corrupt that has ever existed. In 1163, the Vizier Shawar had just been ousted by one of his own creatures, the Great Chamberlain Dhirgam. Anarchy was rife everywhere. Egypt was ripe for the plucking.

Faced with this spectacle, Amalric I clearly understood that a new phase in the history of the crusades was opening. The Frankish drives toward Aleppo and Damascus were finished forever. The era of crusades into Egypt could now begin. And resolutely anticipating John of Brienne and Louis IX, Amalric turned Frankish expansion in the direction of the Nile Valley.

His first campaign in this direction, in September 1163, was a simple reconnaissance expedition. He thrust as far as Bilbeis, which he made a semblance of besieging, and then retired before the inundations which the Vizier Dhirgam directed against him with the aid of the flooded Nile. But he had collected a substantial amount of intelligence for a larger scale undertaking, and, for the rest, the Egyptians themselves were to bring about a fresh intervention on his part. In fact, it was the arbitration of Nur ed-Din which was sought in the first place. The former Vizier Shawar, displaced by his competitor Dhirgam, took refuge in Moslem Syria and implored the puissant atabeg to send an expeditionary force to restore him to the vizierate. In April 1164, Nur ed-Din assigned this mission to his best general, the Kurdish Emir Shirkuh, the uncle of the great Saladin.

He was a stout warrior, Shirkuh. In spite of his age and his physical handicaps—he was short, obese, almost blind in one eye—the old Kurdish chief knew how to animate his troops by his own example. He was well aware that Amalric would try to bar his route, but so rapid was his march across the desert that he had already reached the delta before the Franks had had time to mobilize. In May 1164, he appeared before Cairo, defeated Dhirgam, who was killed in flight, and reinstated Shawar as vizier. But the accord between the two allies did not last long. Shawar soon found Shirkuh's protection an intolerable burden. In fact, Nur ed-Din's lieutenant no longer spoke of leaving Egypt. As the reward for services rendered, he demanded a war contribution, whole provinces, and constantly protracted his stay in the country at the head of his troops, behaving like a master. Exasperated by his attitude and anxious to be rid of him, Shawar had no hesitation in appealing to the Franks. This approach raised the whole Egyptian question: was Egypt to become a dependency of Nur ed-Din's Moslem Syrian kingdom or a Frankish protectorate?

Amalric hastened to answer Shawar's call. At his approach, Shir-kuh, afraid of being caught between the Frankish army and the Egyptian army, evacuated the Cairo region and sought the shelter of the stronghold of Bilbeis. He was besieged there by the united forces of Amalric and Shawar and was in a somewhat parlous state when the king of Jerusalem received bad news from Syria: in the absence of the Frankish army, Nur ed-Din had captured the fortress of Harim from the principality of Antioch and the frontier fort of Baniyas from the kingdom of Jerusalem (August and October 1164). This diversion had the expected result. By continuing to besiege Bilbeis, Amalric risked losing the Holy Land. He therefore proposed to Shirkuh that he would evacuate Egypt if Shirkuh himself would do the same. Shirkuh, at the end of his tether, was happy to accept these conditions. The two expeditionary forces returned simultaneously to Syria, Amal-ric following the coast and Shirkuh crossing the desert of Idumaea, while Shawar remained in peaceful possession of the country (November 1164).

The Egyptian campaign of 1164 thus ended in a draw. On reflection, however, it was no small success for Amalric to have prevented Egypt from becoming a vassal to Nur ed-Din's men. That was what Shirkuh himself began to think. Back in Syria, the old Kurdish captain was champing at the bit. He had taken the measure, even better than Amalric, of the irremediable decadence of the Fatimid dynasty, at the same time that he had sounded out this rich land of Egypt, a defenseless prey, foredoomed to fall into the power of the boldest. Moreover, in the eyes of orthodox Sunnite Moslems, such as Shirkuh and his master

Nur ed-Din, the Shiite Moslem doctrine, as professed by the Fatimid Caliphs, was pure heresy. Political interest was thus reinforced by confessional zeal, and it was for all these reasons that, in January 1167, Nur ed-Din ordered Shirkuh to undertake a fresh campaign for the conquest of the Nile Valley. The terrified Shawar called upon the Franks for the second time.

At this news Amalric convened the "parliament" of the Palestinian barons at Nablus and told them how things stood. If Nur ed-Din, already master of all Moslem Syria were to lay hands on Egypt as well, that would mean the encirclement and soon the ruin of Frankish Syria. At all costs, they must fly to the aid of Shawar and safeguard Egyptian independence. A third expedition was therefore decided upon; but before it could move off, Shirkuh and his army had already covered the distance between Damascus and Cairo. It is true that Amalric with the Frankish army arrived almost on his heels (February 1167). Shawar welcomed the king of Jerusalem as a savior, while, in the face of the junction of the Egyptian and Frankish forces, Shirkuh, abandoning the siege of Cairo, put the Nile between himself and his adversaries and posted himself opposite at Giza. Shawar established his Frankish allies in the eastern suburbs of the city to defend him against any surprise attack from the enemy.

To seal the alliance with his Frankish friends, Shawar arranged for his master, the Fatimid Caliph, to give audience to an embassy from King Amalric led by Hugh of Caesarea. The chronicle of William of Tyre describes for us the amazement of the Latin baron as he passed through this Arabian Nights palace: "They traversed galleries of marble columns all paneled with gold; they passed by marble pools filled with running water; they heard the song of a multitude of marvelously colored tropical birds; after the aviaries, they were shown menageries filled with quadrupeds unknown in our climates. After passing through an infinity of corridors, they reached the palace itself. A curtain woven of gold, heavy with precious stones, was drawn, and the caliph appeared on his golden throne, robed in a costume of unimaginable richness." For a moment, the courtiers were embarrassed by a difficulty of protocol. To seal the pact of Frankish-Egyptian alliance, Hugh of Caesarea, in Frankish fashion, wished to take the caliph's hand. At first, the courtiers were scandalized at such sacrilege. The caliph ultimately condescended, having the wit to smile at this barbarian extravagance—the salvation of the dynasty was well worth the sacrifice—and Hugh of Caesarea returned to the Christian camp, enchanted with his mission.

The Frankish-Egyptain army sought to end the war at a single stroke by crossing the Nile unexpectedly and surprising Shirkuh at Giza, but the cunning captain extricated himself and reached Upper Egypt. Amalric and Shawar pursued him and compelled him to accept battle at Babein (March 18, 1167). In the center the Franks, under Amalric himself, drove back the enemy, but they made the mistake of allowing themselves to be enticed too far in the pursuit of the fugitives. When they got back to the battlefield they found that, on their left wing, Shirkuh had scattered the Egyptian army, in spite of the support elements which Amalric had taken care to reinforce. Night fell. The broken detachments of the Frankish-Egyptian army were looking for each other among the maze of dunes. To assemble them, Amalric raised his banner on a mound which dominated the terrain. When he had re-formed his forces, he drew them up in close column and, at marching pace, made straight for Shirkuh's army which was trying to bar his way to the Nile. Faced with these resolute men, Shirkuh dared not join battle again; he left the road open. More experienced than the Franks, he did not even try to head them off on the road to Cairo; but as they were going down to the Egyptian capital, he hastened, by the master stroke of a great captain, to seize Alexandria.

The occupation of Alexandria gave Shirkuh a solid base in Egypt. Amalric and Shawar realized the full gravity of the event. They immediately invested the great seaport. Menaced with starvation, Shirkuh took a bold course. Entrusting the defense of Alexandria to his nephew, Saladin, he sallied out at night with the rest of his troops and went to forage in Upper Egypt. But the rich merchants of Alexandria, vexed at the destruction of their suburban villas and the naval blockade which was ruining their trade, thought only of yielding. Saladin, with that persuasive eloquence which we shall meet so often, succeeded in persuading them to be patient. Shirkuh, briefed by him, offered terms of peace. He would restore Alexandria to Shawar and return to Syria provided that Amalric followed suit. Agreement was reached on this basis (August 1167). It gave rise to picturesque scenes of fraternization before Alexandria, between yesterday's besiegers and besieged, the townsmen making sightseeing visits to the

Frankish camp, where they were graciously welcomed. In return, the Frankish soldiers were completely free to wander about the town. Saladin paid a courtesy call on Amalric, whose guest he was for several days. Shawar and his friends, once masters of Alexandria, set about revenging themselves on those citizens who, during the siege, had shown their devotion to Saladin. Saladin appealed to Amalric, and the king of Jerusalem chivalrously obtained from his allies full amnesty for the whole population. At Saladin's request, Amalric even provided ships to carry the wounded of Shirkuh's army back to Syria. With the rest of his troops, Shirkuh set off overland for Damascus. Even more than the first time, he was inconsolable at having so nearly missed the conquest of Egypt. In contrast, Amalric, who had balked him, returned to Jerusalem in triumph. Not only had the shrewd monarch saved the independence of Egypt and halted the unification of the Moslem world, but, into the bargain, the Cairo government, in gratitude for his intervention and to ensure his future support, had agreed to pay him an annual tribute of 100,000 pieces of gold. In this autumn of 1167 a veritable Frankish protectorate, freely accepted and even solicited, had been established over Egypt.

To consolidate these magnificent results, Amalric resolved to strengthen the Frankish-Byzantine alliance. Following the example of his predecessor, he sought the hand of a Byzantine princess. The Emperor Manuel gave him his great-niece, Maria Comnena, who landed at Tyre in August 1167, and whose marriage was celebrated at Jerusalem on the twenty-ninth of the same month.

The court of Constantinople had followed Amalric's campaign in Egypt with great interest. It had concluded from it that nothing would be easier than for the Christians to seize the country. In 1168 it proposed to the king of Jerusalem a joint expedition for this purpose. On the request of Manuel Comnenus, Amalric immediately sent William of Tyre to Constantinople, where he drew up a concerted plan of action with the emperor. It was understood that in the following year the Byzantine forces would join up with those of the king of Jerusalem to undertake the conquest of the delta.

It was by no means certain that such an expedition, in the then state of the Moslem world, was preferable to the Frankish protectorate as it was by then operating in Egypt. In spite of the expected support of the Byzantines, it might have been a question of losing the substance for the shadow. In any event, the support must be waited for. By a fatal error, the Franks, in October 1168, decided to act on their own. We know that, in the Crown Council of the Hospitalers, part of the barons and all the newly landed pilgrims were violently in favor of this course. For a long time Amalric challenged this view, but unfortunately he finally allowed himself to be won over. It may be said in his defense that, according to reports received from Cairo, the Vizier Shawar was beginning to weary of the Frankish tutelage, to the point of contemplating a fresh reversal of alliances and a secret approach to Nur ed-Din. Amalric may have wished to forestall some treachery on that side, which would explain why he acted without waiting for the arrival of his Byzantine allies.

Be that as it may, once the expedition was decided upon, he conducted it with his customary energy. He left Ascalon on October 20, arrived before Bilbeis on November 1, and took the town by storm on the fourth. On the thirteenth he appeared before the old town of Cairo, Fostat. Shawar then took a desperate course, the same course that Rostopchin took in Moscow in 1812. To stop the Franks from installing themselves in Fostat, he set fire to the town. As the first fires reddened, his envoy presented himself before Amalric: "Look, O king, at that smoke mounting to the sky; Fostat is burning. We have thrown in 20,000 jars of naphtha and 10,000 torches. In a few hours it will be nothing but a heap of ashes. You have nothing to do but turn back!" The king of Jerusalem realized that his enterprise had missed its mark. All he could do was to try to bargain his retreat against a sizable war indemnity. As soon as the first installment was paid, he quit the country and went back to Palestine.

He could now measure the full extent of the mistake he had been induced to make. This attack on his old protégé Shawar, an attack which, in the eyes of the public, savored of treachery, had wrought the union of the whole Moslem population against the Franks. Shawar now found himself delivered up, without any counterbalancing force, to the tutelage of Nur ed-Din. As soon as the Frankish aggression was known, Nur ed-Din had in fact ordered Shirkuh back to Egypt. This was all that the old captain had been waiting for, and he set off at full gallop. On January 8, 1169, he made his entry into Cairo, where Shawar professed to receive him with unalloyed pleasure. In reality, the restless vizier was seeking to recommence his double game and to gain time, but the moment for ruse had passed. On January 18, Shawar rode out to visit the tomb of a Moslem saint. Saladin, Shirkuh's nephew and lieutenant, offered to go with him. The two men were riding side by side when suddenly Saladin seized his traveling companion by the throat, unhorsed him, and placed him under arrest. A few hours later, the unhappy man was beheaded and Shirkuh installed himself as vizier in his place. Shirkuh dying a couple of months later (March 23, 1169), Saladin succeeded him in the vizierate. Under this modest title, which respected the theoretical authority of the fainéant caliphs of the Fatimid house, the young Kurdish hero was master of Egypt.

Thus, the ill-fated Frankish expedition of 1168 had merely led to a diplomatic disaster with incalculable consequences. Instead of being a vassal, and in any event harmless, Egypt now had at its head a young chief whose genius was to be revealed by his whole subsequent history, a warrior and statesman of the front rank, the strongest personality produced by Moslem society during the whole epoch of the crusades. And Saladin, master of Egypt, still looked upon himself as Nur ed-Din's lieutenant there. Moslem unity was thus restored from the Euphrates to Nubia. If Frankish Syria was not to be stifled, this situation must be ended at all costs before it had time to become consolidated; Saladin must be overthrown. Amalric, reverting hastily to the project of collaboration between Franks and Byzantines, turned to the Emperor Manuel Comnenus for help. In July 1169, the emperor sent him a powerful fleet with an expeditionary force under the orders of the Grand Duke Contostephanos. On October 16, the Franco-Byzantine army, commanded by Amalric and Contostephanos, set off from Ascalon to conquer the delta. At the end of the month it opened the siege of Damietta. But by prodigies of skill, Saladin succeeded in revictualing the town, while in the Christian camp misunderstandings were rife between Franks and Byzantines. The disagreements between the allies soon became so grave and paralyzed their efforts to such an extent, that on December 13 the whole Christian army raised the siege and evacuated the delta.

This withdrawal had the result of finally confirming Saladin in the possession of Egypt. He took advantage of it to threaten the kingdom of Jerusalem from the direction of Gaza, while Nur ed-Din harassed the great Frankish fortress of Kerak of Moab. In the face of these blows, Amalric I, no doubt regretting the misunderstandings of the siege of Damietta, resolved to revive the Franco-Byzantine alliance and on March 11, 1171, himself set sail for Constantinople.

Manuel Comnenus received the Frankish sovereign with magnificence. It is impossible to read the recital in the contemporary chronicle of William of Tyre without a touch of sadness, for it was truly the encounter of the last great Byzantine *basileus* with the last king of Jerusalem worthy of the name. On landing, Amalric was conducted with great pomp to the palace of Bucoleon dominating the port. "It is reached by a marble stairway going right down to the shore, flanked by lions and columns, all marble, of a prodigious luxury. Ordinarily, this way is reserved for the emperor alone, but by special favor the king made his entry by it." Then came the reception of Amalric by Manuel in the great hall of honor of the Chrysotriklinion, followed by a private talk between the two princes until finally the curtains of this sanctuary of the Byzantine imperial cult were drawn and the Frankish barons beheld their king seated in glory on a throne of honor beside the throne, a little higher, as protocol demanded, of the *basileus*.

For several weeks, Amalric was the guest of the Byzantine monarch who showed him in detail the honors of his palaces and his churches. One day Manuel invited the king and the barons to the races in the Hippodrome, to the performances of dancing girls and mimes. "Our folk were dazzled," avows the good William of Tyre. Finally, Amalric took a fancy to visit the Bosphorus by boat and sailed up the "Straits of Saint-George" as far as the entry to the Black Sea, observing and inquiring into everything with all that mental curiosity for which he was famed.

These feastings were the outward decoration of serious diplomatic talks between Amalric and Manuel. Recent experience had taught both men that the old quarrel, between Greek orthodoxy and Latinity was solely to the profit of Islam. Learning from the lesson of the failure at Damietta, they decided to mount a better prepared expedition to seize Egypt from Saladin. It was this great project which Amalric, taking leave of the *basileus* with renewed hope, brought back to Palestine with him.

The chances on this side again seemed to be becoming more favorable. To please Nur ed-Din, Saladin, it is true, had in September 1171 suppressed the Fatimid caliphate of Cairo, ending at one stroke the great religious schism which had divided Islam for two centuries and, as the Sunnites said, stifling heresy. But this act, which deprived the Franks of the opportunity of profiting from confessional rivalries in the Moslem world, had its obverse side. Saladin, once the caliphate of Cairo was abolished, found himself in fact, if not in name, the sole master of the country, the real king of Egypt. Now that he had grown too powerful not to aspire to complete independence, relations between him and Nur ed-Din, who continued to treat him as a simple lieutenant, were not long in deteriorating. The old atabeg began to take umbrage at his dazzling ascent and seriously thought of mounting a punitive expedition against the rebel general. Saladin, informed of these intentions, now courted the Franks. When Nur ed-Din invited him to cooperate in a common offensive against them, he temporized; the kingdom of Jerusalem seemed to the new master of Egypt to be a providential buffer state against the vengeance of Nur ed-Din. A politician like Amalric I could therefore see new possibilities of maneuver here. These prospects widened even further when, on May 15, 1174, Nur ed-Din died at Damascus, leaving as his only heir a child of eleven, Malik as-Salih. It needed no prophet to foretell that this young boy would not preserve his father's empire. The king of Jerusalem could either act as his protector against the covetousness of Saladin or partition Moslem Syria with Saladin. Amalric was turning over these thoughts and, with the agreement of his Byzantine allies, preparing a new solution to the Eastern question, when the evil fortune of Frankish Syria struck him down in full course. On July 11, 1174, he was carried off by typhus at Jerusalem, at the age of thirty-nine.

10

THE DRAMA HEIGHTENS
Baldwin IV, the Leper King

THE DEATH of Amalric I, coming at that moment, was a disaster. No man's sudden end ever had graver consequences for the destinies of a state. This daring politician had directed the crusade along new lines, toward enterprises from which it must emerge eternally triumphant or mortally wounded. After succeeding for an instant in restoring the Frankish protectorate over Egypt, he had seen his venture turn against him and Egypt fall precisely into the power of the most redoubtable of the Moslem chiefs, the great Saladin. But the last word had not been spoken and everything could still be put right; Amalric had not given his full measure when destiny, at the decisive moment, snatched him brutally from his work. His death left the field open for Saladin. He took immediate advantage of it to settle Nur ed-Din's succession to his own liking. On November 25, 1174, he appeared before Damascus, made his entry unresisted, and annexed the great city. Homs and Hama suffered the same fate. Except for Aleppo, which he left in the hands of Nur ed-Din's feeble successors until 1183, he was master of Moslem Syria, as he was of Egypt.

It was a catastrophic reversal of the situation! Only the day before, the Frankish kingdom of Jerusalem, profiting from the political and confessional split between the Fatimid caliphate of Cairo and the Turkish kingdoms of inland Syria, favored in Syria itself by the providential fragmentation between Turks and Arabs, playing at will on the Moslem anarchy, had appeared to be the arbiter of the East. And now, overnight, it found itself encircled by a powerful military monarchy, directed by a chief of genius, ready to profit in his turn from all the divisions of the Franks. And to reap this dire inheritance, Amalric I left an only son of thirteen, the young Baldwin IV.

The boy on whom the destinies of Frankish Outremer reposed in these dark hours gave every promise, it is true, of being one of the most brilliant representatives of that dynasty of Anjou which was then blossoming in the East with the Plantagenets. He was, William of Tyre tells us, a charming and remarkably gifted youth, handsome, lively, frank, skilled in bodily exercises, already a perfect knight. With a very quick mind and an excellent memory ("he never forgot an insult, still less a good deed"), he appears to us as the most cultivated of the princes of his house. From the age of nine, he had been given as tutor the future Archbishop William of Tyre, humanist and Arabist, historian and statesman, who was later to become his chancellor, and we know from the testimony of the master that the pupil profited admirably from his lessons, especially in Latin letters and in the study of history, for which he had a passionate enthusiasm.

But from the first lines of the moving portrait which William of Tyre thus paints of his royal pupil, we sense an underlying profound sadness. This child, so handsome, so promising, and so cultivated, had already been attacked in secret by the horrible evil which earned him his surname of Baldwin the Leper. William tells us how the evil was discovered one day when the young prince was playing with other children, the sons of the barons of Jerusalem. "It happened that in the heat of the game they grazed their hands and the other children cried out. Only the young Baldwin made no complaint. William was astounded. The child replied that he felt nothing. Then it was realized that his skin was really insensitive. He was entrusted to the *mires*, but their art proved powerless to cure him." They were indeed the first symptoms of that terrible malady which, year by year, was to turn this youth so full of valiance into a living corpse. . . .

The reign of the unfortunate young man, from 1174 to 1185—accession at thirteen, death at twenty-four—was therefore in the end to be nothing but a long agony, but an agony on horseback, in the face of the enemy, firm in the sentiment of royal dignity, of Christian duty and the responsibilities of the crown in those tragic hours when the drama of the king matched the drama of the kingdom. And when the evil grew worse, and the Leper could no longer mount his horse, he had himself carried onto the field of battle in his litter, and the appearance of this dying man on that litter put the Moslems to flight.

On the very morrow of Amalric's death, after the coronation of his successor at the Holy Sepulcher, around the sick child the struggle for power began. The seneschal Miles of Plancy, who had assumed the government, displeased the barons with his arrogance and harshness. In the closing months of 1174, during a visit to Acre, as he was crossing the main street one evening at nightfall he was riddled with dagger strokes and no man ever discovered the assassins. His death delivered the regency to Count Raymond III of Tripoli. A strange figure, this last representative of the Toulousain dynasty which, three quarters of a century earlier, had come to found a Languedoc lordship on the Lebanese riviera. Not only was he the most powerful vassal of the kingdom (to his county of Tripoli, he joined in his wife's right, the lordship of Tiberias or Galilee) but also the king's cousin and indeed one of his closest kinsmen; the grandson, through his mother, of King Baldwin II, he could, in the event of the death of the leper child, claim the crown. William of Tyre, who appreciated the politician in him, has left us a very living picture of him. Slight to the point of thinness, though fairly broad-shouldered, with a big handsome face, a rather long nose, straight black hair, keen and penetrating eyes, he was measured in everything, in speech as at table, full of sense, wise and clear-sighted in affairs, free from pride, more generous with strangers than in privacy, and with all that, very well read. He followed with the closest attention everything that happened in the lands of Islam. Himself thoroughly familiar with the Moslem world (he had spent eight years prisoner in Aleppo), he had maintained friendly relations there which he was to turn to the benefit of the Christian lands. Saladin himself was his personal friend. Behind the calumnies of the Templar party and the Lusignan party, the historian can discern in this born statesman the true heir of the Boulogne, Ardennes, and Angevin kings whose shrewd policy in the first half of the twelfth century had founded the kingdom of Jerusalem. The most that can be said about him (but in the face of the military superiority of a now unified Islam was there any other alternative?) is that he completely subordinated the spirit of chivalry and the whole romance of the crusade to the most circumspect realism.

For the instant, in this imperiled kingdom, realism was imperative and it was this instinct of self-preservation which, at the "parliament" held in Jerusalem at the end of 1174, ensured that Raymond III was unanimously elected regent by the prelates and the barons "and all the people had great joy of it." But in this unhappy Frankish Levant, sick with politics, party strife was not long in ruining these favorable prospects. Because in the event of the death of the leper child the count of Tripoli might legitimately aspire to the crown, his loyalty was suspect. His diplomatic caution, his valuable relations with Saladin earned him the accusation of being pro-Islam, even of treason. Immediately on assuming power, however, he dealt a master stroke against Islam. In the winter of 1174–1175, Saladin laid siege to Aleppo. We have seen that this city was the only part of Moslem Syria which the Kurdish conqueror had left to Nur ed-Din's family. If he succeeded in capturing this stronghold, if to Egypt and Damascus he added Aleppo, Moslem unity would be achieved from the Sudan to the Euphrates. Faced with this threat, the Aleppo Turks appealed to the Franks. The count of Tripoli hastened up and, by a swift diversion against Homs, forced Saladin to cry off (February 1175). While the regent was doing his job in the north, in Jerusalem the boy-king was not remaining inactive. In this same year of 1175, at harvest time, he took the head of his people (he was now fourteen, and the evil had not yet undermined his physical strength) and led a brilliant expedition over the massif of Mount Hermon as far as Dareiya, two or three miles from Damascus. Saladin, faced with the prospect of a war on two fronts, in the north against the Aleppo Turks and in the south and west against the Franks, made up his mind to make peace with the Franks.

But it was no more than a breathing space. In his desire to perfect the unity of Moslem Syria, Saladin, in July 1176, again laid siege to Aleppo. The young Baldwin IV immediately mounted a new diversion, this time against the fertile valley of the Bekaa, "a land so delectable," says the *Eracles*, "that it is flowing with milk and honey." After defeating a Damascene army corps near Andjar, Baldwin led his chivalry "with great joy" back to Tyre, where the booty was shared. Thus, even under the reign of this poor leper boy, even in the face of Moslem unity, three fourths restored, the Franks kept Islam at bay.

The brilliant victory of the young sovereign in the Bekaa could only increase the general sorrow at the incurable disease by which he was attacked. As his leprosy grew worse, leaving him no hope of marriage, he found himself, on the morrow of his triumph, bound to arrange for his succession, like a dying man. True, his cousin, Count Raymond III of Tripoli, would have had all the necessary qualities to take over this burdened inheritance; but as the Salic Law did not run here, his rights were postponed to those of the two sisters of Baldwin IV, Sibylla and Isabella. On Sibylla, the elder, in particular, the future of the dynasty reposed, and on the choice of her husband depended the destiny of the realm.

The choice of Baldwin IV and his counselors fell on the Piedmontese baron, William Long-Sword, son of the marquis of Montferrat. At the beginning of October 1176, the fair-haired young man, one of the most handsome and valiant knights of his time, landed at Sidon, and, with magnificent feasting, wed the Princess Sibylla. But fate was cruel for Frankish Outremer, and within a few months William was dead of malaria at Ascalon and the whole question of the succession was thrown open again (June 1177).

At this juncture, an illustrious crusader, Philip of Alsace, count of Flanders, landed in Palestine with an imposing escort. Baldwin IV, his first cousin, welcomed him as a savior. From Robert II, the hero of the First Crusade, down to Thierry of Alsace, Flanders had played a magnificent role in the history of Frankish Syria. At that very hour, the Byzantine Emperor Manuel Comnenus, fulfilling his promises to the late King Amalric, announced the dispatch of an armada to cooperate with the Franks in a new raid on Egypt. But Philip declined to take part in an expedition which he deemed hazardous. No doubt the final setback of King Amalric was hardly encouraging. It was nonetheless true that only in Egypt could Saladin's empire be shaken, on condition, naturally, that this time Franks and Byzantines cooperated with equal ardor in the operations. The court of Constantinople, alerted by events, had finally made up its mind to exert every necessary effort; but in spite of the pathetic supplications of the Leper King, Philip of Alsace persisted in his refusal. The Byzantine admirals re-embarked in disgust. As for Philip, instead of attacking Saladin at the vulnerable point, in the delta, he set off campaigning in northern Syria, not without first autocratically borrowing from Baldwin IV the best troops in the kingdom. Saladin realized that Palestine was thereby stripped of defenders. Quitting Egypt immediately with his cavalry, he conducted a lightning raid on Ascalon, the main bulwark of Frankish power in the southwest.

In this agonizing situation, the young king proved heroic. His army, lent to the count of Flanders, was waging distant battles, somewhere between Antioch and Aleppo. He had no more than four hundred men at hand. Rallying all that he could, he went to meet the invader, accompanied by the True Cross. So fast did he march that he outstripped Saladin to Ascalon. Scarcely had he entered the city when it was invested by the Egyptian army, twenty-six thousand strong. The Frankish situation seemed so desperate that Saladin, disregarding the contemptible little army whose surrender appeared only a question of hours, decided to leave only a thin screen of troops before it at Ascalon and march straight on Judea, perhaps even on Jerusalem, devoid of defenders. On his route across the plain which stretches from Ascalon to Ramleh, he burned the townships and pillaged the farms, letting his troops enrich themselves with the loot of a whole countryside. In his triumphant and unopposed march, he had arrived, according to some chroniclers, near Tel-Jezir, the Montgisard of the Franks, or according to others, only at Tel as-Safiya, the Blanchegarde of the crusaders, at the mouth of the valley of Terebinthes, and was setting about taking his army across the bed of a wadi when, to his stupefaction, he saw rising before him, on the side where he least expected, that Frankish army which he believed reduced to impotence behind the walls of Ascalon (November 25, 1177).

He had indeed reckoned without Baldwin IV. As soon as the king, from the height of the towers of Ascalon, descried Saladin's departure, he had led his little army into the field; but instead of following the enemy on the high road to Jerusalem, he had swung northward along the coast and then dropped straight down to the southeast on the track of the Moslems. In crossing the countryside devastated by the Moslem scouts, the little troop was animated by a burning desire for vengeance. Near Ramleh they came up with the Moslem columns strung out in the bed of the wadi. In other circumstances, the Frankish chivalry would no doubt have hesitated in the face of its incredible numerical inferiority, but the ardor of the first crusaders burned in the Leper King. "God, who manifests his strength in the weak," writes

Michael the Syrian, "inspired the sick king. He dismounted, prostrated himself on the ground before the Cross, and prayed in tears. At
this sight the hearts of all the soldiery were moved and they swore on
the Cross not to give way and to hold as a traitor any man who turned
his bridle. They remounted and charged." In the van went the True
Cross, borne by Bishop Albert of Bethlehem; once again it was to
dominate the battle, and the Christian combatants were later to have
the impression that in the midst of the fray it seemed to grow immense
and reach the very sky. The chroniclers show us Baldwin IV and his
three hundred knights plunging in and losing themselves for an instant
in the throng of Moslem forces who tried to rally in the middle of the
wadi. The Moslems, who first thought to crush them by sheer weight
of numbers, soon began to lose countenance before the Frankish fury.
"The passage," says the *Book of the Two Gardens*, "was encumbered
with the baggage of the army. Of a sudden the Frankish squadrons
appeared, quick as foxes, baying like hounds; they charged in mass,
ardent as flame. The Moslems gave ground." Saladin, sultan of Egypt
and Damascus, with his thousands of Turks, Kurds, Arabs, and Sudanese, fled before the three hundred knights of the leper boy.

It was a headlong flight. Casting away their baggage, their helmets,
and their arms, they galloped across the Amalek desert straight for the
stream of Egypt and the delta. For two days Baldwin IV gathered in a
prodigious booty on all their tracks and then returned to Jerusalem in
triumphant array. No finer Christian victory had ever been won in
the Levant; and in the absence of the count of Flanders and the count
of Tripoli, all the merit redounded to the heroism of the king, whose
seventeen years, triumphing for an instant over the evil which was
eating away his body, equaled the maturity of a Godfrey of Bouillon
or a Tancred.

Baldwin profited from his victory to place Galilee under protection
against incursions from Damascus. In October 1178, he erected at
Jacob's Ford, on the banks of the Upper Jordan, a powerful fortress,
designed to command the historic route which runs from Tiberias to
Qoneitra. Further north, by the sources of the Jordan, he disputed
with the Damascenes the region of Baniyas, the old frontier marches
recently lost. In April 1179, as with his constable, Humphrey of
Toron, he was conducting a somewhat hazardous raid in this direction,
he was surprised by the Damascene troops. The old constable, respon-

sible for the imprudence committed, saved the young king. Shielding
the prince's retreat with his own body, he was riddled with wounds
but held off the enemy and returned to die, his honor saved, in his
fortress of Hunin. Meanwhile Saladin, returned from Egypt with a
new army, was preparing to invade Galilee from Baniyas. Boldly,
Baldwin IV resolved to stop him. At the head of his chivalry, and
accompanied by the count of Tripoli, he galloped as far as the entry to
Marj Ayun, the prairie lying between the great bend of the river Litani
and the forest of Baniyas, where, from the heights of Hunin, he
descried the enemy masses in the process of concentration, while their
forage parties returned from fruitful raids into Phoenicia. Repeating
the surprise attack of Montgisard and Blanchegarde, Baldwin fell on
these isolated detachments and routed them. Unfortunately, in their
too rapid descent from the mountain, the knights had become somewhat dispersed. From his headquarters at Baniyas, Saladin had time to
come up with his main body. Rallying the runaways, he fell on the
breathless French cavalry and, after a furious melee, routed it in turn.
Baldwin IV and the count of Tripoli managed to escape, but many
others were killed or captured (June 10, 1179). A few weeks later
Saladin razed to the ground the fortress of Jacob's Ford. But hostilities stopped there. The following year Saladin and Baldwin IV concluded a renewable truce, which under the Frankish-Moslem law of
the time, was equivalent to peace. In sum, during these three years the
Leper King had stood up to the redoubtable sultan, and the agreement
of 1180 confirmed the *status quo*.

Unfortunately, Baldwin's condition was growing worse. The leprosy was manifesting itself in its full hideousness. With his stigmata,
the character of the heroic young man became darker. He now had
fits of mistrust toward his entourage. In 1180, when the prince of
Antioch and the count of Tripoli set out to perform their devotions at
the Holy Sepulcher, he imagined that they wanted to take advantage
of his physical incapacities to depose him. A sick man's fancies, but
they showed how necessary was an official settlement of the succession
to the throne. The heiress was still his eldest sister, Sibylla, whose
husband, William of Montferrat, had died after a few months of
marriage, leaving a posthumous son, the future Baldwin V. As the
Leper King might quit the scene at any moment, and a long regency

was to be foreseen, it was important to marry the princess again in all haste. The king and the court were therefore seeking a suitable match for Sibylla among the sovereign families of the West, when she let it be known that her heart had chosen with little heed for political calculations.

The happy subject of her choice was a simple Poitevin younger son, without fortune or personal distinction, Guy of Lusignan. Ever since his arrival in Palestine, his handsome bearing and elegant manners had made the most favorable impression on the young widow. Her idle hours and her romantic and passionate crossbred Frankish character did the rest. If the malevolences of the chroniclers are to be believed, she had even committed such indiscretions with Guy that the marriage was inevitable. Baldwin IV, at the height of his personal crisis, had no strength to resist the pressing solicitations of his sister. He gave his consent to the lovers' union and enfeoffed Guy with the county of Jaffa and Ascalon (1180).

This romance was to have disastrous political consequences. A penniless younger son, unconnected with the Syrian nobility, who always regarded him as a foreigner and an upstart, designated by the whim of an amorous woman and the lassitude of a moribund sovereign, with no other claim to his elevation except that of being the handsomest man of his time, Guy was badly served even by his negative qualities. His natural naïveté, as sung by the poet Ambroise, passed for "simpleness." In his own family, he was thought to be a bit of a simpleton; and when they learned that "Guido," the little brother, was about to win a crown down there thanks to the infatuation of a fanciful queen, his eldest brother burst out laughing: "If Guy can become a king, why cannot I become a god?" Indeed, such a frivolous choice, at such a tragic moment, when the Leper King was traveling fast to the grave, when Egypt and Damascus were united under the iron hand of Saladin, was a veritable gamble. Into the bargain, Isabella, the younger sister of Baldwin IV and Sibylla, shortly afterward married another stripling, Humphrey IV of Toron, who, although the heir of a line of heroes, was an even more insignificant *"poulain,"* as weak morally as he was physically and quite incapable, as we shall see, of playing any role at all.

In the meantime, the state of the Leper King worsened from day to day; "he seemed already quite rotted away and his limbs like to fail him." At this stage of his illness, he could no longer, in spite of his energy, deal with business, except in spasms. His immediate entourage took advantage of it to hoodwink him and pocket the benefits. His own mother, Agnes of Courtenay, the repudiated ex-wife of King Amalric, "who was scarce a woman of good repute," distinguished herself by her thirst for power and her greed. Her brother, Joscelin III of Courtenay, seneschal of Jerusalem, allied himself with her in cynically exploiting the pitiful condition of the king and the kingdom.

Let us sum up the details which the chroniclers give us on this subject. A decadent court. The heiress to the throne conveying the heritage to a worthless pretty boy. The king's other sister about to marry an insignificant lordling. The queen mother, flighty and rapacious, intervening solely in favor of the caucus. Finally, the king dying of leprosy and, in spite of his great worth, most frequently reduced to helplessness by his hideous disease. All the elements for the fall of a state.

Only one man could save the kingdom, Count Raymond III of Tripoli. But it was precisely he who was the bugbear of the caucus. And he went from Tripoli to visit his estates in Galilee, the queen mother and the seneschal Joscelin persuaded the unhappy king that the count was coming to snatch away his kingdom, and Raymond was forbidden to enter Galilee. The count returned to Tripoli, humiliated and furious. The wisest of the barons had great difficulty in appeasing his wrath and later reconciling him with the king.

The count of Tripoli being cold-shouldered and power being in the hands of such colorless individuals as Joscelin III and Guy of Lusignan, a new actor, or rather an old one come back, was to cast himself in a leading role in the affairs of the kingdom, the old prince of Antioch, Reynald of Châtillon, finally released from the Turkish prisons and invested, thanks to a second marriage, with the lordship of Transjordan and Wadi Musa. We have already seen the savage character of this brigand-knight, a typical representative of the pillaging and sanguinary feudalism of the West, become in the East a sort of Frankish Bedouin who regarded war merely as a looting expedition. Twenty years earlier he had, by his brigandage and even atrocities in the island of Cyprus, almost roused up the Byzantine Empire against the Franks.

But what would happen if he renewed the same acts of banditry against an adversary like Saladin? Now that Egypt and Damascus were united under the scepter of the great sultan, if he obeyed any principle it was above all the freedom of communication between his two kingdoms. But Reynald's new fief, with the district of Moab (Kerak) and Idumaea (Wadi Musa), precisely cut the route from Damascus to Cairo. At least it was necessary that, from his citadels of Kerak and Montreal, Reynald should refrain from any attacks on the Moslem caravans so long as the truces remained in force. But who could stop him? The eclipse of royalty during the crises of the Leper King, the boycott of the count of Tripoli, the insignificance of the other Frankish dignitaries, all conspired to highlight the harsh personality of the lord of Transjordan. Suddenly placed in this situation without a peer, free to involve all the Franks by his personal initiatives, without countercheck and without bridle, the old adventurer was to drag the kingdom into adventure with him. During the summer of 1181, at the height of the peace, without even entertaining the idea of denouncing the truce, he penetrated Arabia in the hope of thrusting into the Hejaz as far as Mecca. He was unable to carry out his projects, but he surprised a great caravan which was quite tranquilly traveling from Damascus to Mecca and carried it off.

The news of this senseless agression plunged the court of Jerusalem into consternation. Baldwin IV, in particular, seems to have felt violent indignation at the conduct of his vassal. The peace, so essential to the Franks, was now broken by their fault, in odious circumstances, which made them appear in the eyes of all Islam as breakers of the plighted truce. Baldwin, who always reasserted his kingship in the hour of peril, addressed an energetic remonstrance to Reynald and summoned him to restore all the prisoners and booty to Saladin forthwith. But the lord of Transjordan laughed at the royal authority. Every appeal to honor or duty addressed to him he answered with a blank refusal. The unhappy king was forced to admit to Saladin that he was powerless to enforce obedience. It was the signal for general war.

It was at the same time the collapse of royal authority or, in other words, of the Frankish state. The most powerful of all the feudal lords took advantage of the physical breakdown of the Leper King to proclaim implicitly the breakdown of the monarchy. Openly flouting his sovereign, he committed king and kingdom, without their warrant and against their will, to the road to suicide.

Coming out of the blue, without any preliminary warning, the rupture of the peace had immediate and highly painful consequences for the Franks. Saladin hastened up from Cairo to Transjordan with the whole Egyptian army. Reynald of Châtillon, who had so lately flouted the royal authority, implored the help of Baldwin IV to save his fief. The young king, whose sanctity equaled his heroism, had the generosity to respond to this appeal and, at the risk of leaving Palestine unmanned, went down with the Frankish army toward Moab; but Saladin, avoiding a clash, made straight for Damascus, while other Moslem detachments made raids across Galilee, leaving fire and blood behind them. The sultan, crossing the Jordan in full strength, then invaded Galilee in his turn, where he attacked the stronghold of Beisan and then the Frankish fortress of Belvoir (the modern Kaukab), which protected the route to Nazareth. The Frankish army, back from Moab, took up its position facing him. In spite of their numerical inferiority, the Franks bore themselves so stoutly that Saladin, under the teeth of their counterattack, fell back across the Jordan, defeated (July 1182).

The sultan then devised a daring project: to cut the kingdom of Jerusalem off from the county of Tripoli by taking Beirut. In August 1182, he crossed the Lebanon at full speed and appeared unexpectedly before the town, while an Egyptian squadron hastened up, plying every oar. Once again, the Leper King was the savior of the country. From Galilee, where he was camping, he galloped up with his chivalry, not forgetting, on the way, to order all Christian ships anchored off the coast to set sail for Beirut. His movement was so rapid that Saladin found all his plans thwarted. The people of Beirut had, moreover, defended themselves stoutly. When the sultan learned of the king's approach he realized that his stroke had failed, and he withdrew across the Lebanon after sacking farms and crops.

The brilliant relief of Beirut proves that, in spite of a situation full of peril, the Frankish state was standing its ground against the enemy all around. Even represented by an ill-fated leper, the Angevin dynasty was vigilantly fulfilling its tutelary role. And what an epic character —from a Christian epic, where spiritual values prevail—was this young chief who, his limbs eaten away by ulcers, his flesh falling from his bones, still had himself borne at the head of his troops, galvanized them by his martyr's presence, and in the midst of all his sufferings again had the pride of putting Saladin to flight!

The hero in Baldwin was coupled with the statesman. Pursuing the old Moslem policy of his predecessors, now that the kingdom was freed from invasion, he set about defending the secondary Islamic dynasties, the Turkish atabegs of Aleppo and Mosul and the family of Nur ed-Din, against the annexationist and unitary designs of the sultan. As Saladin attacked those two cities, Baldwin had no hesitation in making a powerful diversion in their favor in the Hauran and Damascene Sawad (September to October 1182). Better still, in the course of a third expedition, Baldwin advanced into the suburbs of Damascus, as far as Dareiya, where, moreover, he respected the mosque. After this brilliant expedition right up to the gates of Saladin's capital, the Leper King returned to celebrate Christmas 1182 at Tyre in the company of his old tutor, our historian, Archbishop William.

But, with an adversary of Saladin's activity, the Leper King would have had to be constantly in the saddle to thwart the enemy's plans. In the autumn of 1182, the Frankish diversions had saved the independence of Aleppo from the attacks of the sultan. In the following year, the ineptitude of the last local Turkish kings delivered the city up to him (June 1183). This time the whole of Moslem Syria as well as Egypt belonged to the great sultan. The situation of the Franks, in spite of the desperate efforts of Baldwin IV, was becoming blacker and blacker. Saladin, after the annexation of Aleppo, had returned to his faithful city of Damascus to mount the invasion of Palestine (August 1183). At this news, Baldwin summoned all the Frankish forces to the fountains of Sephoria, the usual rallying point of the Christian armies. It was there that his malady triumphed over his heroism.

After a halt of some months, the terrible evil had resumed its progress. Baldwin IV was now in the last phase. "His leprosy," says the chronicler, "weakened him so that he could no longer use his hands or his feet. He was all rotted away and on the point of losing his sight." In this condition, almost blind, immobilized for long periods on his couch, a living corpse, he still struggled against his destiny, and anyone who has followed his activity since his accession can understand his pathetic and painful inner conflict. Even in this state, with his heroic spirit, he still wished to govern. In vain his entourage counseled him to withdraw from public affairs, to retire to some palace "with a good income, to live honorably." He refused, says the chronicle, "because, though feeble of body, he was lofty of soul and his will was greater than human strength. But bouts of fever finally brought him down. Around his bed at Nazareth his nearest kin assembled, his mother, his brother-in-law Guy of Lusignan, the Patriarch Heraclius. In this family council the unhappy sovereign delegated Guy as "bailiff" or, in other words, as regent of the realm.

The new bailiff immediately proved himself a poor chief. "Vain and puffed up with pride at his new dignity," writes the chronicler, "he behaved like a madman; he was, in any event, a man of little sense." His lack of authority became apparent when, in October 1183, Saladin again invaded Galilee. Guy, who had advanced to meet him, allowed himself to be encircled between Sephoria and Ain Jalud and, in spite of a terrible inferiority of numbers was about to order a charge, which would have been suicide. The count of Tripoli stopped him. Thanks to the count, the Frankish army, compact and bristling, refused battle and remained intact. This purely defensive strategy got the better of Saladin's patience. He struck camp and went back to Damascus.

Throughout the campaign, Guy of Lusignan had distinguished himself only by his irresolution and his inexperience. The old Palestinian barons had nothing but scorn for this newcomer whom the favor of the Princess Sibylla had forced upon them as chief. Profiting from this state of mind, some zealous courtiers set about embroiling Baldwin IV and his brother-in-law. Guy was foolish enough to resent the king's request for an explanation; and the Leper, egged on by the barons, and whose actions, owing to his torments, had now become spasmodic and almost breathless, felt himself threatened. He immediately deprived Guy of the "bailiwick" of the realm and, at the same time, of all hopes of the succession. To bar the way to this incompetent youth, a child of barely five was proclaimed king, as partner to the throne and heir presumptive, the young Baldwin V, the son of Guy's wife, Sibylla, by her first marriage to William of Montferrat (November 1183). To match Saladin there were now two kings, a poor, almost blind leper, practically bedridden, and a five-year-old child! The feudal party, it is true, seemed to temper these disadvantages by reserving the regency

for the count of Tripoli, the only statesman capable of replacing
Baldwin IV.

They had reckoned without Reynald of Châtillon. The lord of
Transjordan had not joined in the maneuvers of the great vassals who
had snatched the regency from Guy of Lusignan to guard the reversion for the count of Tripoli. He was bound to prefer the feeble
Lusignan, whom he hoped to dominate easily, rather than that shrewd
politician, Raymond III; moreover, the prudent methods of Raymond,
the inheritor of the traditions of the royalty of Jerusalem, were bound
to hinder his pillaging enterprises.

The lord of Transjordan was, indeed, reviving his old designs on the
holy cities of Arabia, Mecca and Medina. Having built a small fleet, he
transported the dismantled parts by camel from Transjordan to the
Gulf of Akaba on the Red Sea. Once launched, this surprise squadron
conducted a running warfare along the coasts of Egypt and the Hejaz,
seizing Moslem ships and sacking the ports, capturing caravans and
stopping all traffic. The aim of these Frankish corsairs was twofold.
Their object was to cut the pilgrim route to Mecca, by sea as well as
overland by the Hadj road, and strike at the head of the Moslem world,
and secondly, by the conquest of Aila in the north and the projected
conquest of Aden in the south, to hold the commerce of the Indian
Ocean for ransom.

It was a project beyond all measure, which would have called for the
full force of the Frankish monarchy at its zenith but which in the
precarious state of Baldwin IV's kingdom could only rouse the una-
nimity of Islam against the Franks. The patient policy of the kingdom
of Jerusalem, playing on the dissensions of the Moslems, had had the
constant aim of getting the Frankish state accepted as a valuable factor
in maintaining the equilibrium of the East. The Moslem princes had
grown so used to this idea that we have seen them constantly appealing
to the king of Jerusalem against their own fellow believers. In contrast, Reynald's sacrilegious enterprise made the Franks appear as the
inveterate enemies of the faith of the Koran. By directly threatening
Mecca and Medina, their corsairs again provoked that wave of indignation throughout all Islam which had flooded it before, in 1099, after the
massacre of the Mosque of Omar. Reynald's lair, the fortress of Krak
of Moab, suddenly cast its long shadow as far as the sands of the Hejaz

and, in the imagination of the Moslems, assumed the monstrous aspect of an Apocalyptic vision. It became, says an Arab historian, "the anguish that grips the throat, the barrier that closes the way, the wolf that lurks in the valley. Men thought that the day of the Last Judgment was come and the earth would return to chaos."

Saladin, spurred on by the unanimous sentiment of Islam, acted with decision. A strong Egyptian squadron, launched by him in the Red Sea, destroyed the Frankish flotilla, and in November 1183, he came in person, at the head of a powerful army, to lay siege, in Transjordan, to Reynald's fortress, the famous Krak of Moab (Kerak). The walls were threatening to crumble under the incessant bombardment of his mangonels, when once again royalty saved its imprudent vassals. The beacon fire lit on the lofty Tower of David in Jerusalem found its answer from tower to tower across the fortress keeps of southern Judaea and announced to the besiegers of the Krak of Moab on the other side of the Dead Sea that relief was on the way. Baldwin IV, the living corpse, again proved himself a king. Blind, paralyzed, dying, he summoned his troops, placed the count of Tripoli at their head, and followed them himself in his litter as far as Kerak. Once again Saladin withdrew without waiting for him. The Leper King made a triumphal entry into the fortress, welcomed as a savior by the throng of the besieged. He put new heart into the garrison, had the damaged parts of the ramparts rebuilt, and did not return to Jerusalem until he had done his duty as a chief to the end (December 1183).

The last months of the reign of Baldwin IV all but witnessed the outbreak of a civil war in the face of the enemy. We have seen the king's conduct toward Guy of Lusignan. Since he had penetrated his brother-in-law's incapacity and discerned the peril for Christendom represented by the man who was to be the grave-digger of the Frankish state, his indulgence for Guy had changed to a clear-sighted aversion. Not only had he deprived him of the office of bailiff but he sought to have Sibylla's marriage annulled. Guy profited from an absence of Baldwin's to hurry to Jerusalem, where Sibylla had stayed behind, and to take her back with him before the king's return. Taking refuge with her in his fief of Jaffa-Ascalon, he refused to obey the king's orders summoning him to appear before him. It was an open fight. The king marched against Ascalon only to find the gates

closed against him, but he succeeded in laying hold of Jaffa. He then
called a parliament at Acre to have done with the rebel. The Patriarch
Heraclius and the grand master of the Temple tried in vain to intercede
for him. Guy was all the less deserving of pardon since he had just
been guilty of an abominable act. In the neighborhood of Ascalon a
party of Bedouin nomads, tributaries to the king and under his protection, were peacefully grazing their flocks in full confidence when Guy,
in order to harm his sovereign, fell upon them and massacred them.

Baldwin's wrath in the face of this act of felony was tremendous. It
was then that he finally conferred all power on the count of Tripoli,
Lusignan's enemy (1185). For the rest, events came thick and fast.
The Leper King was on his deathbed. He summoned his great vassals
and repeated his will that the count should hold the regency until the
majority of the young Baldwin V.

The heroic prince whose reign had been a long slow agony gave up
his soul to God on March 16, 1185. When one remembers that he was
only twenty-four and when one thinks of all he was able to accomplish
during those short years, in spite of his leprosy and his ultimate
incapacitation and blindness, one is filled with respect and admiration.
Knowing how to maintain to his last breath the royal authority and the
integrity of the realm, he knew too how to die like a king. The
chronicles depict for us the dramatic scene in which, knowing that the
end had come, he summoned all the grandees of the realm. "Before he
died, he summoned all his vassals before him at Jerusalem and all came
and when he left this world below, all were there at his death." Like
the Frankish chroniclers, the Arab historians bow before his memory.
"This leper child knew how to make his authority respected," writes
Imad ed-Din of Isfahan, almost with a swordsman's salute. He was a
stoic and dolorous figure, perhaps the noblest in the history of the
Crusades, a figure whose heroism, beneath the sores and scales which
covered him, borders on sanctity, the pure image of a Frankish king,
whom I have tried to rescue from an unjust oblivion to place alongside
a Marcus Aurelius or a Louis IX.

Delivered from his long martyrdom, the Leper King was entombed
near Golgotha and the Holy Sepulcher, where the Man of Sorrows, his
God, had died and where He had rested.

THE DISASTER OF TIBERIAS
Guy of Lusignan

Aᴄᴄᴏʀᴅɪɴɢ to the last wishes of the Leper King, his
nephew, Baldwin V, aged five or six, "Baudouinet" as the Frankish
chroniclers call him, succeeded him under the regency of the count of
Tripoli, Raymond III (March 1185).

During his regency, Raymond, profiting from his Moslem friend-
ships, made peace with Saladin, a welcome peace which gave the
kingdom time to breathe. The year 1185 had been marked by a
terrible drought and the country was threatened with famine, when
Saladin, at the request of the count, revictualed the Franks, a gesture
which, by the confession of the chroniclers, was their salvation. The
country, then, was in good hands when, after a few months, the young
Baldwin V died at Acre (about September 1186).

The death of the child-king reopened the whole issue. Who was to
have the throne? By rights, the Princess Sibylla, Baldwin IV's sister,
and her husband, Guy of Lusignan. But Guy had been disinherited by
Baldwin IV, who seemed to have designated Raymond of Tripoli as
the choice of the barons if young Baldwin were to die. Raymond was
connected with the reigning dynasty as the grandson, through his
mother, of Baldwin II. He had the great majority of the barons on his
side. In the present plight of the country he represented the party of
prudence and peace.

But Sibylla and Guy of Lusignan had found four powerful protectors, the Patriarch Heraclius of Jerusalem, the grand master of the Temple, Gerard of Ridfort, Reynald of Châtillon and the former guardian of the young Baldwin, Joscelin III of Courtenay.

Heraclius was the reverse of a saint. The Christian chroniclers paint an indignant picture of this dissolute beau, who was less at home with the Scriptures than with women. The Queen Dowager Agnes had favored him for the patriarchal see over that saintly prelate, Archbishop William of Tyre. In this high station, far from reforming, he continued to lead a life of scandal. He set up his mistress, Paschia de Riveri, in Jerusalem, so that when she passed through the streets, weighed down with silk and pearls, the people irreverently cried, "Here comes Madame la Patriarchesse!" Though despised by the religious-minded, Heraclius wielded all the authority of his office. To please his old friend, the queen dowager, he threw the whole weight of his influence behind Guy of Lusignan. As for the grand master of the Temple, he was estranged from the count of Tripoli by an ancient quarrel. Long before, as a young Flemish knight, he had come to seek his fortune in the East and had entered the service of the count, who had befriended him; but, having failed to obtain from the count the reversion of the fief of Botrun, he had sworn inveterate hatred against his old master. Having entered holy orders and become grand master of the Temple, Gerard was to use the enormous power of these knightly monks to serve his personal vengeance. Reynald of Châtillon was no less hostile to the count of Tripoli. The count's prudent and temporizing methods, his preference for a policy of peace with Saladin thwarted the anarchical fire, the adventurousness, the robber habits of the lord of Transjordan. He declared with violence for Guy of Lusignan, indecisive and weak as he was, because Lusignan seemed to him singularly easier to handle. But the one of the four accomplices who carried the day was Joscelin III.

Like so many third-generation "*poulains*," Joscelin was an intriguing Levantine, without either heart or faith. The child Baldwin V had died under his care and custody at Acre. Feigning to enter into the projects of the count of Tripoli, Joscelin himself undertook to conduct the body to Jerusalem, the scene of the royal burying grounds, while the count assembled his forces at Tiberias. While Raymond trustingly set out for Galilee, Joscelin, Sibylla, and Guy of Lusignan hastened to Jerusalem to seize power under cover of the obsequies.

Furious at finding himself tricked, Raymond summoned the barons to a "parliament" at Nablus. All of them, except Reynald of Châtillon, attended, firmly resolved to oppose Guy's *coup d'état*. But it was too late. Installed in Jerusalem, Sibylla acted as the legitimate heiress of the ancient kings. The Patriarch Heraclius brought her the support of the clergy. Summoned by her, Reynald hastened from Kerak to place his sword at the service of the young woman. Gerard of Ridfort's hatred for Raymond did the rest. Fortified by the principle of legitimacy which she represented in strict law, she summoned Raymond and the barons of Nablus to attend her coronation. The barons, on their side, recalled the express will of the Leper King and forbade the patriarch to proceed with the crowning.

The patriarch, the grand master of the Temple, and Reynald overrode this veto. In defense against any attack mounted from Nablus, they had the gates of Jerusalem closed. The grand master of the Hospitalers, asked for the keys of the treasury containing the royal crowns, refused to yield them without a mandate from the assembly of Nablus. He shut himself up in the house of his order, unyielding, inaccessible. The time went by. They begged him, they pleaded with him. Worn down at last, he flung the keys in the midst of the hall and they fetched the regalia. The patriarch crowned Sibylla, and she, in turn, crowned her husband. "She took the crown and summoned her lord, Guy of Lusignan, saying, 'My Lord, come, receive this crown, for I know no man to whom I may better offer it.' Then he knelt before her and she placed the crown on his head." It is a pretty picture of womanly love, but the grand master of the Temple, Gerard of Ridfort, savoring his vengeance against the man who had once thwarted him of the fief of Botrun, murmured between his teeth, thinking of the absent Raymond III: "This crown is well worth the reversion of Botrun!" A revealing word; the whole affair had been mounted as a foul blow. But those who knew Guy's incompetence were under no illusion about the future of the Holy Land. The old Baldwin of Ramleh, the most valiant baron in the land, greeted the news of the coronation by saying: "He will not last a year as king! The realm is lost."

Nothing was achieved, however, so long as the assembly of barons meeting at Nablus did not give its assent. But it had just devised a solution. As we have seen, Sibylla's younger sister, Isabella, had married the son of one of the leading families of the kingdom, Humphrey, lord of Toron, whom the memory of his heroic grandfather, the old constable, rendered dear to all the Franks. The assembly therefore offered the throne to Humphrey and Isabella. Unfortunately, Humphrey was nothing but a timid, good-looking lad, who was frightened of the role they wanted to force upon him. That very night he fled secretly from Nablus to Jerusalem. Queen Sibylla, when he presented himself before her, received him coolly enough, which completed his discomfiture. All penitent, says the chronicle, he began to scratch his head "like a child caught in the act" and to excuse himself pitifully: "It is not my fault, madame, they wanted to make me king by force." Sibylla, knowing whom she was dealing with, and ending by taking advantage of the situation, replied: "Then I forgive you; and now go and do your homage to the king!"

The defection of their candidate threw disorder into the barons' camp. Deprived of any legal grounds for excluding Guy, they were forced to fall into line with more or less good grace. Only Raymond III, in his county of Tripoli and his lordship of Tiberias remained in a state of dissidence. For a moment Guy thought of marching against him, and it took all the wisdom of the old "wise men" to prevent such a criminal combat. Under the menace, moreover, Raymond became closer to Saladin. Without betraying the Frankish cause, as his adversaries alleged, he began to negotiate a pact of security and guarantee with the sultan. In any event, the situation became troubled, the path of duty uncertain. The hour seemed propitious for the worst adventures.

It was that moment that Reynald of Châtillon chose to provoke a war.

After the disaster of the squadron which he had launched on the Red Sea, Reynald too had made a truce with Saladin. It was all grist to his mill, since, thanks to the peace, he levied handsome customs duties on the Moslem caravans which were bound to traverse his lands of Wadi Musa or Transjordan to get from Damascus to Cairo or from Cairo or Damascus on the pilgrimage to Mecca. But the old robber-knight could not long resist the temptation to pillage. At the end of 1186 or the beginning of 1187, as an exceptionally large caravan, laden with enormous wealth, was announced, coming from Cairo and traveling toward Damascus, he could no longer restrain himself. He set an ambush, surprised the convoy, laid hands on the merchandise, and flung merchants, caravaners, and escorting troops into the dungeons of Kerak.

At this news, Saladin summoned Reynald to return the booty. The lord of Transjordan replied with a peremptory refusal. Saladin then appealed to King Guy of Lusignan. Guy, who at least understood the gravity of the situation, begged Reynald to give the sultan satisfaction; but he too was met with a blank refusal. Such disobedience shows how little the new king was respected, even by those who had forced him on the country. Flouted by his own partisans, while the principal vassal of the crown refused to recognize him, he proved himself, from the very first steps, incapable of organizing the defense of the realm in a state of war.

For general war it was. From the month of May 1187, Saladin, drunk for vengeance, blockaded Reynald in Kerak and pillaged all of Transjordan. Then he resolved to invade the kingdom of Jerusalem itself and, for that purpose, asked his new-found friend, the count of Tripoli, for free passage across the land of Galilee, which, it will be remembered, indeed belonged to Raymond. This demand plunged the count into the most cruel embarrassment. So far he had played off Saladin's protection against Guy. But the game could not go on. If he refused the right of passage, he embroiled himself with the redoubtable sultan. If he granted it, he placed himself under the ban of Christendom. He tried to escape with a half-measure. He authorized Saladin's advance guards to make a demonstration on Frankish territory, on condition that they entered at sunrise and returned across the Jordan before night, and contented themselves with reconnoitering the country without harming any village or attacking any town. In this way, he thought to observe the letter of his treaty with Saladin, while at the same time tempering the clash between the Moslems and the king.

At this juncture, Guy, desiring to unite the Frankish forces in the face of the enemy, sent a delegation to Raymond, then installed at Tiberias, among whom, by misfortune, was the count's personal enemy, the grand master of the Temple, Gerard of Ridfort. As soon as Gerard learned that on the morrow Saladin's troops were to make a demonstration, by way of Galilee, as far as Samaria, he alerted the Templars of the region and, himself at their head, advanced against the

Moslems. He came up with them near Sephoria. The Moslems, faithful to their pact with Raymond III, were returning peaceably, their demonstration made, and having done no serious harm to Christian lands. Against this expeditionary force of many thousands, the grand master had no more than a hundred and fifty knights. In vain did his own lieutenant, the marshal of the Temple, James of Mailly, try to convince him of the rashness of an attack. He turned on Mailly with insults, accusing him, before the others, of cowardice: "You set too much store by that fair head you are so determined to keep!" "I know how to die as becomes a gentle knight," retorted Mailly. "It is you who will turn tail!" After that, there was nothing left but to seek death. The hundred and fifty knights hurled themselves against the Moslem army with such fury, says the Arab chronicle, "that the blackest of hair would have turned white with fear." But they were overwhelmed by numbers. Three only of the Templars escaped alive, among them, as Mailly had foretold, the grand master, Gerard of Ridfort.

After this unexpected victory, the Moslem column returned from Sephoria toward the Jordan, brandishing on their lances the heads of the slain Templars. From the ramparts of Tiberias Raymond III and his companions saw this macabre cavalcade defile before them. Raymond was dumbfounded. Forthwith, he submitted to be reconciled with the king and even set out to meet him. The encounter took place at Saint-Job, near Jenin. The count bent the knee; Guy raised him up, embraced him, and, making the first advance, apologized for the circumstances of his precipitate coronation. But the time for discussions between Christians was past. Guy and Raymond agreed to concentrate all the Frankish forces at the rallying point of Sephoria, in the center of Galilee, halfway between Tiberias and the sea. This "general mobilization," once completed, yielded some 1500 knights and 20,000 infantry or native auxiliaries.

It was high time. Saladin, "with a numberless army, like the Ocean," was invading Galilee in the direction of Tiberias. The lower town of Tiberias was taken in an hour and the Countess Eschiva, Raymond III's wife, found herself besieged in the citadel. It was Raymond's first interest to rescue her. But as a cool politician, he was also the first to be ready to sacrifice Tiberias and his family rather than risk an ill-considered march. The Franks were numerically inferior.

The month of July, torrid in those regions, favored the Moslem light cavalry over the ironclad knights. They must decline battle, remain on the defensive, wear down the adversary, whose contingents, mobilized for a short campaign, must ultimately disperse. It is a moving exchange that the chronicle of Ernoul recounts here. "Sire," said the count of Tripoli to the king, "I would fain give you counsel, but I know in advance that you will not heed me!" "Speak on." "Well, then, I counsel you, sire, to let the citadel of Tiberias be taken. Tiberias is mine; the lady of Tiberias is my countess; she is in the fortress with my children and all my fortune. I am therefore the first to be concerned and no one will lose as much as I by the fall of the citadel. But I know that if the Moslems take it, they cannot hold it. If they raze the walls I will build them again. If they capture my wife and my children I will pay their ransom. But I would rather see my wife captive and my city taken than the whole Holy Land lost. For lost you are, if you march against Tiberias at this moment. I know the country. Along the whole route there is not a single water point. Your men and your horses will all be dead of thirst even before they are surrounded by the multitudes of the Moslem army!" At this warning cry the grand master of the Temple replied that such words savored of treason: "I smell a wolf!" Spurning the insult, the count of Tripoli held his ground. Toward midnight, when the council of war broke up, he seemed to have carried the day.

But the grand master of the Temple was on the watch, and his hatred with him. After the barons had left the royal tent, he returned on his own, and his evil genius was quick to sow discord in Lusignan's mind. "Sire, do not listen to the count; he is a traitor whose counsel aims at dishonoring you by keeping you in craven inactivity." Alarming Guy by these perfidious insinuations, he induced the feeble monarch to change his mind within a few hours and finally wrung from him the marching orders.

In the dead of night the barons heard the call to arms sound through the camp. Dumbfounded, they asked one another whence came the counterorder, and finding themselves all equally amazed, they hastened to the king's tent to ask the reason for this sudden change. Guy, singularly embarrassed to justify his change of face and yielding to the brutality of the weak, refused all explanation; it was theirs only to obey.

The Frankish army thus moved off, at dawn on July 3, from Sephoria toward Tiberias. The day broke torrid. The army was in poor heart, for even to the simple knights who had not heard the adjurations of Raymond III, the absurdity of the march imposed by the arrogance of the Templars on the incapacity of Guy was evident. The predictions of the count of Tripoli were fulfilled at every point. They left the waters of Sephoria for the zone of stony, arid, bare hills which spread south and east of the Jebel Turan. In contrast, Saladin's army, based on the shores of Tiberias, enjoyed the coolness of the lake. His whole tactics were to stop the Franks from reaching the banks and hold them in the furnace. In these circumstances the upshot of the battle was written in advance on the terrain. Saladin read it clear, as Raymond III had done. On the news of the Frankish move, he could not contain his joy: "Allah has delivered them into our hands!"

On the evening of July 3, the Franks halted for the night on the heights of Hattin. A tragic night during which men and horses were tortured by thirst. Not a drop of water on the fatal mound. When day broke, Saladin's army entirely encircled the position. Profiting from an easterly wind, the Moslems fired the dry grass. The gusts of smoke, blowing in the eyes of the Franks, added to their torture. "On these ironclad men," says the Arab chronicle, "the midsummer sun shed its burning rays. Cavalry charges followed each other thick and fast in the midst of the dust and smoke and hail of arrows. These dogs howled with their parched tongues under the blows. They hoped to reach the water, but before them were flames and death."

In this desperate plight, if the foot sergeants, tortured by thirst, yielded fairly quickly, the Frankish chivalry saved their honor. Twice they charged, drove back the enemy, and almost reached Saladin. But, in the end, numbers prevailed. Raymond of Tripoli, with a few barons, succeeded in breaking through the Moslem masses and reaching the coast. All the rest were killed or taken. The three men responsible for the catastrophe, Guy of Lusignan, Reynald of Châtillon, and Gerard of Ridfort, whose incapacity had led the Christians into the butchery, were taken prisoner. Neither the arrogant Templar nor the robber-knight had succeeded in winning a noble death. Saladin had all three brought to his tent. Guy of Lusignan, tortured by thirst, broken with exhaustion, fever, and terror, was on the point of collapse.

Chivalrous as ever, the sultan seated him at his side. Speaking to him gently, calming his fears, he handed him a goblet of rose water cooled with Hebron's snows. "It is a noble custom of the Arabs that the life of a captive is spared if he eats and drinks with his captor." But Guy having passed the cup to Reynald of Châtillon, Saladin violently refused to extend the benefit of royal immunity to him. He taunted Reynald with his brigandage, his perjury, the broken treaties, the capture, in the midst of peace, of the Mecca caravan. To which the lord of Transjordan insolently replied that such was the custom of kings. Such arrogance finally enraged Saladin. Falling upon Reynald of Châtillon with drawn scimitar, he severed his shoulder. The body-guard finished him off. The headless body was dragged to the feet of Guy of Lusignan, who trembled with terror. Saladin again seated him at his side and reassured him: "A king does not kill a king!" After the execution of Reynald, Saladin's only example of severity was the execution of the Knights Templar and Knights Hospitaler, with the sole exception, curiously enough, of the grand master, Gerard of Ridfort.

The Frankish "colonization" had never been very dense. The massacre of Hattin and the capitulation of the survivors wiped out the chivalry at a single stroke. Overnight, the country was stripped of defenders. Exploiting his victory at once, Saladin hastened to conquer the principal strongholds. Instead of marching directly on Jerusalem, he dashed for the sea, to secure the ports. It was, indeed, important for him to cut the Franks off from their naval bases and to deny ports of landing for any future crusade. On July 10 he forced the capitulation of Acre, where, for the rest, he accorded the Christian population exceptionally favorable terms. They had complete freedom to stay in the city, under Moslem domination, keeping all their wealth, or to emigrate in complete security. History must bow before the lofty and chivalrous figure of the great Kurdish sultan, so different from the pitiless Turkish atabegs, his predecessors, as well as from the brutal Mameluks who were one day to succeed his dynasty. But wherever Saladin was not present in person, his lieutenants reduced the whole Christian population to slavery. The historian Ibn al-Athir received a young Frankish slave girl in the share-out, taken prisoner at Jaffa with her year-old child. "The child fell from his mother's arms and scratched his face. The mother wept sorely at this accident, and I sought to calm her by showing her that the baby was not badly hurt. 'It is not for him alone that I weep,' she answered, 'it is for all of us. I had six brothers who have all perished, and a husband and two sisters whose fate I do not know.' " A little further on, the same Ibn al-Athir evokes the sad encounter of two other young Frankish women, sisters, captives in the harems of Aleppo. "I saw at Aleppo a Frankish woman who went with her master to visit one of his neighbors. The master knocked at the door and the neighbor opened it. With him too there was a Frankish woman. As soon as they saw each other, they both began to cry, embracing each other and weeping, and flinging themselves to the ground to talk. They were sisters and they had many kinsfolk of whom they had no news." The men killed or prisoners of war, the women dispersed throughout all the harems of the East, such was the liquidation of that brilliant Frankish colonization, the work of so many heroes and saints. It is easy to understand the wrath of the chroniclers against the insensate chiefs who had staked and lost everything on the throw of the dice at Hattin. After Acre and Jaffa, Saladin took Beirut (August 6, 1187) and the other ports of the Lebanon. Guy of Lusignan, more lamentable than ever, agreed to act as his factotum; the sultan had promised him his freedom in return for the surrender of the last Frankish strongholds. In fact, the ex-king and the grand master of the Temple came, in company with Moslem troops, to invite the defenders of Ascalon to surrender. The men of Ascalon indignantly overwhelmed Lusignan with insults and continued to resist. Saladin was only able to take Ascalon after a month of efforts (September 5). He then turned against Jerusalem.

Among the prisoners taken at Hattin was one of the leading barons of Palestine, Balian of Ibelin. Balian was the very pattern of the "courteous knight," according to the ideals of our twelfth century, cautious and wise as well as valiant. He had married, as his second wife, the ex-queen of Jerusalem, Maria Comnena, the widow of Amalric I. Like many of his peers, he had never ceased to maintain relations of chivalrous amity with the Moslem princes. Thus, when he begged for his liberty to go to Jerusalem to look after the safety of Maria Comnena, Saladin granted his prayer. At Jerusalem Balian found a frantic people. Nearly all the knights were dead or captive. Balian knighted all their sons over fifteen as well as the leading burgesses of the Holy City. But such makeshift forces were obviously not capa-

ble of defending the fortifications of this city into which all the refugees
from Judaea and Samaria were streaming, a weeping mob of resource-
less women and children, who had to be fed and who added to the
chaos. At this juncture Saladin arrived to invest Jerusalem (September
20, 1187). Gallantly, he allowed Maria Comnena to leave the city in
good time and even gave her an escort to Tyre. Then the parleying
began.

In his heart Saladin would have wished to spare the Holy City the
destructions of a siege. But the burgesses of Jerusalem could not,
without losing honor in the eyes of Christendom, capitulate without a
fight. In the face of their resolution, the sultan launched his assault, a
terrible assault, supported by the bombardment of twelve great siege
engines. The Franks held out, and at several points even launched
counterattacks. But the Egyptian sappers, working under cover of
perriers and mangonels, succeeded in breaching the walls. Rather than
submit to the law of the victor, knights and burgesses then formed the
desperate resolution to try a sortie under cover of darkness, to break
through or die, arms in hand.

The Patriarch Heraclius dissuaded them. This worldly prelate and
servile politician set no great store by the martyr's crown. He was,
moreover, able to find the loftiest moral justifications for his defeatism.
He represented to the fighting men that their heroic gesture, if they
perished, would deliver their young children into the hands of the
enemy and that the Moslems would not fail to bring them up in the
faith of Islam. Had they the right to compromise the eternal salvation
of so many young souls for the pleasure of rushing to their own death?
Another argument in favor of yielding was the more than equivocal
conduct of the native Christians of the Greek rite. In their hatred of
the Latin Church, the Greek element were taking sides with Saladin.

Balian of Ibelin then sought an interview with the sultan. He
offered to surrender the city in return for the free departure of the
population. But Saladin, irritated by the Frankish resistance, now
insisted on unconditional surrender. The champion of Islam recalled
terrible memories. He spoke of the massacre of the Arab population
of Jerusalem on the entry of Godfrey of Bouillon. "I shall not behave
any differently to you than your fathers behaved to our fathers, whom
they all massacred or reduced to slavery!" Balian of Ibelin then spoke
the language of despair. "In that case, we shall slay our sons and our

wives, we shall burn the town, we shall overthrow the Temple and all those sanctuaries which are also your sanctuaries. We shall massacre the five thousand Moslem captives we hold, then we shall sally forth in mass and none of us will fall without slaying one of your people!"

This fierce resolution made Saladin think again. He agreed that the Christian population of Jerusalem could redeem themselves at a ranson of ten bezants for a man, five for a woman, and one for a child. "Since God has inspired you with pity for these unfortunate people," said Balian, "then think of all those poor people who cannot pay their ransom, that multitude of women and children who have nothing left because you have slain or captured their husbands and their fathers!" Saladin then agreed to accept a lump sum for the ransom of the poor.

Unfortunately, the avarice and hard-heartedness of the Templars and Hospitalers, who were naturally called upon to raise the sum required, only allowed the ransom of seven thousand, so that sixteen thousand Christians still remained unredeemed in the Moslem prisons. Even so, in order to force the grand master of the Hospital to pay this first installment, the burgesses of Jerusalem had to threaten to deliver up his treasure to the sultan.

Saladin, in contrast, kept his word with a loyalty, sense of humanity, and chivalrous good grace which won the admiration of the Latin chroniclers. On the entry of his troops he had the main streets guarded by trusted men, responsible for preventing any violence against the Christians. At the prayer of the patriarch, he freed five hundred poor Christians. His brother, Malik el-Adil, obtained the grant of another thousand, whom the avarice of the Temple had also omitted to redeem and whom he freed. Heraclius had dismantled, in order to carry them off, all the gold and silver plate, the precious metals, hangings and carpets of the sanctuaries. The historian Imad ed-Din reminded Saladin that this wealth was deemed to be immovable property and should stay where it was. The sultan agreed, but rather than embark on a legal argument, preferred to shut his eyes. Some fanatics also asked Saladin to raze the Holy Sepulcher and put an end to Christian pilgrimage. He stopped them with a word: "Why raze and destroy, when the object of their adoration is the place of the Cross and the Sepulcher and not the outward building. Let us imitate the first Moslem conquerors who respected these churches."

The instances of liberality of the great sultan are beyond counting.

There were two old Franks at Jerusalem, both centenarians, who had known Godfrey of Bouillon. Saladin, moved by pity, ordered that they should be allowed to end their days in peace and provided for them. He provided a guard of honor to escort the three princesses, Sibylla of Jerusalem, Maria Comnena, and Stephanie of Transjordan, to the coast. He showed no less courtesy to the simple noblewomen. A delegation of those who had lost their families in the war came to see him. "When he saw them, he asked who they were and he was told that they were the wives and daughters of knights who had been slain or taken in battle; and he asked them what they wanted; and they asked him, in God's name, to have pity on them, who had their lords slain or in prison and their lands lost, and to give them aid and counsel. When Saladin saw them weep, he had great pity for them and told them to find out whether their lords were living, and all those who were in prison he would free and all those who were found were faithfully freed. After, he ordered largesse to be given from his own store to the dames and damsels who were widowed or orphaned. So much were they given that they praised God and proclaimed to the world the good which Saladin had done them."

It remained to conduct all this population to the coast, or rather to that part of the coast which was still in the power of the Franks, Tyre and Tripoli. Saladin divided the emigrants into three convoys, faithfully escorted by his troops to protect them against the attacks of the Bedouin. "When the Moslem horsemen of the rearguard saw a Latin woman or child exhausted with fatigue, they made them mount in their place and led them by the bridle." Part of the refugees were handed over to the barons of the Tripoli coast, who, unfortunately, were not slow to profit from their distress to exploit them. The luckiest were those who went to embark in Egypt. Continuing in this way to benefit from Saladin's protection, they were housed all under his care the winter at Alexandria. In March they were able to embark for the West. They owed it to the sultan's energetic intervention that they were able to do so, for the masters of the Genoese, Pisan, and Venetian vessels which put in to Alexandria at first refused to encumber themselves with a penniless crowd. To compel these heartless men to ship the fugitives, the cadi of Alexandria had to threaten the Italian captains with an embargo on their vessels. The Italian sailors then formed the project of getting rid of their pitiable passengers on some desert coast.

Learning of this dastardly plan, the Egyptian officials made the Italians personally responsible for the lives of the emigrants; fearing the denunciation of their trade treaties, the Venetians and the Genoese complied.

Meanwhile, Saladin had made a memorable entry into Jerusalem. Conscious of his historic role, he had solemnly restored to Islam the great sanctuaries of the Haram es-Sherif, the "Temple of the Lord," once again become the Mosque of Omar, and Solomon's Temple, the Temple of the Templars, once again become the Mosque al-Aqsa. In a dramatic scene described for us by Ibn al-Athir, the great gilded cross which the crusaders had raised above the dome of the Mosque of Omar, was felled before Saladin's army and before the Frankish population setting out on its exile. "When the Cross fell, all those who were there, Franks as well as Moslems, uttered a great cry. The Moslems cried, 'Allah is great!' The Franks uttered a cry of sorrow. So great was the clamor that the earth shook therewith."

After the fall of Jerusalem, Saladin made for the Lebanon coast. His efforts against Tyre failed, the city, as we shall see, having received unexpected reinforcement in the person of Conrad, marquis of Montferrat. At Tripoli, Count Raymond III, escaped by a miracle from the carnage of Hattin, had just died from despair as much as illness. But the fortress was in a state of defense, and Saladin could do nothing against it. In the mountains, the celebrated fortress of the Hospitalers, the Krak des Chevaliers, also defied all assault. In return, Saladin occupied Jabala and Latakia, ports which the prince of Antioch had had the imprudence to entrust to a Moslem officer who hastened to defect. This prince of Antioch, Bohemund III, was a poor creature, whose mistress was at the same time flirting with Saladin, to whom she disclosed the Frankish defense plans. The result was that the sultan, continuing to mop up the Christian possessions, had no difficulty in capturing from the principality most of the fortresses on the coast as well as on the Orontes. The Frankish state of Antioch thus found itself virtually confined within the limits of its capital itself.

Was this, in Syria as in Palestine, the end of the Frankish settlements?

12

THE THIRD CRUSADE

Conrad of Montferrat, Philip Augustus,
and Richard the Lionhearted

FRANKISH SYRIA, around 1188, apart from a few mountain fortresses like the impregnable Krak des Chevaliers and Marqab, was practically reduced to the fortified enclosures of Tyre, Tripoli, Tortosa, and Antioch, the last islands which the rising tide of Moslem reconquest seemed bound to submerge in their turn. There was no longer any Frankish royalty, since Guy of Lusignan, though freed at this juncture by Saladin, was too discredited, since the disaster of Hattin, to command any obedience; there was no more Frankish settlement to give support. But at this very moment a new fact emerged. A man appeared who, well before the Third Crusade, crystallized resistance around himself. Because he was a newcomer, he escaped the demoralization which had become general since Hattin. Not having known Frankish Jerusalem, not being paralyzed by invincible despairs, he took up the crusade again from scratch. This providential newcomer was Conrad of Montferrat.

The Piedmontese Marquis Conrad of Montferrat, after a long stay in Constantinople, had set sail for Syria shortly before the disaster of Hattin. Arriving off Acre on July 13, 1187, he was greatly astonished. Ordinarily, when Christian ships entered the roadsteads, the port authorities pealed the bells and sent out boats to welcome the pilgrims. This time there was nothing of the kind. Surprised at this omission,

Conrad and his men were even more surprised when they looked more attentively at the appearance of the crowds which thronged the beach; they were Arabs and Turks, for Saladin had just taken the town. The marquis of Montferrat thus learned at one stroke of the disaster at Hattin and the fall of the kingdom. He set sail again and was fortunate enough to reach Tyre, a stronghold still in Christian power.

Tyre, together with Tripoli, had been the refuge of most of the Franks who had escaped the disaster. But these demoralized mobs, already besieged by Saladin's army, were on the point of capitulating in their turn, when the marquis of Montferrat's ship appeared in port. His arrival changed the whole posture of affairs. Conrad was truly the strong man needed to cope with a desperate situation, "a man like a demon," says the Moslem chronicle, "full of prudence, vigilance, and bravery." Greeted like a savior by the Tyrians, who supplicated him to defend them, he frankly stated his terms: he insisted on being recognized as sovereign lord of the city. These proposals, which were immediately accepted, made a clean sweep of all prior rights, even those of King Guy of Lusignan, and established a new right, founded on services rendered. Now assured of his position, Conrad assumed the defense. It was high time. Traitors were already hoisting Saladin's standard on the ramparts. Conrad flung the banner into the fosse. Now Saladin had, among the prisoners taken at Hattin, precisely in his power the old lord of Montferrat, Conrad's father. He brought the old man before the walls of Tyre and offered to free him in return for the surrender of the city. But Conrad was not a man to yield to sentiment. He answered that he would see his father slain rather than render up a single ashlar of the walls. Saladin, taking the measure of his man, withdrew, and Conrad remained the peaceful possessor of Tyre. With the wealth he had brought with him, the marquis, setting all the refugees to work on the fortifications, soon made the city into an impregnable stronghold.

Tyre thus became the bulwark of Frankish resistance. Saladin, who had now completed the conquest of Palestine, made one more effort against it. But his enormous numerical superiority was of no avail to him, since Tyre was linked to the mainland only by a narrow neck of land, which Conrad had taken the precaution of cutting by a sea-water canal. After a Frankish naval victory in the roadsteads on January 2, 1188, the sultan resigned himself to raising the siege.

But "the Gibraltar of Tyre" was too confined, its garrison too small, to mount a reconquest. There must be a Third Crusade. Once firmly in possession, Conrad of Montferrat charged the archbishop of Tyre to go and preach it in the West.

The three greatest sovereigns of the West at this moment were King Philip Augustus of France, King Henry II Plantagenet of England, and the German Emperor, Frederick Barbarossa. On the news of the fall of Jerusalem, all three took the Cross; but the first two, divided by an ancient rivalry, could not agree and indefinitely postponed the performance of their vow. Frederick Barbarossa showed greater zeal. On May 11, 1189, he left Ratisbon with a remarkably well organized and disciplined army which, according to some chroniclers, started off at nearly 100,000 strong. He took the road for Constantinople, through Hungary. On reaching the Byzantine Empire he encountered the ill will of the Emperor Isaac Angelus. The Byzantine court, feeling itself menaced by the rancor and covetousness of the Latins, had made a pact against them with Saladin, whom they kept informed of the progress of the crusade. Frederick, indignant at the obstacles clandestinely placed in his way, sacked Adrianople and was on the point of assaulting Constantinople itself. However, he had enough "Christian patriotism" to master his wrath and, at the end of March 1190, he crossed over into Asia Minor with his army.

To cross Asia Minor, Frederick followed the old route of Godfrey of Bouillon, crossing the peninsula diagonally from northwest to southeast, from the Sea of Marmara to Cilicia. The Seljuk Turks, who tried to stop him before Konya, their capital, were defeated and Frederick entered the city, where he rested for five days. The difficult crossing of the Asia Minor plateau, fatal to so many earlier crusades, was therefore effected without hindrance, thanks to the discipline and the excellent victualing arrangements of the German army. After crossing the Taurus, Frederick moved down into the Cilician plain, where he was welcomed as an ally by the Armenians.

The approach of the German grand army filled the Moslem world with terror. Saladin's lieutenants were so disconcerted that they evacuated the fortresses on the frontier between Syria and Cilicia, such as Baghras, lately conquered by their chief. Saladin himself precipitately had the defenses of Sidon, Jaffa, and Caesarea dismantled, regarding them as indefensible. "If Allah," says the Arab historian, Ibn al-Athir, "had not deigned to show his goodness to the Moslems by willing the death of the king of the Germans at the very moment he was about to penetrate Syria, men would say today, 'Syria and Egypt once belonged to Islam . . . !'" Indeed, between the German grand army debouching from the north and the French and English armies about to land at Acre, Moslem Syria must inevitably have been crushed. But on June 10, 1190, Frederick Barbarossa was drowned in the waters of the Calycadnus, a little Cilician river, and the whole face of the Eastern question was changed.

The superiority of the German army lay in its methodical organization, but also in a sense of collective power, symbolized in the person of Frederick Barbarossa. Once the great emperor was removed from the scene, it went to pieces and became demoralized; deprived of the driving force of a single man, this immense army became a spiritless rabble, whole detachments of which were captured by the Moslems without offering any resistance. The late emperor's son, Frederick of Swabia, proved incapable of halting this moral and material disintegration. Without ever having been defeated, after taking the impregnable Konya, the German Crusade, at the very moment of arriving on the scene of action, thus lost its impetus. Some of the princes took their men back to Europe. The rest went on by sea to join the Christians at Tyre or before Acre.

The German Crusade had faded away. The French and English Crusade, as we shall see, tarried for months to come in Sicilian waters. The Syrian Franks, reinforced by sundry groups of crusaders, set about reconquering the coast on their own.

The regrouping of the Syrian Franks was apparently aided, but in reality complicated, by the reappearance on the scene of Guy of Lusignan, freed by Saladin. It was on the personal approach of Queen Sibylla that the sultan, always courteous to the Frankish ladies, had liberated the loser of Hattin. In reality, knowing Guy's ineptitude, from which he believed he had nothing to fear, he had been well content to let him loose, as it were, under the feet of the redoubtable Conrad of Montferrat. Scarce liberated, Guy in fact made straight for Tyre, the only stronghold of the old kingdom still in the hands of the Franks, but where Conrad now commanded as master. He found the

gates closed against him "and forthwith cried for them to be opened."
"The marquis of Montferrat came out upon the battlements and demanded who dared to speak in that fashion. They answered him that
it was Guy, the king, and Sibylla, the queen, who were minded to
come again to their faithful city of Tyre. The marquis retorted that
the place was his, because he it was who had saved it and that never in
their life should they set foot therein again."

Guy of Lusignan, a king without lands and a captain without troops,
renounced by most of his former subjects, who rightly blamed him for
the disaster, then formed a resolution whose energy is astonishing for
such a weakling: he decided to win back the second city and principal
port of the old kingdom, Acre. Assembling all the old Palestinian
knights and newly landed pilgrims whom he could find, he set out for
Acre on August 20, 1189. A week later he pitched his camp east of the
city on the knoll of Tel el-Fukhar.

It was an enterprise of noble daring. His little army was a quarter
the size of the Moslem garrison of Acre. Furthermore, on the news of
the arrival of the Franks, Saladin, hastening to Acre, took up his
position in their rear, so that from besiegers they soon became besieged. But the arrival of new crusaders from the West diminished the
dangers of this situation. First came a fine Pisan squadron of fifty-two
sail, followed by a Genoese squadron and a Venetian squadron, and
finally five hundred Danish, Frisian, and Flemish ships with ten thousand men. In mid-September the first French contingents arrived with
the count of Bar, Everard II of Brienne, Robert of Dreux, and his
brother, Bishop Philip of Beauvais, two valiant captains who were to be
heard of again at Bouvines, followed in October by Guy of Dampierre,
Narjot of Touvy, Raymond of Turenne, and Geoffrey of Joinville
with a contingent of knights from Champagne.

Thus reinforced, Guy of Lusignan, before pressing the siege, tried to
rid himself of Saladin, whose army, still camped on the heights east of
Acre, encircled the besiegers. On October 4, 1189, he made a sudden
attack on the Moslem camp, took it by surprise, and penetrated as far
as the sultan's tents. Unfortunately, the victors tarried to pillage;
Saladin was able to recover and drive the Franks back to their own
camp. In brief, forces were balanced. Saladin could not stop the
Franks, on the coast side, from investing Acre; and they themselves, on
the landward side, could not shake off his pressure. Operations then

began to assume the aspect of siege and trench warfare, immobile, exhausting, a war of attrition which might last two years. The garrison of Acre behind its walls, the Franks behind their entrenchments, continued to struggle by dint of perriers and mangonels, crossbow shafts, fireballs, and sheets of Greek fire. Thanks to their mastery of the sea, the Franks sought to reduce the garrison of Acre by famine, while they themselves were harassed, starved out, and, as it were, besieged at a distance by Saladin's army.

This war of position fostered curious relations of military courtesy between the Franks and the soldiers of Saladin. "A sort of familiarity," notes the Arab chronicle, "grew up between the two camps. When the fighting was done, they engaged in conversation, and after this long frequentation, they ended by singing and dancing together, and then, an hour later, began to fight again." During these hours of truce the children of the two armies could even be seen playing "Franks and Saracens" in no-man's land. There were less innocent pastimes: the Arab chronicle, highly scandalized, reports that Saladin's Mameluks could not resist the fascination of the wenches who followed the French camp and that more than one deserted for a pair of fine eyes.

Saladin himself continued to give the example of the most chivalrous conduct. They brought to him from among the prisoners one day a decrepit old man who, in spite of his infirmities, was determined to make the pilgrimage to the Holy Land. Taking pity on him, the sultan gave him a horse and had him returned to the Frankish army. One night, Moslem raiders carried off a three-month-old child from the Christian camp. In the morning, the mother discovered her loss and was in despair. The Frankish knights counseled her to appeal to Saladin's generosity. She ran to the enemy outposts and begged an audience of the sultan. "The Sultan," writes Imad ed-Din, "was on horseback, surrounded by a numerous escort, of which I was one, when the mother presented herself, moaning, and threw herself at his feet, her face in the dust. The sultan informed himself of her plight, and when he learned it, his eyes filled with tears. He sent for the child. As it had already been sold in the market, he redeemed it from his own purse and would not depart until the child had been restored to its mother. She took it and pressed it to her heart in a flood of tears. All who saw the scene, and I among them, wept too. After she had suckled the child the sultan had her led on horseback, with her child, to the Christian camp."

But famine was beginning to rage in the Frankish army. Conrad of Montferrat made it his duty to conduct a supply fleet to Tyre. On March 4, 1190, this fleet of fifty vessels appeared off Acre. The Moslem squadron put out from the port of Acre to stop the landing. "You would then have seen," says the epic of Ambroise, "something like ants issuing from an anthill. Such were the 10,000 Turks who put out from Acre in their galleys, bedecked, like themselves, with silken stuffs, buckram, and velvet. They all set upon our fleet which the north wind bore along the coast. They began to fire their crossbows and the naval battle was joined. The hue and cry was unceasing in both squadrons. Each gave way in turn. Of a sudden, they came together and launched the Greek fire; the decks took flame and when two ships grappled, blows rained on either side." Meanwhile, on land, the Moslem army made a sortie against the Christian camp. "The whole plain, right up to the foot of the mountains, was covered, like a field of corn, with Turks attacking without respite and flinging themselves into our trenches in such numbers that they overthrew each other. They were a great mass of hideous black men, and their headgear was all red. The sight of these serried ranks, all crowned with red, reminded you of a cherry orchard in full fruit." In the end, the Moslem attack was repelled by land while the supply squadron, forcing the blockade, landed its chests of stores in the Christian camp.

While the two armies, pending the arrival of the kings of France and England, were bogged down in static warfare, the dynastic question once again split the Franks. In October 1190, Queen Sibylla of Jerusalem, the wife of Guy of Lusignan, through whom he held his rights to the crown, had died childless at Acre. Under the Frankish law of Syria, she alone was queen *de jure*, Guy being merely associated to the throne in the capacity of prince consort. The inheritance fell not to him but to the dead queen's younger sister, Isabella.

Isabella, it will be remembered, was married to a young native-born baron, Humphrey of Toron, a very good-looking youth (the Arab chronicles themselves surrender to his beauty), very cultured (he knew Arabic so well that he acted as interpreter with Saladin), but mild, timid, unambitious, in spite of the illustrious name he inherited, and worse than weak in character. It will be recalled that in 1186 the barons of the anti-Lusignan party had wanted to proclaim him king in spite of himself, and in order to escape this dangerous honor he had, somewhat ridiculously, slipped through their hands and rushed, with childish excuses, to beg the pardon of Sibylla and Guy. The barons who had counted on him and whose hopes he had disappointed from lack of character had not forgiven him this lamentable attitude. For the rest, at a moment when it was a question of winning back the kingdom from Saladin, Humphrey had none of the qualities of a chief. With his effeminate appearance, his vague gestures and hesitating speech, it was hard to imagine him standing up to the great sultan. The realm needed a strong man, capable of founding a new dynasty. And such a man was there on the spot, the new master of Tyre, Marquis Conrad of Montferrat. The barons' party therefore resolved to make Isabella divorce Humphrey of Toron and marry Conrad.

One obstacle remained. Isabella, who was barely twenty, adored the handsome boy she had been given as husband. From the very first words, she would hear nothing of a divorce. But the Montferrat party had powerful support—the queen mother, Maria Comnena. The queen mother set about lecturing the recalcitrant girl: Isabella had a duty to the kingdom and to the dynasty of which she was the sole heiress. Since Humphrey of Toron had proved himself incapable of reigning, state reason demanded that his young wife should sacrifice him, even if she sacrificed herself at the same time. Isabella, worn down, harassed by her family, consented "under duress" (the poor child expressly proclaimed it) to separate from her beloved Humphrey and marry Conrad. It remained to find a pretext to annul the marriage. One was found: Isabella had been married too young, without her consent, a hasty marriage, which was not valid. The lamentable Humphrey tried to protest, but appeal was made to the argument of force. One of the barons of the Montferrat party, Guy of Senlis, "flung down his gage" to challenge him to single combat. Courage had never been the strong point of the last of the Toron family. "His heart failed him." He did not take up the challenge and allowed his wife to be snatched away from him. She was married to Conrad on the spot. For all that, Conrad was not thereby recognized as king by the friends of Guy of Lusignan. The two princes each kept their partisans and awaited the arrival of the kings of France and England to decide between them.

It will be remembered that King Henry II of England and King Philip Augustus of France, long at war, had at one moment called a truce to their quarrel to take the Cross. But as they had started to fight again, and were in no hurry to fulfill their vows, Henry died before the preparations were completed. His son, Richard the Lion-hearted, renewed his vows, but it was only on July 4, 1190, that, with Philip Augustus, he set out from Vézelay for the Holy Land. Philip sailed from Genoa and Richard from Marseilles. They joined up in Sicily but tarried in the island for another six months, in somewhat inexplicable inaction, while the Christian army besieging Acre fever-ishly awaited their arrival. In reality, the Capetian and the Plantage-net, though allied for the holy war, suspected each other, watched each other, and hampered each other. After incidents which almost pro-voked open war between the two crusader princes, Philip Augustus set off first from Messina on March 30, 1191, to land before Acre on April 20. As for Richard, leaving Messina on April 10, he was not to land in Syria until June 7. In the interval, he conquered the island of Cyprus.

It was a storm which cast the king of England on the Cypriot coasts. The island belonged to the Byzantines, specifically to the Byzantine Prince Isaac Comnenus. Isaac having shown a hostile attitude to the English ships which chanced to be at his mercy, Richard landed, beat him at Tremithus, took him prisoner, and entered Nicosia, the island's capital (end of May 1191).

The unexpected conquest of Cyprus by Richard the Lionhearted was to change the course of Frankish history. The Latin East, which Saladin had driven back into the sea, rose again from the waves. It may be noted, without anticipating, that as soon as Richard had landed in Cyprus, Guy of Lusignan had hastened up from Acre to crave his support against the pretentions of Conrad of Montferrat to the crown. Guy placed his sword at the service of the king of England and helped him to conquer the island, thus laying the first foundations of the future "Lusignan kingdom of Cyprus."

Meanwhile, Philip Augustus had brought new blood to the siege of Acre. He had pitched his camp opposite "La Tour Maudite," the Accursed Tower, the main defensive tower of Acre. On June 7 he was joined by Richard the Lionhearted, landing from Cyprus. That night the whole Frankish army was a blaze of illumination. "The night was clear and the joy was great," sings Ambroise. "They

"After burying Baldwin II, Fulk was crowned king at the Church of the Holy Sepulcher with Melisende on September 14, 1131." (*Les passages d'Outre-Mer*, by Sébastien Mamerot, from a fifteenth-century ms.)

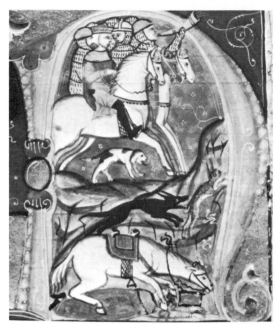

"While he was out hunting, Fulk's horse stumbled and fell on top of him, crushing his skull." The death of Fulk of Anjou. (Chronicle of William of Tyre, from a thirteenth-century ms.)

"On the very morrow of the death of Almaric I, his successor, Baldwin IV, the Leper, was annointed king." (*Les passages d'Outre-Mer*, by Sébastien Mamerot, from a fifteenth-century ms.)

Arrest and imprisonment of the patriarch of Antioch, Aimery of Limoges, by Reynald of Châtillon. (*Les histoires d'Outre-Mer* from a fifteenth-century ms.)

Almaric I at the head of the first expedition to Egypt. (*Chronique de la conquête de Jérusalem*, by William of Tyre, from a fifteenth-century ms.)

"The assassination of the seneschal Miles of Plancy delivered the regency to Count Raymond III of Tripoli." (*Chronique de la conquête de Jérusalem*, by William of Tyre, from a fifteenth-century ms.)

Baldwin V, a child barely five years old, is proclaimed king. (*Chronique de la conquête de Jérusalem*, by William of Tyre, from a fifteenth-century ms.)

After the death of Baldwin V, "the patriarch crowned Sibylla, and she, in turn, crowned her husband." (*Chronique de la conquête de Jérusalem*, by William of Tyre, from a fifteenth-century ms.)

"The garrison of Acre behind its walls, the Franks behind their entrenchments, continued to struggle by dint of perriers and mangonels." (*Histoire de la Guerre Sainte*, by William of Tyre, from a thirteenth-century ms.)

Saint Louis set sail on August 25, 1248.
(*Vie de saint Louis*, from a fifteenth-century ms.)

"Saladin inflicted reprisals on the Frankish captives, with which history has no right to reproach him." (*Roman de Godefroi de Bouillon*, from a fourteenth-century ms.)

Disembarkation of the crusaders at Damietta. (*Grand Voyage de Hiérusalem*, printed in 1522 by François Regnault, facsimile of a woodcut—library of A. Firmin-Didot.)

The capture of Damietta by the crusaders. (*Vie de saint Louis*, from a fifteenth-century ms.— photo. Giraudon.)

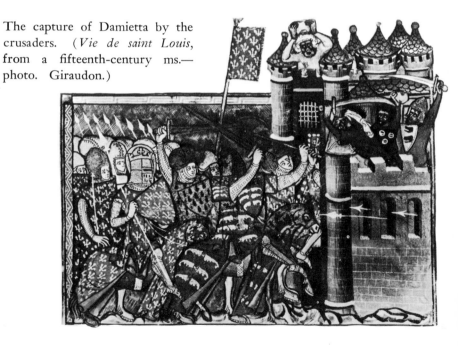

sounded the timbrels, the trumpets, and the horns. In the camp they sang fine songs and brave tunes. The stewards served wine to great and small alike. All were full of confidence. I do not think you could ever have seen so many torches and so much light, so that it seemed to the enemy army that the whole valley was ablaze with fire."

Each of the two kings took over the attack of a sector. Philip Augustus undertook to demolish the Accursed Tower, which protected the stronghold of Acre on the east. Against it he had erected a powerful perrier or stone-thrower called "Male voisine," the Evil Neighbor, which bombarded the city with enormous blocks of stone but to which the defenders replied with another catapult, which the Frankish good humor dubbed "Male cousine," the Evil Cousin. Alongside the Evil Neighbor the king of France stood his turn as a simple soldier, drawing his crossbow with the rest. An angle of the wall adjoining the Accursed Tower was breached and on July 2, Philip Augustus launched an assault on the breach which was only halted by a diversion by Saladin against the crusader camp. But the besieged passed word to Saladin that they could only hold out for one day more. The next day, July 3, Saladin made a desperate attempt against the camp. It was driven back. "The Franks," says Beha ed-Din, an eyewitness, "were as solid as a wall. One Frank, of enormous stature, standing on the parapet, held the Moslems at bay single-handed. At his side, his comrades passed him blocks of stone which he hurled at us. He was struck by more than a score of stones and arrows, without even seeming to notice. To have done with him one of our officers had to burn him alive with a flask of flaming naphtha." The same writer tells us of a Frankish heroine, clad in a green mantle, who launched a stream of arrows and laid many Moslems low. "Finally she was overwhelmed by numbers. We slew her and bore her bow to the sultan." While the defenders of the camp were thus repelling Saladin's counterattack, Philip Augustus renewed his assault on the Accursed Tower. He was within an ace of success. The marshal of France, Aubrey Clement, who had sworn to take Acre or die in the attempt, flung himself into the breach in the tower, but the scaling ladders broke and he was killed.

Nevertheless, the day of July 3 had been decisive. If Acre was not taken that day, it had indeed been given the death blow. On July 11 a furious assault by the English finally shattered the morale of the garrison. On the twelfth they capitulated and the crusaders made their entry into the town. From the heights on the east of the plain of Acre, Saladin was compelled to look helplessly on at this spectacle. "This Friday, at noon," writes his historian, Abu Shama, "we saw the crosses and flags of the Franks raised on the walls. An immense clamor of enthusiasm rose from the Frankish army, while our camp rang with groans and sobs. It was a hateful sight for us when the marquis of Montferrat entered Acre with four banners of the Christian kings and placed one on the citadel, another on the minaret of the great mosque (and it was a Friday!), and a third on the blockhouse in place of the flags of Islam . . ."

To capture Acre, Richard and Philip Augustus had called a truce to their quarrel. Their rivalry revived on the morrow of the victory. In the competition for the crown of Jerusalem, Richard had taken the side of Guy of Lusignan, and Philip that of Conrad of Montferrat. To put an end to a controversy which paralyzed the army, the Syrian barons, meeting in "parliament" on July 28, forced a compromise: Guy, crowned in the Holy Sepulcher, would keep the crown for life but would be succeeded by Conrad of Montferrat as husband of Princess Isabella of Jerusalem.

Once this agreement was reached, Philip Augustus announced his intention of returning to Europe. On August 2 he set sail from Tyre for Brindisi, leaving in Palestine the whole Capetian contingent—10,-000 knights, not counting infantry—under the orders of Duke Hugh III of Burgundy. His departure was nonetheless regarded by the Plantagenet party as a desertion. It is true that Philip had done his duty magnificently before Acre and the recapture of the city was his doing as much as Richard's. But it was undeniable that in the eyes of this realistic politician the crusade was infinitely less important than the consolidation of French territory; and it was without remorse that, believing his vow fulfilled by the victory of Acre, he left the liberation of Jerusalem in the hands of Richard.

The departure of Philip Augustus was certainly a misfortune for the Syrian venture. Richard would have profited from the counsels of the Capetian whose cool intelligence would have saved him from many mistakes. The king of England was, indeed, the most magnificent soldier of his time but singularly lacking in political sense and liable to be carried away by his violence on the least occasion. Saladin was ready to pay very dear to redeem the garrison of Acre, held prisoner by the Franks, although in oriental fashion he insisted on haggling. Did Richard think he was being duped? Did he want to strike terror into Islam like the crusaders of 1099? The fact remains that, on August 20, before Acre, he assembled three thousand prisoners in front of his troops and had "all these dogs" done to death.

This act of barbarism, into the bargain, was a great mistake. Saladin had hitherto made war with feelings of humanity which merited a different response. Toward Richard himself, his attitude had been impeccably courteous. When the king of England fell ill during the siege of Acre, the sultan had been quick to send him sherbets cooled with the snows of the Lebanon, to hasten his convalescence. The massacre of the prisoners put an end to the chivalry of war as well as throwing away a means of pressure and a precious bargaining counter. Saladin, in his indignation, inflicted reprisals on the Frankish captives, with which history has no right to reproach him.

Richard the Lionhearted rehabilitated himself happily in the course of the campaign which followed, for he immediately set about winning back the Palestine coast from Acre to Ascalon.

The first thing was to snatch the army away from "the fleshpots of Acre." Indeed, the great port, as the poet Ambroise avows, was filled with taverns flowing with excellent wine and crowded with trollops, "some of whom were ravishingly well made." To prevent the column's being encumbered with wantons, the barons wisely ordered that no woman should follow the troops, "save only good and ancient pilgrims, serving women and washerwomen to wash their linen and their heads, and who are worth their weight in monkeys when it comes to delousing."

The Frankish column, moving southward, progressed along the coast, revictualed from stage to stage by the Christian fleet, mistress of the seas. Saladin's army marched parallel, along the line of the hills, hoping to profit from the slightest error to harass or surprise Richard. "The Frankish cavalry and infantry," writes Imad ed-Din, "advanced along the shore, with the sea on their right and our army on their left. The infantry formed a sort of rampart around the horse, the men being clad in corselets of felt and coats of mail so closely made that arrows could not penetrate them. Armed with powerful crossbows, they kept our horsemen at a distance." The cadi Beha ed-Din tells of seeing a Frankish soldier receive as many as ten arrows in the back of his corselet without flinching in the slightest. As for the knights, they rode in the center of the column, leaving it only for sudden charges to clear the infantry or force a passage. "The Turks, the children of the devil, were enraged," recounts Ambroise, "because with our armor we were almost invulnerable; they called us the iron men." If the superiority of the Franks lay in their armor and their discipline, the Moslems had extreme mobility on their side. At every instant, Ambroise's epic shows us the Turkish horsemen riding up at full gallop, on their horses as fast as lightning, launching a salvo of arrows against the Frankish column, and disappearing, uncatchable, in a cloud of dust.

In spite of being harassed in this way, the Frankish column advanced in strict order, without allowing itself to be broken or lured far from its route. They skirted Carmel and reached Caesarea, which Saladin, in despair of defending it, had destroyed; they arrived before Arsuf: it was there, in the gardens at the approaches to the town, that the sultan had decided to stop the Franks. In an instant the Christian army found itself encircled by the Mameluks. "The trumpets and drums advanced before the emirs, drums beating and howling like demons; you could not have heard God's thunder. After the Turkish cavalry came the Negroes and the Bedouin, agile and rapid footmen, behind their light bucklers. They all aimed at the horses to unhorse our knights."

On this torrid day of September 7, in the palm groves of Arsuf, the Franks, surrounded by Saladin's army, their horses slain, themselves riddled with arrows, thought for an instant that all was lost. As in 1187, on the fatal expedition of Hattin, battle seemed to have been joined in the worst conditions. After describing the whirlwind attack of the Islam mounted archers, the hail of arrows which fell upon the Frankish column in a suffocating dust cloud, the infernal row of the Egyptian drums, the howling of all these "dogs," Ambroise avows that "there was no man in the Christian army so hardy that he did not wish to have done with his pilgrimage." In the heat and dust of this torrid September, it was indeed the foretaste of a new Hattin. . . .

But Richard the Lionhearted was no Reynald of Châtillon or Guy of Lusignan. A poor politician in council, he became on the field of battle the very incarnation of the spirit of war. The Hospitalers of the rearguard confessed to him that they were at the end of their tether; imperiously, he ordered them to hold fast—and they held. But the defensive was too costly and the Moslem archers slew the Frankish horses at long range. Richard planned an enveloping charge which should have led to the capture or annihilation of the whole Moslem army. "It was agreed that before the action six trumpets would be posted in three echelons who would sound a sudden charge for all our cavalry." The precipitation of a Hospitaler prevented the maneuver from developing. There was a simple direct charge. It is true that it was a charge like a tidal wave, which swept all before it. Beha ed-Din, who was at Saladin's side, has left a terrifying picture of the scene: "The Frankish cavalry then formed in mass, and knowing that nothing could save it except a supreme effort, decided to charge. With my own eyes I saw these knights, all massed around a square formed by their infantry. They seized their lances, and all together uttered a terrible cry, the line of infantry opened to let them through, and they fell upon us. One of their divisions fell upon our right wing, another on our left wing, a third upon our center, and all among us were put to rout . . ."

It was a revenge for the old defeats which earns us an epic page from the pen of Ambroise: "The Knights Hospitaler, who had suffered much, charged in good order. Count Henry of Champagne with his brave companions, James of Avesnes and his lineage, charged too. Count Robert of Dreux and the bishop of Beauvais charged together. By the sea, on the left flank, charged the earl of Leicester with all his echelon among whom there were no cravens. Then charged the Angevins, the Poitevins, the Bretons, the men of Maine, and all the other army corps. Like brave men they attacked the Turks with such fury that each of them picked his man, ran him through with the lance, and flung him from the stirrups. When King Richard saw that the charge was launched without waiting for his orders, he pricked spurs and hurled himself upon the enemy at full gallop. He displayed such prowess that day that all around him, on both sides, before and after, there was a trail of Saracens slain, and at sight of him the survivors scattered to give him a wide berth. The bodies of the Turks, with their bearded heads, lay thick as swaths at harvest time."

The victory of Arsuf was resounding. It effaced the disaster of Hattin. It restored military superiority to the Frankish banners.

Power had once again changed sides, together with morale, tactical
skill in battle—in short, all that constitutes military potential. Saladin
was the first to realize it. Refraining henceforth from meeting Richard
the Lionhearted in open country, he contented himself, Bedouin fashion, with laying waste the country before him. With despair in his
heart, he had the coast towns, and even Ascalon, evacuated by the
Moslem population; and while the dismal processions of refugees
streamed along the road to Egypt, he razed the walls of the cities to the
ground. Richard, disconcerted by these tactics, was nevertheless able
to rebuild Jaffa, particularly important as the "pilgrim port," the
landing point for Jerusalem. As for Jerusalem itself, the unanimous
feeling of the army was a determination to resume the siege at once.
Three times did Richard approach so near that the marvelous hours of
July 1099 seemed to have come again. At Christmas 1191, he was only
a dozen miles from the Holy City. Already, Ambroise tells us, the
soldiers were burnishing their coats of mail, the sick were already
declaring themselves cured, so that they too would be among the first
to see the dome of the Temple, when, to the general surprise, Richard
turned around.

The truth was that the strategic circumstances were no longer by
any means those of the First Crusade. Godfrey of Bouillon, in the old
days, had been able to set tranquilly about the siege of Jerusalem
because there was no Moslem army to distract him from his task. This
was no longer true. Saladin, with a field army of superior numbers,
held the countryside; he followed Richard's tracks; his troops crowned
the heights, ready to fall on the rear of the Frankish column if it
assaulted the walls of Jerusalem. As an experienced captain, Richard,
in spite of his fire, refused to mount an operation of this kind so far
from his base, in the hostile environment of the Judaean plateau. He
led his army back to the coast and, from that moment, opened informal
talks with Saladin.

In default of winning back the Holy Places by force, there was,
indeed, nothing left but to negotiate. A *modus vivendi* must be found
between the Franks, again masters of the coastal strip, and the Moslems, still in possession of the hinterland. Some people (including for a
moment Richard himself) contemplated a romantic solution. Saladin's
brother, al-Adil, who had always shown a certain liking for the Christians, should marry Richard's sister, Queen Joanna of Sicily, and this

hybrid couple should reign over a neutralized Jerusalem. The project was obviously not feasible, if only because of Joanna's religious scruples; but it nevertheless foreshadowed a happy softening of confessional hatreds and the birth of a spirit of reciprocal religious toleration which was to be that of Frederick II and the successors of Saladin.

Nevertheless, as the negotiations dragged on, Richard, in June 1192, made a second demonstration toward Jerusalem. On the morning of June 12, as he was chasing a Moslem patrol with a platoon of his vanguard, he came in sight of the Holy City. But once again he refused, with Saladin on his flanks, to attack such a stoutly defended stronghold. The morale of the army being shaken by this failure to follow through, he set about restoring it by a spectacular raid. The Bedouin (for he had taken Bedouin into his service) had just informed him that an enormous Moslem caravan coming from Egypt was headed for Syria, and, under the protection of a squadron of Mameluks, was now traversing the desert of Juda. At this news Richard leaped to the saddle with the duke of Burgundy and five hundred knights and galloped off southwestward. It was the evening of Sunday, June 20. They rode all night by the light of the moon and only dismounted on arriving south of Ascalon. There, a Bedouin warned them that the caravan was halted at the water point of the Round Tank in the heart of the Negeb Desert. Richard made his knights bind their heads with a kaffieh, Bedouin fashion and then, at nightfall, again pricked due south, himself leading the van, the duke of Burgundy bringing up the rear. They rode throughout the night, a beautiful Palestine summer night, which led the column without mishap through the dunes to the Round Tank, where the caravan, men and beasts alike, was peacefully slumbering in the midst of their unloaded bales of merchandise. Shortly before dawn, Richard ordered the attack. The surprise was total. The Mameluk escort was the first to disband. The caravaners, abandoning beasts and merchandise alike, followed them in flight into the Negeb. "Like greyhounds coursing the hare in the plain, so our people hunted theirs." The prize was endless files of camels, laden with gold, silks, velvet, and purple stuffs, copper bowls and ewers, silver candlesticks, Damascene armor, ivory chessmen, bales of sugar and spices, all the treasures, all the delicacies of old Islam.

But these brilliant master strokes could not mask Richard's embarrassment. He failed either to force Saladin into some decisive action or to win from him a compromise peace. In July 1192, the king went back up to Beirut, leaving Jaffa with only a feeble garrison. Profiting from his absence, Saladin made a surprise attack on the city (July 26). On the very next day, the Moslem sappers succeeded in breaching the curtain wall, but the Franks lit great fires behind the breach; protected by the flames and smoke, they held the Moslems off. Beha ed-Din, an eyewitness, could not refrain from exclaiming: "What admirable warriors they were, what courage!" On July 31 the curtain wall finally fell. "When the dust cloud cleared, we saw a rampart of halberts and lances where the fallen wall had stood, closing the breach so well that not even the eye could penetrate it; we beheld the frightening spectacle of the intrepidity of the Franks, the calm and precision of their movements." When they could no longer defend the lower city, they retired in good order into the citadel. In spite of everything, toward evening they had begun to parley, and the next morning, August 1, they were preparing for the inevitable capitulation, when, at the first light of dawn, a Christian fleet suddenly appeared off Jaffa. It was King Richard, who, alerted by a miracle, arrived with all speed in Genoese galleys, with the first troops he could muster.

It was then that the king of England showed what manner of man he was. The epic of Ambroise has left us an unforgettable picture of the scene. Without waiting to make shore, Richard, his shield slung around his neck, a great Danish battle-axe in his hands, leaped into the sea up to his waist, ran to the shore, cleared it of Moslems, penetrated the city, surprised the throngs of enemies looting the houses, wrought terrible slaughter among them, and then, joining forces with the liberated garrison, flung himself with them on Saladin's army, overran his camp and put him to flight as far as Assir. "The King," sings Ambroise, "pitched his tent on the very spot from which Saladin had fled. There camped Richard the Great. Never, even at Roncesvalles, did Paladin do such a doughty deed." Beha ed-Din, for his part, has preserved the king's mordant jests with the conquered Moslems: "Your sultan is the greatest sovereign that Islam has ever had, and yet my mere presence is enough to make him decamp! Look, I am not even in armor; I am wearing simple sea boots. So I did not come to fight him! Why has he fled?"

And yet, Richard had only two thousand men in Jaffa, of whom not more than fifty were knights, who in any event were horseless. His numerical weakness inspired the enemy with the hope of wreaking their revenge.

Once it had gained a breathing space at Assir, the Moslem army began to feel the full shame of its panic of August 1. It learned that Richard's little troop, with crazy indifference, was camping outside the walls of Jaffa. It seemed easy to cut down these footmen. On the night of August 4–5, the Moslem cavalry set off by moonlight toward the English camp. Some dispute which arose among the Mameluks somewhat delayed the march, so that when they arrived within sight of the camp, it was already first light. A Genoese who had wandered onto the heath saw the glint of arms and gave the alarm. Wakened with a start, Richard and his men barely had time to leap to arms; several of them had to fight half-dressed. In serried ranks, kneeling on one knee in order to resist more stoutly, their shields implanted before them, their lances couched, they withstood without flinching, in the clear light of dawn, the furious charge of the Moslem squadrons. Hastily, Richard had posted crossbowmen between the spearmen. As soon as the enemy horsemen, their first charge broken on the pikes, wheeled about to re-form, the bowmen fired, killing the horses and throwing disorder into the squadrons. All Saladin's charges broke before these precise tactics. In vain, behind the ranks, the sultan tried to rally his men. "So brave were the Franks," notes Beha ed-Din, "that our troops, discouraged, contented themselves with keeping them in sight, but at long range . . ."

Then, Richard the Lionhearted turned to attack this demoralized army. "He hurled himself into the midst of the Turks and clove them to the teeth. He charged so often and struck so many blows, striving so hard, that all the skin of his hands was torn off. He smote before him and behind and cut a passage with his sword wheresoever he plied it. Whether he struck at a man or a horse, he cut them all down. At one stroke he severed the head and arm of an ironclad emir and sent him straight to hell. And when the Turks saw this blow they gave him such a wide berth that he returned, thank God, unharmed. But his person, his horse, and his caparison were so full of arrows that he looked like a hedgehog."

The battle lasted all day on August 5. By nightfall, the crusader

victory was total. In the face of the king of England and his little
band of heroes, the Moslem army beat its retreat with Saladin humiliated and discouraged.

So great was the admiration of the Moslems for the extraordinary
courage of the great Plantagenet that at the height of the battle,
al-Adil, seeing him fight on a wretched nag, already foundered, had
sent him a new courser. Parting the crowd of combants, a Mameluk
galloped up and halted before Richard leading two magnificent Arabian steeds, "for it was not fitting that the king should fight on foot."
A few days after the battle, the king fell ill at Jaffa, and Saladin again
sent him peaches and sherbets cooled with the snows of Mount Hermon.

But events in Europe required the presence of the king of England.
In his absence, Philip Augustus and John Lackland had begun to
despoil him of his realm. Impatient to return, he concluded a compromise peace with Saladin on September 3, 1192, based on the situation
map. The Franks obtained the territory reoccupied by their armies—
that is to say, the coast zone from Tyre to Jaffa. The interior, with
Jerusalem, remained in the power of Saladin, but the sultan guaranteed
the Christians free pilgrimage to the Holy City. Saladin inaugurated
the new regime by welcoming at Jerusalem, with magnificent courtesy,
the bishops, barons, and knights, his erstwhile enemies, who came,
before re-embarking, to fulfill their vows at the Holy Sepulcher.

After all the fighting, the tumult, and the drama, all was now calm.
The adversaries had learned to esteem each other. Since the Franks
had been unable to drive the Moslems out of the interior, and the
Moslems had been equally unable to stop the Franks from regaining
their foothold on the coast, the best thing for both of them, as they
well realised, was this friendly understanding, which was favored
by the existence, in both camps, of a very similar spirit of chivalry, as
well as by the interlocking of trade interests at this Levantine crossroads. It is a striking fact that it was a Richard the Lionhearted who,
after the initial brutalities, was the initiator of this policy. When he
set sail again for Europe, on October 9, 1192, the fiery Plantagenet
found that, at the end of all his prodigious swordplay, he had replaced
the holy war with an understanding between Franks and Moslems. It
was, nevertheless, obviously not without sadness that he left without
having been able to deliver the Holy Sepulcher. He punished himself

for it by refraining from accompanying his knights on their visit to the Holy Places.

His chivalrous adversary, the Sultan Saladin, who could also add to his glory in arms the merit of having (and for much longer) favored this understanding, equally had to satisfy himself with a half success. No doubt he enjoyed throughout the world of Islam the incomparable prestige which he had won by the reconquest of Jerusalem; but after having, on the day of Hattin, been within an ace of total victory, he had known the dark days of Acre and Jaffa, and, while preserving the Mosque of Omar for Islam, he had had to yield back the Palestinian coast to the Christians. It is equally true that his generosity, his profound humanity, his Moslem piety, devoid of fanaticism, that flower of liberality and courtesy which had been the marvel of our old chroniclers, won him no less popularity in Frankish Syria than in the lands of Islam. By living at his side in those circumstances of high tragedy in which a man shows the whole of his true being, the Franks had learned that Moslem civilization too could produce genuinely superior types of humanity, just as the Moslems, a little later, were to have a similar revelation of Christian civilization from the presence in their midst of Saint Louis.

But all this travail and all this anguish had exhausted the great sultan. He had dreamed of profiting from the peace to visit his beautiful land of Egypt, which he had not seen for so many years, and above all of returning thanks to God in the pilgrimage to Mecca. The time was not granted to him. On the night of March 3–4, 1193, he died in that city of Damascus that he had loved so well and where, grand and simple as the Moslem faith itself, his tomb still rises today.

13

THE MEN OF
CHAMPAGNE AND POITOU
Henry of Champagne
and Amalric of Lusignan

AT THE moment when the kingdom of Jerusalem was beginning to rise again in the diminished form of a kingdom of Acre, the dynastic question arose more acutely than ever. Toward the end of his sojourn in the Levant, Richard the Lionhearted, in spite of his own preference for Guy of Lusignan, had been obliged to yield to the wishes of the Palestinian barons, who nearly all came out in favor of Conrad of Montferrat. In April 1192, the king of England had therefore rallied to the eventual nomination of Conrad as king of Jerusalem. As for Guy of Lusignan, he intended to compensate him by granting him the island of Cyprus.

Conrad of Montferrat, in his faithful city of Tyre, was preparing to assume this royal crown, so long the object of his covetous desires and which, it must be recognized, could not have gone to a better chief, when an unexpected drama threw everything back into the melting pot, including the very destiny of Frankish Syria.

A few weeks earlier, Conrad had caused to be flung into the sea some traffickers who proved to belong to the sect of Assassins. We have already spoken of this redoubtable Moslem secret society, which professed in the bosom of Islam a profoundly heretical doctrine and which, to gain its ends, resorted to terrorism against anyone, Moslem or Christian, who dared oppose it. Learning of the execution of his creatures, the grand master of the Assassins, the sinister Sinan, from his eyrie of Qadmus in the Alaouite Mountains, demanded satisfaction from Conrad. Conrad gave him no answer and thought no more of it, preoccupied as he was with the preparations for his coronation. One evening, April 28, 1192, as his young wife, the Princess Isabella, lingered in the bath, tired of waiting, he went off and invited himself to dinner with his old friend, the bishop of Beauvais. After dinner, leaving the bishop's residence, in the narrow lanes of ancient Tyre he was accosted by two of Sinan's bravos, who, to create a false scent, had just had themselves baptized. They presented him with a petition, which he accepted without mistrust. While he was reading it, one of them plunged a dagger in his side, and he died almost at once.

The death of Conrad of Montferrat, the strong man, at the very moment when he was at last in a position to give of his best, was a sad loss for the Latin East. The Syrian barons once again had to start suddenly casting around for a new chief. Their choice fell on a French crusader, Count Henry II of Champagne, who had the advantage of being nephew both to Philip Augustus and to Richard the Lionhearted. It was only with mixed feelings that Henry greeted an offer which would compel him to end his days in the East. The memory of his lands of Champagne filled him with nostalgia. Furthermore, Conrad's widow, Queen Isabella, whom he was expected to marry in order to link himself with the ancient dynasty, was a beauty who had passed through many hands. First married while still almost a child to the handsome Humphrey of Toron, whom she still regretted, separated from Humphrey by force, remarried equally by force to Conrad of Montferrat, and now widowed, she was left with child by Conrad. That was indeed a mortgage on the dynastic succession which encumbered the future of the prospective husband and wife, as the chronicler recalls with relish. Richard, for the rest, had indeed invited his nephew to marry Isabella, but without dissimulating that she was pregnant by the marquis and that, if the child was a boy, he would inherit the crown. "And in that case," riposted the count, "I shall be stuck with the lady!"

The reply was not very gracious, but no doubt Henry had not yet had a good look at Isabella. He changed his mind as soon as he came into the presence of the young widow. "And, by my soul," says the good poet Ambroise, "I would have done the same, for she was marvelously fair and full of charm. And so in the end, he was well content to wed her." We shall see that, on her side, she too became very attached to Henry. The wedding was celebrated on May 5, 1192, in the city of Tyre itself, in the midst of a rejoicing people.

Henry of Champagne, who had not at first shown any greater enthusiasm for the offer of the kingdom than for the offer of the queen, proved himself, once in power, as good a head of state as he was a good husband. This young man, thoughtful and confident, was able, after the departure of Richard the Lionhearted, to rule the kingdom of Acre with prudence and firmness. He restored the monarchic authority which Guy of Lusignan had allowed to decline. He remained on good terms with the house of Saladin. Intervening, like the former kings of Jerusalem, in northern Syria, he arbitrated in a serious quarrel between Bohemund III, prince of Antioch, and the Armenian prince of Cilicia, Leo III. Leo having captured Bohemund, Henry of Champagne journeyed to Cilicia, restored concord between the two men, and obtained the liberation of the prisoner. In the course of his journey, he even went to visit the grand master of the Assassins in the fortress of al-Kahf; the Assassins (as we have seen, alas! in the death of Conrad of Montferrat) constituted a force which, in the event of fresh Frankish-Moslem hostilities, it was better to have as ally than enemy. The grand master, who laid no less store by Frankish amity as a guarantee against orthodox Islam, gave Henry the warmest welcome. In honor of his visitor, he offered him, as the most natural thing in the world, the spectacle of some of those mass suicides which proved the blind obedience imposed on the sect. "Let us wager, sire," he said lightheartedly to Henry," that your knights will not do for you what my faithful will do for me." Whereupon he waved a scarf, and two of the sectaries, who had stationed themselves on the battlements of the topmost tower, immediately hurled themselves into the void. The wretches were scarcely dead when he offered the count the suicide of a dozen others. The good Henry, horrified, begged him to call a halt. Before taking leave of him, the Grand Master overwhelmed him with presents and, as a parting gift, gallantly offered to arrange the assassination of any of his enemies he cared to name.

The Latin East was at peace under the sage administration of Henry of Champagne when the Germanic Emperor, Henry VI, who had just added the Norman Kingdom of the Two Sicilies to the German realm, announced his intention of resuming the crusade of his father, Frederick Barbarossa. Pending his own departure, he dispatched to Syria an advance guard of German crusaders, who landed at Acre in September 1197. But these crusaders, if we are to believe the chroniclers, behaved very badly. They billeted themselves on the population by force, turned the owners out, insulted the Frankish ladies, and acted just as though they were in a conquered country. The burgesses of Acre complained to Henry of Champagne. A Syrian baron, Hugh of Tiberias, recommended to him the only effective line: "I know the Germans well," he said, as the Frankish chronicle reports. "With them you must use force; it is the only thing they understand." He therefore counseled that the women and children should be placed in safety with the Knights Hospitaler and that the men should then be called to arms to drive out the soldiery. But, as he had foreseen, it was not necessary to go to those lengths. The chiefs of the Germanic army, getting wind of the project, evacuated their men from Acre and encamped them in the suburbs. The landing of the German Crusade nevertheless had unfortunate results. It provoked a breach of the truce with the Moslems, all the more inopportune since the Germanic crusaders were no more than an advance guard, too few for any effective action. The sultan of Damascus, Malik al-Adil, Saladin's brother and successor, deeming himself threatened, responded by surprising and pillaging Jaffa.

At the precise moment when this regrettable event occurred, in the midst of the troubles caused both by the German threat and by the resumption of the Moslem war, a new drama intervened, which plunged all Frankish Syria into mourning. On September 10, 1197, from the balcony of his palace at Acre, Henry of Champagne had been watching the march past of the reinforcements dispatched to Jaffa when, stepping back mechanically to receive a delegation, he fell backward through an open window and broke his skull. His dwarf, Scarlet, tried to catch him by his clothes but was dragged down and

killed with him.   The chronicle describes in pathetic terms the sorrow
of Queen Isabella, warned by the cries of the servitors.   "She ran up
like a madwoman, tearing her face and snatching her hair.   At the
castle gate she met the bearers.   She fell on the lifeless body of her
husband, covering it with kisses and tears so that it was a pitiful sight to
see."

Henry of Champagne followed Conrad of Montferrat from the
scene. . . . A strange fate seemed to dog not only the unhappy Queen
Isabella but the whole kingdom.   But it was no time for lamentations.
The war had broken out again, sparked off by the untimely German
Crusade, and a new chief had to be found without delay.

The eyes of the Syrian barons turned toward the island of Cyprus,
where Guy of Lusignan, on his death in April 1194, had been succeeded by his brother Amalric.   He was a very different man from
Guy, if not his exact opposite.   A prudent and firm politician, ruth-
less enough on occasion, indifferent to unpopularity if the interest
of the country so required, knowing how to make himself obeyed by
all men, breaking down, if need be, the cabals of the barons and the
arrogance of the commons—no better guide could have been found in
these uncertain times.   For the rest, he had already proved himself in
Cyprus.   In less than three years he had organized the new island state
so solidly that, at his request, the Emperor Henry VI had erected this
lordship into a kingdom; in this very month of September 1197,
Amalric of Lusignan had received the royal crown of Cyprus from the
hands of the imperial chancellor and the papal legate in the cathedral of
Nicosia, thus founding a dynasty which was to last for three centuries.

The barons of Syria therefore made a very judicious choice when,
after the death of Henry of Champagne, they offered, together with
the hand of his widow Isabella, the crown of Jerusalem, to the new
king of Cyprus, Amalric of Lusignan, a choice which, in addition to
the sterling qualities of the prince, had the advantage of concentrating
the Christian forces of Acre and Nicosia.   Amalric, becoming by this
designation Amalric II of Jerusalem, accepted, landed in Syria, and
married Isabella.   It must be confessed that there is a strangeness in the
destiny of this young woman, barely twenty-six and already married
for the fourth time.   By now resigned to her fate, she does not seem, in
spite of the sorrow of her latest bereavement, to have raised any

objection, since, after all, state reason demanded that, as the sole heiress of the dynasty of Jerusalem, she should marry the successive war leaders chosen by the barons and thus confer on them legitimate monarchy.

Amalric of Lusignan celebrated his marriage and inaugurated his reign at Acre by a brilliant conquest. On October 24, 1197, he won back from the Moslems the city of Beirut, a precious acquisition which restored communications between the kingdom of Acre and the county of Tripoli. He next profited from this success, as well as from the lamentable failure of the German Crusade before Tibnin, to conclude a welcome peace with al-Adil, which left the Franks in possession of their latest conquests, Beirut and Jebail.

The West, at that moment, was headed by one of the greatest popes of the Middle Ages, Innocent III. In 1199, Innocent set about preaching a Fourth Crusade. In his mind, this expedition was no doubt intended to make a raid on Egypt to seize pledges and a bargaining counter for the recovery of Jerusalem. We know how this crusade was diverted from its aims by the Venetians, and instead of contributing to the deliverance of the Holy City, resulted in an "impious war" against the Byzantines, the conquest of Constantinople, and finally the foundation of an unexpected Latin Empire on the Bosphorus (1204). We know that, after being on the brink of excommunicating the main actors responsible for this "corruption of a crusade," Innocent III ended by accepting the accomplished fact, in the hope of at least making the best of it in the interests of the Holy Land itself. It might indeed have been hoped that, now in possession of the bridgehead of Constantinople, the Franks would be in a better position to throw reinforcements into Syria. In fact, it was the reverse which happened. After shattering the Byzantine power, the victors of 1204 put nothing in its place; for this artificial empire, hanging in mid-air, improvised in the midst of a completely hostile Greek and Slav world, was not to be a source of strength but, on the contrary, of constant weakness, to the Latin world. Above all, the foundation of a Latin Empire in the Balkans ended by depriving Frankish Syria of the immigration on which it could reasonably count. The new Frankish states of Romania and Greece, by diverting the knights who would normally have sought their fortune in the Levant, cut off the life blood of the kingdom of Acre. This already anemic colony became even more bloodless.

Frankish immigration, dispersed from Constantinople to Jaffa, from Athens to Antioch, ended by being insufficient everywhere; the result was that before the end of the century Byzantine revenge drove the Franks out of Constantinople and Moslem revenge drove them out of Acre.

The Fourth Crusade was already for a moment in danger, by inspiring the Franks of Syria with false confidence, of inciting them to incautious acts against Islam. Indeed, the few crusaders who, instead of making for Constantinople, had taken the road for Syria, thought of nothing but falling upon the Moslems. Amalric of Lusignan was wise enough to restrain this ill-considered zeal. In September 1204, he renewed the truce with al-Adil. On this occasion, he even got the sultan to accept the peaceful handing back to "the kingdom of Jerusalem" of Sidon in the north and Lydda and Ramleh in the south. The whole of the coastal plain was thus restored to the Christians.

When Amalric of Lusignan died at Acre on April 1, 1205, he had therefore labored manfully for the Frankish settlements. Unfortunately, under the constitutional assizes of the Frankish lands, the two kingdoms of Cyprus and Jerusalem (that is, of Cyprus and Acre) were once again separated after him. Cyprus went to his son by his first marriage, Hugh I of Lusignan. On the contrary, Amalric having left no male heir by Queen Isabella of Jerusalem, the crown of the Holy Land reverted to Isabella's daughter by Conrad, the young Mary of Montferrat. As Mary was till only fourteen, the regency was conferred upon her maternal uncle, John of Ibelin, lord of Beirut, one of the wisest barons of the country. John, "the old lord of Baruth," as the chronicles call him, ruled with great prudence and was able to maintain the truce with Saladin's dynasty.

14

THE FIFTH CRUSADE

A Knight-King: John of Brienne

IN 1208, the young Queen Mary of Jerusalem-Montferrat being now seventeen, John of Ibelin began to think about having her marry. In agreement with the prelates and the barons, he remitted the choice of the royal groom to King Philip Augustus of France. The king designated John of Brienne.

John of Brienne was a baron of Champagne, getting on for sixty. The choice of the king of France might have seemed strange, if the first consideration had not been to entrust the Holy Land to an experienced statesman. For the rest, John, a big handsome man of Herculean strength, was still full of fire, as is proved by the insinuation, garnered by the chroniclers, that Philip Augustus only designated him in order to separate him from Countess Blanche of Champagne, who was greatly enamored of him. Be that as it may, this accomplished knight combined the bravery of the ancient crusaders with a wisdom which made him one of the best kings of his time. It was in the midst of universal joy, "with a great concert of pipes and tabors," that on September 14, 1210, he was welcomed at Acre and married Queen Mary and on October 3, at her side, was crowned king of Jerusalem in the cathedral of Tyre.

Meanwhile, Innocent III, whose projects had been thwarted by the diversion of the Fourth Crusade, had no intention of renouncing the reconquest of Jerusalem. The great pope was preparing to preach a new holy war, and perhaps even to place himself at the head of the expedition, when death overtook him on January 16, 1216. His successor, Honorius III, carried on his work. Not only did he cause the crusade to be preached in the West, but he charged the eloquent archbishop of Acre, James of Vitry, to reawaken the zeal of the Franks of Syria themselves. If we are to believe James of Vitry (whose picture in any case seems to be painted too black) the Frankish settlers had shown a tendency to let themselves be influenced by the Levantine environment, and even by Moslem customs. These native-born Franks —or *"poulains"* as they were then called—enamored of the easy life in their fair cities on the Lebanon coast, had no difficulty in adjusting themselves to the Frankish-Moslem *modus vivendi* of 1192. The peace brought unprecedented wealth to the ports of Tripoli, Tyre, and Acre, once again become, as in Phoenician days, marts for the whole trade of the Levant. This was the terminus of the caravans which brought all the produce of the Moslem world and of the Indian Ocean; and the thriving settlements of Venetians, Pisans, Genoese, Marseillais, and Catalans who had set up there were more interested in the price of spices than in the deliverance of the Holy Sepulcher. The picture which James of Vitry paints of these great ports plunges us back into the habitual environment of the Levantine ports of call, medieval forerunners of the modern Hong Kong or Singapore. It is understandable, that before again fanning the flame of 1099 in the West the pope should first feel the need to revive the crusading spirit in Frankish Syria itself. We know too that James's preaching achieved its end, at any rate temporarily; in Acre, Beirut, Tripoli, Tortosa, Antioch, crowds thronged to take the Cross. In Tripoli, his sermons were translated into Arabic for the Maronites and the other Christians of the Syrian rite.

It now only remained to wait for the Western crusaders. They came in several waves. In September 1217, two pilgrims of great mark landed at Acre, accompanied by noble chivalry, King Andrew II of Hungary and Duke Leopold VI of Austria. The king of Cyprus, Hugh I of Lusignan, and the prince of Antioch-Tripoli, Bohemund IV, came to join them. The army thus mustered under the orders of Andrew II and John of Brienne represented a fairly imposing force. To use it to maximum effect, there should have been a unity of command, obviously under Brienne, who knew the country better. Andrew II would not agree. Aware of this rift, the Sultan al-Adil was careful not to encounter the crusaders in the field. He systematically avoided them, seeking only to wear down the adversary's morale by marches "into the blue" or tedious sieges. His calculations succeeded, especially with the Hungarians. When the crusade was halted at the Moslem fortress of Mount Tabor, they lost heart. Having come out in the hope of spectacular actions and heroic charges, they lost interest in the sustained operations; and at the beginning of 1218, King Andrew II, in any event weakened by illness, went back to Europe.

Nevertheless, in spite of the abortive issue of the Hungarian Crusade, other crusaders, French, Italian, or Frisian, continued to land at Acre. On the initiative of John of Brienne, it was decided to use these reinforcements for a great expedition to Egypt.

It was an excellent idea. In this year 1218, the keys to Jerusalem were to be found in Cairo. The Moslem Empire, as Saladin had constituted it by uniting Aleppo and Damascus with Egypt, was invulnerable on the side of Syria: with enemy armies holding the country-side, it was too dangerous for the Christians to venture, for months on end, far from the coast, on the arid plateau of Judaea, in order to undertake the long and arduous siege of a stronghold such as Jerusalem. Richard the Lionhearted, with all his fire, had been forced to recognize this in the face of Saladin, as the king of Hungary had just found in the face of al-Adil. It was not in Judaea, but in Egypt, in the fertile plains of the delta, that the Moslem empire was vulnerable. Masters of the sea, the Franks could, without undue difficulty, lay hands on the great Egyptian ports, Alexandria or Damietta, and with this counter in their possession, bargain for the return of Jerusalem in exchange. This policy of seizing ports as bargaining counters was later very often followed in the nineteenth century by the powers in the Ottoman Empire as well as in the Far East. It is interesting to note its first application in the midst of the Crusades.

Damietta, being nearer to the Palestine coast than Alexandria, was chosen as the first objective. On March 29, 1218, the crusading army, commanded by John of Brienne, landed opposite the town, on the other side of the mouth of the Nile. To defend the access to Damietta and at the same time to block any attempt to sail up the Nile, the Egyptians had barred the river with enormous iron chains, riveted to a

central tower. On August 24, after three months' effort, John of
Brienne succeeded in capturing the tower and cutting the chain. In
the words of the *Book of the Two Gardens*, it was the keys of Egypt
which fell into the hands of the Franks. Three days after, the old
Sultan al-Adil died of chagrin.

The sultan's eldest son, al-Kamil, who succeeded him in Cairo, set
about mounting a counterattack in the utmost secrecy. On October 9,
his army crossed the Nile, the cavalry over an improvised bridge and
the infantry in boats, and launched a surprise attack on the Frankish
camp. This master stroke nearly succeeded, the Franks being caught
completely off guard. It was John of Brienne who restored the
situation. At the first rumor he leaped to horse and with thirty
companions galloped to the outposts. He fell upon the Moslem infantry, who were landing in waves in such numbers "that he was full
dumbfounded." The whole bank of the Nile was covered with them.
If these battalions penetrated the camp on one side, while the cavalry
debouched from the bridge on the other, all was lost. John and his
thirty knights had no time to turn rein and give the alarm. Staking
everything on one throw, the king charged with his thirty heroes,
renewing the exploits of Richard the Lionhearted. "He spurred on his
horse, jumped it over the fosse of the camp at one bound, and hurled
himself at full gallop into the thick of the Moslem infantry. In the
enemy ranks he espied an emir of great height, armed with a halberd
and brandishing a blue standard with a gold crescent. John pricked
spurs, couched his lance, and smote the emir such a deadly blow that
he shattered his halberd, clove his heart, and laid him stone dead. At
this sight, the Moslems withdrew in disorder toward the Nile to swim
back to their boats."

After this setback, the situation soon became very serious for the
Egyptians. During the night of February 4–5, 1219, the Sultan al-Kamil, losing heart, abandoned his camp before Damietta to draw nearer
to Cairo. The next morning, the Franks, finding no more enemies in
front of them, crossed the Nile without opposition and installed themselves in their place on the east bank, at the foot of the walls of
Damietta, to which they immediately began to lay effective siege. The
chroniclers tell us here of John of Arcis, the knight who bore a
peacock's feather in his helmet, whose exploits terrified the besieged.

The expectations of John of Brienne immediately began to come true.

Even before Damietta had fallen, the sultan of Egypt, al-Kamil, in agreement with his brother, al-Muazzam, the sultan of Damascus, offered the Franks the return of Jerusalem against the evacuation of the delta. King John of Brienne, the barons of Syria, and the crusaders were unanimous in favor of accepting these terms. Unfortunately, John was no longer in single command of the crusade. At the end of September 1218, there arrived before Damietta the cardinal-legate, Pelagius, who forthwith claimed the command.

Pelagius comes down to us as the evil genius of the Fifth Crusade. It must be said at once that the holy see, whose confidence he was to betray, was, at the end of the campaign, to censure him severely for all his conduct. At Constantinople, in 1213, his intransigence had already brought to naught the program assigned to him by Pope Innocent III for the reconciliation of the Greek Church and the Roman Church. This intolerant Spaniard, full of pride and fanaticism, now displayed himself under the walls of Damietta in the same colors he had already shown in Romania: "hard-hearted, intolerably severe with all men, ostentatious, insolent, holding himself out as invested with all the prerogatives of the papacy, bedecked from head to foot in red, even to the saddlecloth and bridles of his horse." Broached on the evacuation of Egypt in order to obtain the delivery of Jerusalem, he bridled with indignation. He wanted both Jerusalem and Egypt! With his usual fieriness and intolerance, backed, moreover, and not surprisingly, by the Templars, he silenced John of Brienne and declared that the sultan's proposals were rejected. And he ordered the siege of Damietta to be pushed on with even greater ardor.

At first, the legate's obstinacy seemed warranted by the facts. If the Sultan al-Kamil was trying to ensure the departure of the Franks at all costs, it was because the Moslem garrison of Damietta was really at the end of its tether. The Franks, aware of the position, mounted the assault. On the night of November 5, 1219, they escaladed one of the master towers and by dawn the town itself was taken.

The capture of Damietta was the personal work of John of Brienne, who had mounted and directed the assault. Pelagius was nevertheless able to reap the benefit, since it was his doing that, instead of accepting the sultan's proposals, they had persisted in attacking the fortress. The legate had proved right against the king. His arrogance became all the greater, and with it his pretensions to the sole command. In conquered

Damietta, he gave himself the airs of a master, affecting to override the king's rights, eliminating the royal agents.   Brawls and street fights were rife between his followers, mostly Italian, and the French knights who had taken the side of John of Brienne.   John, his heart full of bitterness, seized the first pretext to quit Damietta and get back to Syria (March 29, 1220).

Pelagius, as he wanted, thus stayed on in Damietta alone at the head of the crusade.   His pride was boundless.   Ever since the conquest of the city, he had fancied himself a great captain.   In reality, his complacency was not long in imperiling the army.   He neglected, among other things, to maintain a lookout squadron off Damietta, a serious mistake, since command of the sea was essential to the success of the expedition.   The Egyptians hastened to take advantage by constructing a fleet to intercept communications between Damietta and Acre. Some informers (no doubt Copts) warned the legate in time, but he would not believe them.   "See these churls!" he is said to have cried. "When they want a free meal they come to us with a bit of news they have made up.   All right, give them something to eat!"   The intelligence was nevertheless so accurate that, a few days later, the Egyptian ships put to sea and began a running warfare between Damietta and the Christian ports, which did the Franks untold harm.

Yet once again, the Sultan al-Kamil offered the Franks the restitution of the whole of the former kingdom of Jerusalem if they would return Damietta.   Once again Pelagius turned him down.   When messages from Egypt brought the news to Philip Augustus, the French king, Ernoul tells us, thought that the legate had gone mad: "He could exchange a single town for a whole kingdom, and he has refused!"

But Pelagius did not stop there.   In the closing days of June 1221, he decided to go and conquer Cairo.   At Acre, John of Brienne summed up the situation at a glance: "The army is being launched on a venture in which all will be lost!"   Despairingly, but obedient only to the call of duty, he set sail at once to join the army, his heart full of sinister forebodings.   On July 7, he landed at Damietta.   Pelagius gave the marching orders.   The whole army set off southward toward Cairo. "The men who forced this decision on the Franks," says Ernoul vehemently, "verily persuaded them to drown themselves!"   The season had indeed arrived when, every year, the Egyptians opened the floodgates of the Nile.   According to the history of the patriarchs of

Alexandria, John of Brienne made one last attempt to dissuade Pelagius. The legate charged him with treason. "So be it, then," replied the king, "I will march with you, but may God judge between us!"

The Frankish army, leaving Damietta, committed itself to the lowland triangle, a veritable "island," bounded on the north by Lake Manzala, on the west by the eastern branch of the Nile, and on the south by the Nile canal known as the Bahr as-Saghir. On the Nile, the Egyptian flotilla, from its moorings between Cairo and Damietta, intercepted communications by water and cut off the crusaders' supply lines. But the legate, convinced that they would be inside Cairo at once, had only arranged for a derisory amount of supplies. Furthermore, at the confluence of the Nile and the Bahr as-Saghir, the Sultan al-Kamil had just raised the powerful fortress of Mansura, which, protected by the canal, denied the crossing and barred the road to Cairo. The crusaders were beginning to realize that they had committed themselves to a blind alley when the final drama occurred: the Egyptians breached the dykes and the water gushed into the plain, leaving the Franks nothing but a narrow causeway in the midst of the floods.

Pelagius—it was now August 26—then decided to beat a retreat. But the floods were rising steadily and on reaching Baramun they were forced to recognize that they could go no further. "The Franks would fain have fought, but their soldiers, in water up to their knees, slithered in the mud and could not get at the enemy, who riddled them with arrows." The legate, out of his wits, then implored the aid of John of Brienne, whom he had thus far treated in such cavalier fashion. "Sire, for the love of God, now show your cunning and your valor!" "My lord legate, my lord legate," answered Brienne, "would that you had never left your land of Spain, for you have led Christendom to its defeat. And now you ask me to save the day, which is no longer in the power of any man, for you can see full well that we can neither come at the enemy to fight nor continue our retreat, nor even encamp in the midst of all these waters. For the rest, we have no provisions, either for our horses or for our men."

Nothing remained for the crusaders but to offer Malik al-Kamil the surrender of Damietta, thinking themselves lucky if they could save their skins on those terms. Fortunately for them, the new sultan of Egypt took rank among the most statesmanlike and most liberal spirits of that glorious Kurdish dynasty; he was as statesmanlike as his father, al-Adil, who had so nearly become the brother-in-law of Richard the Lionhearted, as liberal and as generous as his uncle, the great Saladin. For the rest, al-Kamil had his eyes fixed on the West. He was well aware that the most puissant sovereign of Christendom, Frederick II, Germanic Emperor and king of Sicily, had just taken the Cross. By allowing the Frankish army, held at the mercy of the Egyptians, to perish, he would lay himself open to an even more redoubtable invasion of reprisal. Al-Kamil therefore accepted the crusaders' terms, and the decision once taken, carried it out with a humanity and a courtesy which won the admiration of our chroniclers. John of Brienne, with noble abnegation, had agreed to stand hostage for the evacuation of Damietta. Al-Kamil received him like a king, "overwhelming him with marks of esteem such as he accorded to no other man." In a splendid tent on a lofty mound dominating the theater of operations, flanked by his brothers, al-Muazzam, sultan of Damascus, and al-Ashraf, sultan of the Jezira, he entertained the knightly king at a sumptuous feast. But in the midst of the most flattering attentions, the old warrior could not hold back his tears. The sultan was astonished. "Why dost thou weep? It ill becomes a king to weep." "Well may I weep," replied Brienne, "when I see all those poor folk down there, whom God entrusted to my charge, dying of hunger." In fact, the Frankish army, cut off by the waters and without subsistence on the narrow causeway where it had been forced to lay down its arms, was collapsing from lack of food. Malik al-Kamil, filled with compassion, immediately sent the Franks the supplies they needed. "These same Egyptians, whose families we had lately massacred, whom we had despoiled and driven from home," avows Oliver of Cologne, "now came to victual us and save us when we were dying of hunger and at their mercy. . . ."

The Christian army, thus snatched from destruction, re-embarked without incident after handing over Damietta to al-Kamil. John of Brienne got back to Acre, in the midst of general esteem. As for Pelagius, the author of the disaster, he had to suffer, on his return to Italy, a severe reprimand from the pope, who, after inquiring into the whole incident, found that all the right was on the side of John.

15

A PILGRIMAGE WITHOUT FAITH
The Strange Crusade of Frederick II

T̲HE FAILURE of the Fifth Crusade compelled the Franks to reassess the whole question of the Levant. Since Richard the Lionhearted, a direct assault on Jerusalem had been deemed impossible. Diversion and the capture of pledges in Egypt had merely resulted in the capitulation of the expeditionary force. What was to be done now? John of Brienne traveled to Italy to beg aid and counsel from Pope Honorius III and the Emperor Frederick II (October 1222).

Frederick II was indeed a powerful sovereign, the most powerful since Charlemagne when it is remembered that to the heritage of his ancestor, Frederick Barbarossa—the whole of the Holy Roman Empire, together with Germany, northern Italy, and the kingdom of Arles —he added, through his mother, the heiress of the last Normans of Sicily, the noble kingdom of southern Italy. The dual inheritance of the Germanic Caesars and the Norman Italian princes had made him one of the most complex characters of history, the last of the potentates of the higher Middle Ages through his dreams of universal monarchy, the first man of the Reniassance through his inquiring mind and his completely lay conception of the state. No less strange is his attitude in the dispute between the papacy and the empire, since this scion of the Hohenstaufens, inveterate enemies of the holy see, found himself by force of circumstances the ward of the Roman Church, the adopted child of Innocent III. Innocent's successor, the old Pope Honorius III, who loved Frederick like a son and was to keep so many illusions about him to the very end, counted firmly on him to launch the Crusades anew. These feelings were shared by the grand master of the Teutonic Order, the knightly monk, Hermann of Salza, whose zeal for the Holy Land was equaled only by his devotion to Frederick. Both of them thought they had found a sure way of committing the emperor to the interests of Frankish Syria—by guaranteeing him the crown of Jerusalem.

By his marriage with the queen of Jerusalem, Mary of Montferrat, now dead, John of Brienne had an only daughter, Isabella, now aged eleven. It was this child who, through her mother, was the legitimate heiress to the crown of Jerusalem, John of Brienne having been recognized king merely as prince consort. Now Frederick II had been four months a widower. He was only twenty-eight. Honorius III and Hermann of Salza conceived the idea of marrying him to Isabella.

Frederick welcomed the project with enthusiasm. Under Christian law, the prestigious title of king of Jerusalem added luster, if that were possible, to the title of Emperor of the West. John of Brienne, for his part, was dazzled. The old knight from Champagne whom the favor of Philip Augustus had sent to govern the Holy Land, now found himself the emperor's father-in-law. He consented to the marriage without question. Was it not, moreover, in the interests of the Christian land? Would the sovereign of Germany and Sicily not commit all the forces of the West to the defense and recovery of the Holy Land, to retaking Jerusalem and crushing Islam? Was this not the salvation of the France of the Levant?

So thought the old king, the model knight-errant, as straight and true as his own sword, without mental equivocation or malice. But when, leaving Italy, he came, full of joy, to tell the good news to Philip Augustus, his icy reception by the Capetian began to inspire him with some doubt. The astute politician who had just succeeded in constructing the France of the Gauls was not slow to realize that the imperial wedding bells would sound the death knell of France in the Levant. While the papacy allowed itself to be seduced by the charms of Frederick II, he, for his part, had penetrated the psychology of the young Hohenstaufen. Latin Syria, in spite of its theoretically international character, had long been in practice, both by race and by civilization, a French land; and the marriage of the heiress of its kings with the Swabian Emperor could only rob it of its nationality. Philip Augustus, to whom John of Brienne owed his whole career, blamed him for facing him with an accomplished fact.

For it was too late to go back on the decision. In August 1225, an imperial squadron of fourteen sail escorted Archbishop James of Patti from Brindisi to Acre to celebrate the marriage of Isabella and Frederick II by proxy. The young girl—she was now fourteen—received the wedding ring in the Church of the Holy Cross at Acre and was then crowned empress in the cathedral of Tyre. The chroniclers describe with complacence the feasts which for a fortnight accompanied the ceremony, the streets decorated with the arms of Jerusalem and Swabia, with joustings, tournaments, dancing, and representations of the romances of chivalry, "as is fitting when such a great lady as the queen of Jerusalem weds such a great lord as the emperor." A few weeks later, the young empress said farewell to that land of Syria where she had been born and which she had never quitted, a farewell tinged with a melancholy foreboding. As she left she gazed on the shores, saying, "To God I commend you, sweet Syria, for I shall never see you again." On her arrival at Brindisi, in October 1225, she was received with great pomp by Frederick II, and the marriage was celebrated in that city on November 9.

This whole affair of the marriage was based on a misunderstanding between John of Brienne and his new son-in-law, a misunderstanding the latter had carefully nourished up to this point but which, once in possession of the heiress, he hastened to dissipate. Old Brienne expected to keep the crown of Jerusalem until his death. Frederick intended to make him yield it to him at once. It may be noted that, from the legal point of view (and we know that, like Philip the Fair in France, he had a lawyer's soul), he was strictly within his rights. John of Brienne, as we have seen, had, since the death of his wife, Mary of Jerusalem, exercised power merely as the guardian of their daughter, Isabella; now that, by virtue of her marriage, she was deemed to have reached her majority, the crown reverted to her—that is to say, to her husband. This is what Frederick, on the very wedding night, explained crudely to his simple-minded father-in-law. The old knight, who had always had a quixotic streak, did not immediately get the point. Whereupon Frederick, taking Isabella with him, left Brindisi without telling him, leaving him to his reflections. The unhappy man, swallowing this first insult, hastened to rejoin the emperor at the next staging point, but this time his reception was such that he lost all his illusions: he had been outwitted and despoiled.

The poor little empress-queen was hardly any happier. Frederick, who in spite of his new wife's fourteen years, had hastened to consummate the marriage, was already unfaithful to her. According to the Frankish chronicles, John of Brienne found her one day weeping bitterly because Frederick had just seduced one of her cousins who had accompanied her from Syria. John vented his wrath on the culprit "and told him that were it not for fear of sin, he would run him through the body with his sword." The emperor then forced him to "void the land." The two men were never to meet again except on the battlefield. As for the unhappy Isabella, the young girl precociously initiated into the sorrows of life, she was to die in childbirth at the age of sixteen on May 4, 1228. But as she left a son, the future Conrad IV, the legitimate heir to the throne of Jerusalem, Frederick could continue to administer the overseas territories in the child's name.

For Frederick, after eliminating John of Brienne in such cavalier fashion, had hastened to take possession of Frankish Syria. Only half trusting the French nobility of the country, he sent out as governor of Acre in 1226 his own man, the Neapolitan baron, Thomas of Acerra. This haste to lay hold of his new Syrian kingdom might at least give the Syrian Franks and the papacy the hope that he was about to lead a great crusade. A long time had indeed already elapsed since, at the demand of Innocent III—it was in 1215—he had sworn to take the Cross. Since then he had constantly postponed the fulfillment of his vow. To every papal summons, paternal at first so long as Honorius III was alive and then severe and soon threatening after the accession of Gregory IX, he replied by asking for more time, sometimes on excellent pretexts, sometimes by the most wretched subterfuge. His play-acting ended by exasperating that zealous old man, Gregory, forcing him to a breach from which the empire, the papacy and Frankish Syria were all alike to suffer. And it must be confessed that there was a certain strangeness about the attitude of this chief of the West, this king of Jerusalem, so strict in enforcing all the rights attached to this dual title and so little inclined to discharge the corresponding duties.

The defense of the West, in the thirteenth century, lay on the marches of Syria, face to face with Islam; men called it the crusade.

But Frederick II was anything but the enemy of Islam. He knew all about Islam. Brought up in Sicily, in a land still half Moslem, where the Norman domination was far from having wiped out the traces of the Arab occupation, he found everything in the Arab-Persian civilization flattering to his tastes: Arab philosophy, then at its zenith, which allowed this inquiring and almost free-thinking mind to escape from the circle of Christian thought; the example of the hereditary caliphate which strengthened his tendencies to Caesaro-papism; the blind devotion of his Arab subjects in Sicily who provided him with regiments unmoved by any threat of excommunication; and finally, the Moslem mores with their polygamy. Since the death of his wife Isabella, he had constituted at Lucera, in the kingdom of Naples, a veritable Moslem capital where, in the midst of his Sicilian Mameluks, he played the part of a sultan—a sultan who did not even lack a harem. "The population of Lucera," writes the Arab chronicler Jemal ed-Din, who had visited the city, "was entirely Moslem. The holy day was Friday and the other customs of Islam were observed. Frederick had built a college there for the teaching of the astrological sciences. Many of his intimates and secretaries were Moslems. In his camp the muezzin called to prayer." The Western chroniclers confirm this account. "He had such great love and familiarity for the infidels," confides the Rothelin manuscript, "that he chose among them his most intimate servitors and had his women guarded by their eunuchs"—women who were themselves, as Matthew Paris tells us, Arab or Moorish. "There were many points," continues the manuscript, "on which he had thus adopted Moslem manners. Thus, he was constantly exchanging embassies and gifts with the sultan of Egypt. The pope and the other Christian princes ended by asking whether he had not secretly converted to the religion of Mahomet; but others said that he still hesitated between Islam and Christianity."

What fascinated Frederick was no doubt less the religion of the Koran itself than Arab and Persian science, at that date far in advance of Western science. "He was," the Arab historian Maqrisi tells us, "a prince very learned in philosophy, geometry, mathematics, and all the exact sciences. He sent the Sultan al-Kamil many very hard questions on the theory of numbers. The sultan showed them to the Sheik Alam ed-Din Tasif, and to other learned men. He wrote out their answers and sent them back to the emperor." It may be noted, precisely, that no one was better qualified to understand such preoccupations than al-Kamil. This successor of Saladin was famous throughout Islam for the generous way in which he attracted and pensioned learned men. He always had some of them sleeping in his own palace, Maqrisi tells us, so that he could engage in discussion with them for part of the night. Such a turn of mind in the sultan as well as in the emperor was to introduce quite a new spirit into relations between Moslems and Christians.

But if Frederick II affected such an admiration for Islam, it was rather in the spirit of Montesquieu or Voltaire, not so much for Islam itself as against the Roman Church. Even under the pen of the Arab chroniclers, his praises of Moslem society seem rather like tracts against the papacy. Jemal ed-Din, for example, reports a conversation which would not be out of place in the *Lettres Persanes*. Frederick questioned the sultan's ambassador, the Emir Fakhr ad-Din, about the caliph. "The caliph," replied the emir, "is the descendent of the uncle of our prophet, Mahomet. He received the caliphate from his father, who had it from his father and so forth, so that the caliphate has always remained in the family of the Prophet without interruption." "Now, that is perfect," cried the emperor, "and very much better than what is done by those imbeciles the Franks, who take the first comer as chief (the pope), a man with no kinship to the Messiah, and make him a sort of caliph. This man has no right to such a rank, whereas your caliph, who is of the Prophet's family, has every right." Not many strokes of this kind were needed, when Frederick finally resigned himself to setting out for the East, to make both the surprised Moslems and the scandalized Christians regard the voyage of this strange crusader as a visit by the "sultan of Italy" to his friend, the sultan of Egypt.

This was indeed to be one of the aspects of the "crusade" of Frederick II; even more, it was the decisive reason. It was at the appeal of the sultan that the Germanic Emperor undertook the voyage to Syria. Here is the explanation of this paradox.

Saladin's empire, which still included Egypt, Moslem Palestine, and Syria and southern Mesopotamia, was now divided among three princes of his family, three brothers, his nephews: al-Kamil, who, with the title of Supreme Sultan, had Egypt; al-Muazzam, who had Damascus; and al-Ashraf, who had Mesopotamia. In 1226, the sultan of Egypt, al-Kamil, and the king of Damascus, al-Muazzam, quarreled. To triumph over his elder brother, al-Muazzam called to his aid the redoubtable Turkish conqueror, Jelal ad-Din, who, driven out of Khwarismia or the land of Khiva, his homeland, by the Mongols of Genghis Khan, had carved himself a new kingdom in Persia and Armenia and whose half-savage hordes, massacring all who crossed their path, struck terror into the old capitals of Mediterranean Islam. This was indeed calling in the barbarians. Al-Kamil made no mistake about it. In a flash the philosophic and lettered sultan found his fair land of Egypt invaded by the ferocious Khwarismian squadrons and all Moslem civilization in peril, a peril all the more grave since the Khwarismians were merely the forerunners of the Mongol invasion and behind Jelal ad-Din the terrible Genghis Khan cast his dreaded shadow. For all that Jelal ad-Din was Moslem like himself, al-Kamil, as accommodating on the side of Islam as Frederick II could be on the side of Christianity, felt himself much safer with the skeptical Emperor of the West than with the sanguinary Turkish swordsman. Against the Khwarismian menace, for the defense of civilization, he had no hesitation in appealing to Frederick. "He wrote to the emperor, king of the Franks," attests the Moslem chronicle *The Collar of Pearls*, "bidding him come to Syria, at Acre, and promising, if Frederick helped him against al-Muazzam, to return the city of Jerusalem to the Franks."

The ambassador whom the sultan of Egypt charged to bear this message to Frederick II was the Emir Fakhr ad-Din, one of the strangest figures of these times, as fascinated by Western civilization as Frederick was by Moslem civilization, so that the two men struck up a friendship which ended only with their lives. On one of the two voyages which the emir made to the court of Sicily, in the autumn of 1226 or October 1227, Frederick dubbed him knight with his own hands and thereafter Fakhr ad-Din bore the emperor's blazon on his own banner. On his side, Frederick sent two ambassadors to Cairo, Thomas of Acerra and Bishop Berard of Palermo, who, the Arab chronicler Maqrisi tells us, "presented the sultan with the emperor's own horse, with a golden saddle encrusted with precious stones. Al-Kamil went in person to meet the ambassadors and gave them the palace of the last vizier as their residence in Cairo. He busied himself in turn by sending to the emperor rich gifts from the Yemen and from India." Under the terms of the alliance made with the sultan, Berard of Palermo then proceeded to Damascus to try to intimidate his brother al-Muazzam. As might be guessed, his reception there was very different. "Go tell your master," replied the king of Damascus, "that I am not like some other people, and that for him I have only my sword."

Thus, while the papacy was enjoining Frederick II to go East to direct the holy war against the sultan, the sultan was inviting him to come as a friend and ally to defend him against his own brother and that brother's associates—that is to say, against the eddies of barbarism spread from the depths of Central Asia by the Mongol tempest. This twofold invitation was to enable the Sicilian Emperor to play one of those diplomatic games in which he excelled, a subtle game, complicated and contradictory enough, and even dangerous, in which he succeeded only by a miracle of skill as well as of double dealing.

Let us note one of the first advantages of the situation: Frederick II in his kingdom of the Holy Land could launch a war against the Moslems of Damascus without in any way upsetting the sultan of Egypt, but on the contrary placing him very much at his ease. As early as the beginning of 1227 he sent to Acre a first contingent of Germanic crusaders under the command of Duke Henry of Limburg who recaptured Sidon from al-Muazzam's men, relieved the stronghold of Caesarea, and helped the Grand Master Hermann of Salza to take the fortress of Montfort, subsequently the main seat of the Order of Teutonic Knights. These operations, very useful as they were for the defense of the Holy Land, were merely the foretaste of the great expedition for which the German crusaders awaited the arrival of Frederick II, not without some astonishment that he had not yet landed.

Frederick II's delay in setting off for Syria was explained by the need successfully to complete his negotiations with the sultan. But it also seems that, like Louis XI in France, the German-Sicilian Emperor tried to be too clever. By dint of procrastinating so as to leave at the most favorable moment, he let that moment slip, from the point of view both of the moral effect in the Christian world and of his pact with the sultan. In the first place, the new pope, Gregory IX, who did not have the same fund of patience with him as had Honorius III, ended by demanding his immediate departure; and since Frederick, really delayed this time by the death of the landgrave of Thuringia and by his own illness, asked for one last postponement, the pope, refusing to believe his explanations, excommunicated him (September 28, 1227). It was a grave decision, which seemed to make the emperor's crusade morally impossible: for the rest, Gregory IX understood it in that way, since he expressly forbade him to go to the Holy Land in the future. But Frederick, whose voyage was to be so little like a crusade, paid no attention. In spite of the exhortations of the papacy, he had postponed his departure from year to year. Once excommunicated, in spite of the pope's prohibition, he set sail.

Secondly, even from the point of view of his deals with the sultan, Frederick II had really delayed too long. If al-Kamil had sought his alliance, it was, as we have seen, to fight against al-Muazzam, prince of Damascus, who threatened to unleash the invasion of the Khwarismian hordes against Egypt. But, while the Egyptian ambassador Fakhr ad-Din was still in Italy with Frederick, al-Muazzam died (November 12, 1227). His son, an-Nasir Dawud, who succeeded him in Damascus was only an inexperienced youth, quite incapable of constituting any danger for Egypt. The peril was thus past and it was no longer in the sultan's interest to call in Frederick: why should he still stand by his offer to hand Jerusalem back to the Franks? Repenting his hasty invitation, he now tried to call off the emperor's voyage.

But Frederick had now gone too far to retreat. The pressure of public opinion throughout the West had become irresistible. So he set out, but he set out under the worst conditions, an excommunicated crusader, placed under the ban of Christendom by the holy see, and at the same time, instead of coming as the ally of the sultan of Egypt, now appearing in his eyes as the most unwelcome of intruders. By trying to trim his sails too cunningly between Christendom and Islam, he was now in danger of being disavowed by both.

To all these difficulties, not entirely of his own creation, this strange crusader wantonly added others by his attitude toward the French nobility of Cyprus and Palestine.

The kingdom founded in the island of Cyprus at the end of the twelfth century by the house of Lusignan was, if possible, even more French than the kingdom of Jerusalem. During the minority of the young King Henry I of Lusignan, then aged eleven, the regency was in the hands of an old French baron of Syria, John of Ibelin, lord of Beirut, whose family, originally from Chartres, headed the nobility in Cyprus as well as in Palestine. He was the very pattern of a perfect knight, valiant and wise, prudent and courteous, and with it all, a firm and liberal administrator, learned in the law, fluent in speech; on the marches of the Levant he was the incarnation of the brilliant French civilization of the thirteenth century. When Frederick II stopped at Cyprus on his way to Syria, John of Ibelin received him with the utmost deference at the port of Limassol (July 21, 1228). Frederick, for his part, professed the frankest friendship for him and invited him, with all the Cypriot nobility, to a magnificent banquet in Limassol itself. The lord of Beirut, recalling the troublesome discomfiture of John of Brienne, had some suspicions that these attentions also masked some perfidy; but when his friends tried to dissuade him from accepting the invitation, he replied nobly "that he would rather be made prisoner or slain than hear it said that through his suspicion of the emperor the Frankish forces had been divided and the crusade brought to naught."

Mistrust of Frederick II's attitude, however, was all too well founded. As king of Jerusalem he was determined to establish the same absolutism in his Syrian states as in Sicily. To do that he must break down the franchises and liberties which the French nobility of Palestine had always enjoyed. He must break that nobility itself and, as Philip Augustus had foreseen, transfer the power from the French element to the Italo-German element. To succeed in this it was not enough to assert his authority over Frankish Syria, where his title of king of Jerusalem in fact gave him every right; he must also lay hands on the kingdom of Cyprus by sweeping aside the obstacle put in his way by the regency of John of Ibelin.

This was the sole purpose of the Limassol banquet. The night before, Frederick had secretly manned all the exits from the castle with devoted men-at-arms. When the feast was over these guards suddenly appeared, swords drawn, behind each guest and Frederick himself dropped his mask. Without preamble, he summoned John of Ibelin to render him an account of his administration of the affairs of Cyprus and, on the mainland, to hand over the stronghold of Beirut to the imperialists. The first demand would have been tantamount to conferring on the emperor, king of Jerusalem, suzerainty over the kingdom of Cyprus with the regency of the island state, while the second would have despoiled the head of the French nobility of the Levant of his personal fief. In support of his claims, Frederick cited Germanic imperial law. Nothing could have indicated more clearly that the rights and customs of the two French kingdoms of the East were to be swept away by their attachment to the empire. Then came the threat: "By this head, which has worn many crowns, I shall do my will in these two affairs, or you shall rue it!" Behind the guests, the guards, sword in hand, closed in.

John of Ibelin rose to his feet. With perfect courtesy, but with unshakable firmness, he appealed to the laws of the French kingdoms of the Levant. He would answer for his titles to the lordship of Beirut only before the high court of the notables of the kingdom of Jerusalem, at Acre, and for his administration of the island before the court of Cyprus at Nicosia. Against the projects of imperial absolutism, he proclaimed the rights and liberties of the French nobility, the inheritor of the ancient dynasty of Jerusalem, which had no intention of allowing Levantine France to be treated as a simple Germanic outpost: "I have and I hold Beirut as my own fief of right, and my lady Queen Isabella of Jerusalem who was my own sister and her lord, King Amalric, gave it to me when Christendom had recovered it all destroyed, and it was I who raised its walls and fortified it, and if you allege that I hold it wrongfully, then I call you to account before the high court of the kingdom of Jerusalem. And rest assured that neither fear, nor prison, nor threat of death will make me yield, save by judgment of the court in due and proper form!"

Faced by the clash between feudal law and his theories of Roman law, the Germanic Caesar gave full rein to his brutality: "I have already heard tell that your tongue is mighty fine and courteous and that you are full wise and subtle of speech, but I will show you well that all your eloquence will not prevail against my might!"

In this dramatic dialogue, of which all the cut and trust is preserved for us by the poet-knight Philip of Novara, the lord of Beirut, interpreting the feelings of the French nobility, answered the German Emperor with a bluntness which made men tremble for him and his companions: "Sire, you have heard tell of my courteous words, but for my part I have long since heard tell of your deeds, I and my friends also, who warned me against this trap!" Then came the magnificent declaration which the old knight had already made to the counselors of caution: although he had come relying on the emperor's good faith, he was fully aware of the treachery to which the emperor's well-known character exposed him, but he had preferred to run this risk rather than be accused of defection on the assembly of the crusade. "And I did not want men to be able to say, 'You know, the emperor of Rome went overseas and would have conquered all had it not been for those lords of Ibelin who refused to follow him!'" The magnificent eloquence of this speech, one of the finest in medieval French, comes out best in the text of Philip of Novara. In the powerful spirit which breathes through it, one can feel the noble soul of the old baron and that patriotism of the Holy Land to which the lord of Beirut subordinated his fortune, his liberty, and his life.

"The emperor," continues Novara, "was mighty wroth and changed color," but he dared not go too far. Fearing a general revolt, he let John of Ibelin go. It was just as well for him that he did, for some of the younger Cypriot aristocrats were ready to run him through with their daggers while he was in Nicosia, and it was John of Ibelin, warned of the plot, who stopped them: "He is our liege lord and, come what may, let us preserve our honor!" Agreement was therefore reached. The Cypriot barons agreed to recognize the emperor as suzerain of their king. On the other hand, they refused to add to this eminent suzerainty the direct and personal rendering of homage to Frederick. This sharp legal distinction stopped the emperor from establishing in Cyprus the absolutist government of his dreams.

After the king of Cyprus, the most puissant prince of the Latin East was the prince of Antioch and Tripoli, Bohemund IV. On the news of the emperor's arrival he had hastened to Cyprus to pay his court. But the Limassol incident filled him with the gravest misgivings. Since Frederick sought to dispossess John of Ibelin of the county of Beirut, was he not capable even of seizing Bohemund's person in order to lay hands on Antioch and Tyre? To get out of this wasps' nest, the prince of Antioch pretended to be suddenly struck dumb and out of his mind and "he did nothing," says the good chronicler, "except shout, 'Aha! Aha!' at the top of his voice." Thanks to this subterfuge he was able to slip the watch and fling himself into a boat which took him back to

Tripoli. "As soon as he was on dry land," adds the chronicle slyly, "he found himself cured again, and he rendered thanks to God that he had escaped the emperor." An excellent piece of comedy, smacking of fable, but which clearly shows the deplorable impression produced in the Levant by Frederick II. An impression of fear, but of fear devoid of all respect and, on the contrary, inspiring "our folk" with irreverent and mocking revolt. How far we are from the still Carolingian majesty of a Frederick Barbarossa or the admiration which was to be inspired by the moral grandeur of a Saint Louis! In this instance it must be confessed that the most authentic imperial majesty, in the heir of Charlemagne and the Caesars, sank to the perfidies of a *condottiere*. The very acts by which the emperor tried to realize his dream of a centralized state after the ancient pattern—or already in the modern style—were felt to be misdeeds. Frederick II was a Renaissance tyrant out of time and out of place in the fair Christian society of the thirteenth century.

It was therefore in the wake of the worst of reputations that, on September 3, 1228, Frederick II sailed from Famagusta for Palestine. And yet, as John of Ibelin said, he was still the emperor: the young King Henry and the knights of Cyprus, with John of Ibelin himself, accompanied him to the mainland. On September 7 the whole procession landed at Acre.

As has already been foreshadowed, Frederick II, on landing in Syria, no longer found things as he had expected them. His whole Syrian policy was based on the conflict between the sultan of Egypt, al-Kamil, and his younger brother, the sultan of Damascus. It was at the call of al-Kamil that he had decided to come. He counted on helping the court of Egypt to annex Damascus and on receiving Jerusalem in exchange. And now, the disappearance from the scene of the sultan of Damascus and his replacement by an insignificant youth whom Egypt could call to heel whenever it wished upset the whole plan. At the very moment when Frederick II was making ready to cross over from Cyprus to Palestine, the Sultan al-Kamil set out from Egypt with a powerful army and, without striking a blow, occupied Jerusalem and Nablus in the territory of the young prince of Damascus (August 1128). Soon after, al-Kamil's troops, joined by those of his youngest brother, al-Ashraf, king of Mesopotamia, invested Damascus, a siege which lasted from January to July 1229 and ended, as might have been expected, with the surrender of the town.

These events, which coincided with the arrival of Frederick II in Syria, explain the embarrassed attitude of al-Kamil toward the emperor. It is certain that he bitterly regretted having called him in. The Arab historian, Abul Feda, sums up the situation in a few words: "Al-Kamil had called in the emperor only to embarrass the sultan of Damascus, and once he was dead, the emperor's arrival was to the sultan of Egypt like an arrow which stays in the wound." And another Arab historian, Maqrisi, says: "The Sultan al-Kamil was in the greatest embarrassment, since, under the treaty he had made with the emperor, he could not now go back on his word and refuse to hand back Jerusalem without declaring war on him." For the rest, in the midst of his family quarrels, while he was besieging Damascus, it was not in his interest to push the Christians too far, for then Frederick might have taken the side of the unfortunate young prince of Damascus. Finally, the menace, constantly present on the Upper Euphrates, of the Khwarismian hordes, and behind them, the peril of a fresh Mongol avalanche, of itself still compelled the sultan of Egypt to play a very supple game with the Franks. But, at the same time, he well realized that any too spectacular concession to the Franks would rouse a storm of disapproval throughout the Moslem world, from which the men of Damascus would be the first to profit at his expense.

The situation of Frederick II was no less delicate. Treated since his excommunication as a reprobate by the clergy and by the military orders of the Templars and the Hospitalers, he had also almost wantonly alienated, by the Limassol show of force, the sympathies of the French nobility of Cyprus and Syria. Suspected by the Christians, become a burden to his Moslem ally, he found all his diplomatic preparations reduced to nothing. There remained the way of military intimidation, a way which, with the immense resources of Italy and Germany behind him, no one was better able to use than he. Unfortunately, in his desire to avoid at all costs war with his Moslem friends, in his whim to gain everything by way of negotiation, Frederick had sailed with insignificant forces—not more than a hundred knights—and without the sinews of war—he had had to borrow 30,000 bezants from the lord of Jebail. It was true that since 1227 he had sent ahead contigents of German and Italian crusaders who, with the Templars, the Hospitalers, and the barons of Syria and Cyprus, brought the total strength to 800 knights and 10,000 foot soldiers. But the excommunication under which he lay deprived him of the active support, not only of the Temple and the Hospital, but also of many Italians. The German crusaders, who at least remained faithful to him, were the first to be surprised, as we know, to see him arrive in such feeble strength. Even if all idea of a holy war were dismissed out of hand, even if it was merely a question of a simple military outing in semi-complicity with the sultan, it was mere elementary caution to bring enough troops to back the negotiation.

Frederick was quick to realize this. As soon as he reached Acre, he sent Balian, lord of Sidon, and Thomas of Acerra bearing rich gifts to al-Kamil. The two ambassadors demanded the fulfillment of the treaty concluded with the Emir Fakhr ad-Din, the peaceable return of Jerusalem. The Arab chronicler Dhahabi reveals the gist of the letter in which, as man to man, the emperor begged the sultan to save his face. "I am your friend," he wrote to al-Kamil. "You are not ignorant of how far I am above all the princes of the West. It was you who bade me come hither. The kings and the pope know of my visit. If I were to return empty-handed, I should lose all consideration in their eyes. After all, was it not Jerusalem which gave birth to the Christian religion? With your good grace, give it back to me, that I may hold up my head before the kings. . . ."

The sultan, in reply, pleaded in excuse the changes which had taken place since the death of al-Muazzam, changes which altered the whole face of the problem. He demonstrated how impossible it was for him to surrender Jerusalem without antagonizing public opinion throughout the Moslem world. The Emir Fakhr ad-Din, Fredrick's friend, once again sent to him by the sultan, urged the seriousness of the difficulties: Jerusalem was a Holy City to the Moslems as well as to the Christians; how could the Mosque of Omar, won back by Saladin at the cost of so much effort, be yielded to the Franks without a fight? Not only would it incur the reproof of the caliph of Baghdad, but it was in danger of setting off some pietistic insurrection which would sweep away the dynasty. It is worth adding that, in spite of this refusal to keep his earlier promises, the sultan overwhelmed Frederick with attentions and gifts, silken stuffs, Arab mares, racing camels, elephants, and the rest.

In spite of the courtesy of these proceedings, however, it was clear that, if Frederick wanted to succeed, he must make a show of force. Ending where he should no doubt have begun, he mobilized all the knights of Acre, all his German and Italian contingents, all the visiting pilgrims who were not too scared by the Ghibelline policy, and set off at their head to make a display of arms along the Palestine coast from Acre to Jaffa. The grand master of the Temple, Peter of Montaigu, and the grand master of the Hospital, Bertrand of Thessy, at first refused to be associated with an excommunicated monarch but soon, filled with pity at the sight of these troops of men risking themselves in open country in an area held by several Moslem armies, they followed the imperialists a day's march behind, to protect them in the event of attack. On reaching the "casal" of Montdidier, between Caesarea and Arsuf, Frederick II realized his danger: if an evil temptation came into the mind of the sultan, encamped close by before Gaza, the little imperial army would be surprised and overwhelmed by numbers. Frederick therefore awaited the two military orders before continuing his march. The Templars and the Hospitalers, to save him from disaster, agreed to join his column, but still anxious to avoid contact with an excommunicate, they rode independently, without directly joining his troops. Once at Jaffa, Frederick rebuilt the old fortifications of the city (mid-November 1228). An excellent undertaking, it must be confessed, which by completing the fortification works already carried out by his lieutenants at Sidon, Montfort, and Caesarea, finally restored the mastery of the coast of the Christians. But while he was lingering in Jaffa, the emperor received the most disturbing news from Italy: Pope Gregory IX had just caused the Guelphs to invade his Neapolitan possessions. Frederick's own father-in-law, John of Brienne, was revenging himself for the affronts of Brindisi by leading the papal troops to the attack.

Frederick found himself in the most parlous situation. If he stayed on in Syria to regain Jerusalem, he would lose his kingdom of Sicily, and perhaps even the imperial crown. If he abandoned the East without recovering Jerusalem, he exposed himself to dishonor and made the papal party a present of fresh grievances against him. As was to be feared, his first impulse was to desert the crusade, go back to Italy, and chastise the aggressors. Fortunately, he was stopped by bad weather. And from this dead end, whence he had been driven by fourteen years of misplaced cunning and duplicity, he was able, after tottering on the brink, to extricate himself with sovereign elegance.

In spite of his inferiority of numbers, Frederick had impressed the Moslems by his march on Jaffa. For the rest, reinforcements might still arrive from Italy, which would reverse the balance of power. Moreover, while the imperialists were fortifying Jaffa, the sultan, still at war with his nephew, was opening the siege of Damascus; the conquest of the great Syrian city was far more important to him than the question of the Holy Places. Frederick skillfully profited from this favorable turn of events. On the counsel of his friend, the Emir Fakhr ad-Din, he again sent Thomas of Acerra and Balian of Sidon as ambassadors to the sultan, and after much coming and going, an agreement was concluded at Jaffa on February 11, 1229.

By this treaty, of capital importance in the history of Frankish-Moslem relations, the Sultan al-Kamil restored to the Frankish kingdom the three Holy Cities of Jerusalem, Bethlehem, and Nazareth, together with the lordship of Toron, the modern Tibnin, in Upper Galilee, and, in Phoenicia, that part of the territory of Sidon still occupied by the Moslems. The kingdom of Jerusalem, once again worthy of the name, thus regained, in addition to its capital—a priceless restitution—broad stretches of territory: first and foremost the coast; then, around Nazareth, a great part of Galilee; and finally, from Jaffa to Jerusalem and to Bethlehem, a long strip of land, flanking the Pilgrim Route and including Lydda, Ramleh, and Emmaus. Evidently, the ancient kingdom of Jerusalem was not restored in its entirety, since the sultan still kept East Galilee, Samaria, part of Judaea, and the south of Philistia, but the success was nonetheless resounding. The restitution which Richard the Lionhearted, in the full blaze of his military superiority, had been powerless to exact, Frederick II, without unsheathing his sword, had won from the amity of the sultan.

For the rest, the sultan, be it noted, gave proof of a quite exceptional spirit of conciliation, since, as he had foretold, the peaceable restoration of Jerusalem to the Franks immediately raised a storm of indignation against him in pietistic Moslem circles: this Holy City which the great

Saladin had reconquered with so much difficulty, behold, his nephew handed it back to the "trinitarians" without a struggle. In the great mosque of Damascus, the preacher Chems ad-Din Yusuf drew tears from the crowds by describing the sanctuaries of the Holy City, the precincts of the Haram as-Sherif, again profaned by the "Nazarenes." In the sultan's own entourage the imams and the muezzins publicly treated him as a reprobate.

It is understandable that Frederick had to reckon with this state of mind. If he wanted to avoid a general revolt against his friend al-Kamil, a revolt which would have thrown everything back into the melting pot, he was bound to display the utmost moderation in his success and to refrain from anything which might incite an outburst of fanaticism among the Moslems. The treaty of Jaffa bore marked signs of these preoccupations, or, more exactly, of the preoccupations of both sultan and emperor with public opinion on either side. It was, above all, a compromise, which attests to the anxiety of al-Kamil about the reactions of the Moslem world and of Frederick about the reactions of Christendom. Hence the balance and intricacy of the clauses of the treaty: Jerusalem was politically restored to the Franks but, recognized as a Holy City for both faiths, it was subjected to a sort of religious condominium, which was, moreover, most intelligently designed. The Christians recovered the Holy Sepulcher, but the Moslems kept the whole area of the Haram es-Sherif, with the Qubbat es-Sakhra, or Mosque of Omar, and the Mosque al-Aqsa, the former domain of the Templars. The precincts of the Haram es-Sherif, where the Moslems were licensed to maintain a guard of the faithful—but unarmed, and occupied solely with religion—thus became a Moslem religious enclave in a Jerusalem which was once more Christian, just as Jerusalem itself and Bethlehem became a Christian enclave in a Judaea which remained Moslem. And just as the Moslem populations of the Judaean plateau were required to give free passage to Christian pilgrims on the road from Jaffa to Jerusalem, so the Christians of Jerusalem were required to give full freedom to Moslem pilgrims coming to pay their devotions at the Haram es-Sherif. For the rest, in the Mosque of Omar and the old Temple of Solomon, thus preserved to Islam, Christians too had the right to pray. To avoid any disputes, the Moslem community of Jerusalem remained under the jurisdiction of a resident cadi who acted as an intermediary between them and the new

Frankish authorities. In sum, Frederick II and al-Kamil seem pur-
posely to have bound Christian interests and Moslem interests as closely
together as possible so as to put an end both to the jihad, the Moslem
holy war, and to the crusade, by an agreement acceptable to both
religions. It must be recognized that such an agreement revealed a
spirit of toleration, both in the sultan and in the emperor, singularly far
in advance of their times.

Unfortunately, Frederick II, who had just rendered this immense
service to Christendom, still had to bear the brunt of the fault he had
committed in flouting the papacy to the point of incurring excommunication. Not only did the Templars refuse to recognize the Treaty of
Jaffa, perhaps quite understandably, since in liberated Jerusalem, their
mother house, the Temple of Solomon, had been left to Islam, but,
much more seriously, the Patriarch Gerold placed the Holy City under
an interdict, an act which was to put Frederick and his partisans in a
morally untenable position.

It is evident that Frederick had hoped that the recovery of Jerusalem
would reconcile him with the religious authorities. As soon as the
treaty with the sultan was concluded, he went up from Jaffa to the
Holy City. He made his entry on March 17, 1229, and received the
city from the hands of the cadi, Chems ad-Din of Nablus, representing
the Sultan al-Kamil. The next day, which was a Sunday, he went up
to the Holy Sepulcher. Owing to the patriarch's interdict, the ceremony was purely secular. "To the noise of arms alone," he took a
royal crown from the great altar and placed it on his own head. The
Teutonic grand master, Hermann of Salza, read, first in German, and
then in French, a proclamation justifying the imperial policy.

On leaving the Holy Sepulcher, after holding court in the palace of
the Hospital, Frederick II appeared to busy himself with fortifying the
Holy City, as he was officially entitled to do under his treaty with the
sultan. In any event, he sought to confer on this subject with the
prelates and the grand masters of the three military orders. He seems,
in particular, to have given instructions for placing the Citadel, or
Tower of David, and Saint Stephen's Gate in a state of defense. How
does it happen, then, that the Western chroniclers have doubted the
sincerity of his intentions?

What most shocked Christians in the conduct of Frederick II in
Palestine was obviously his intimacy with the Moslems. It is true that

cordial relations between outstanding personalities in both religions
were far from being a novelty.   Throughout the twelfth century,
Frankish princes and Turko-Arab emirs had maintained relations of
chivalrous courtesy and even of true friendship, as, for example, had
been the case between the king of Jerusalem, Fulk of Anjou, and the
regent of Damascus, Muin ad-Din Unur, or between Richard the
Lionhearted and Saladin's brother.   But with Frederick II, as we know,
it was a question not only of personal friendship with sultans and emirs
but of a veritable leaning toward Islam, and even a leaning of a very
special character, since it was fundamentally anticlerical.   It was this
intellectual approach which most shocked the Latins.   We may also
note in passing that the Moslems, who should have been charmed by it,
were not slow to feel a certain uneasiness as soon as they perceived that
these manifestations of sympathy toward them were accompanied in
the emperor by a skepticism which he hardly took pains to dissimulate.

It is the Arab compilation *The Collar of Pearls* which best reflects
the very complicated impression left in the minds of the Moslems by
the visit of Frederick II to Jerusalem: "This smooth-faced, short-
sighted redhead, whom no one would have bought as a slave for a
couple of hundred dirhams," certainly bore no resemblance to the
Frankish paladins of the old days.   He disturbed the Moslems as much
as he attracted them.   "Judging by his talk," notes Bedr ed-Din, "he
was an atheist and mocked at the Christian religion."   Bedr ed-Din and
Maqrisi cite convincing proof of this religious indifference.   When the
emperor went to Jerusalem, the sultan, as we have seen, sent the Cadi
Chems ad-Din to do him the honors of the city's Moslem monuments.
Under the conduct of this guide, Frederick visited the buildings of the
Haram es-Sherif, "he admired the Mesdjid al-Aqsa, the Dome of
Sakhra (the Mosque of Omar), and climbed the steps of the minbar."
In this same Sakhra, become the most venerable Moslem sanctuary of
Jerusalem, he noticed a Christian priest who had just come in and who,
gospel in hand, seated near the "footprints of Mahomet," began to beg
for alms.   Did Frederick think that this was tactless in the newly
recovered Jerusalem and with the very special status of the Haram
es-Sherif?   If so, his reprimand was even more indiscreet.   "The
emperor," Bedr ed-Din assures us, "bore down upon the priest and
buffeted him till he almost fell to the ground, crying, 'Pig, the sultan
has graciously granted us the right to come here on pilgrimage, and

you are already begging alms! The first one I catch I shall have
executed." Frederick obviously had his reasons for enforcing the
clauses of the Treaty of Jaffa reserving the precincts of the Haram
as-Sherif for the Moslem worship. The manner of it was nevertheless
somewhat surprising. His desire to please the Moslems took such
ostentatious forms, his anticlericalism, exasperated by the interdict
which pursued him, resulted in such brutal outbursts that he almost
seemed like a renegade.

On the cupola of the Sakhra or Mosque of Omar could be read the
inscription set up by Saladin after the reconquest of Jerusalem: "Salah
ed-Din purified this holy dwelling from the polytheists," the name
given by the Moslem to the worshippers of the Trinity. Frederick,
who had no doubt learned a smattering of Arabic in Sicily, deciphered
the inscription, or had it deciphered for him, and asked with a smile
who these polytheists were. When the time came for the Moslem
prayers the bystanders were astounded to see one of his counselors
prostrate himself with the crowd: he was an Arab philosopher from
Sicily, "who taught the emperor logic." The Sultan al-Kamil, incredulous of such religious eclecticism, had, out of courtesy, forbidden the
muezzins to appear on the minarets of Jerusalem throughout the emperor's stay. But at dawn, one of the muezzins, who had not been
forewarned, set about reciting the verses of the Koran, including those
which implicitly deny the divinity of Christ. The cadi having cen-
sured him, the muezzin refrained from saying the next prayers. The
emperor noticed this, sent for the cadi, and forbade him to change the
service of the Koran in any way. "Oh, Cadi, do you change your
religious rites because of me? That is a great mistake."

There was nothing abnormal about this, and Frederick's action fell in
with his policy of detente and religious appeasement. Like William II
at a later date, on his famous pilgrimage to Saladin's tomb at Damascus,
he exerted all his charm to win over Islam. For the rest, in Syria he
seems himself to have felt the attraction of the Moslem land. One of
his sayings, reported by Maqrisi, shows him in a somewhat curious
light in this respect. "My chief aim in coming to Jerusalem," sighed
Frederick, "was to hear the Moslems, at the hour of prayer, call upon
Allah by night": a stroke which puts the finishing touch on the
portrait of this Orientalist and dilettante emperor, the unexpected
forerunner of Chateaubriand and Loti. What is more disturbing and

again gives this figure a somewhat equivocal turn, is the confidence which, according to the Arab chronicle, he confessed to the Emir Fakhr ed-Din: "If I had not been afraid of losing my prestige in the eyes of the Franks, I would never have made the sultan yield up Jerusalem. . . ."

It is even more disturbing—for this was a matter of life or death for the delivered Jerusalem—to note the disagreement between Christian sources and Moslem sources on the capital question of the fortifications of the Holy City. Jerusalem, some years earlier, had been entirely dismantled by the Moslems, in order to deny the imminent crusade a potential stronghold, so that the sultan had merely delivered to Frederick an open city. If this restitution was to be anything more than an episode without sequel, it was essential for the emperor to reconstruct the fortifications without delay. Indeed, according to the French sources, he had obtained the sultan's authorization, and immediately after his coronation, as we have seen, he gave the signal to start work. For a number of Arab chroniclers, on the other hand, this was a mere pretense, since he had secretly promised the sultan not to restore the fortifications, a very grave commitment, which left Jerusalem at the mercy of the first raid. Perhaps, looking at things in the best light, this discrepancy between the Frankish witnesses and the Arab witnesses merely reveals once again the delicate situation both of the sultan and of the emperor. The sultan, in order to appease the wrath of his co-religionists, gave them to understand that Jerusalem would remain an open city which he could reoccupy at will. And Frederick, to appease the legitimate anxiety of the Franks, swore that he would fortify the stronghold. It is, moreover, possible that he really intended to push on at least with the works of the Tower of David and Saint Stephen's Gate, when, hot on his heels, the archbishop of Caesarea arrived at Jerusalem with instructions to apply the interdict launched by the patriarch against the city.

Whatever wrongs Frederick may have committed against Christendom, however two-faced his whole conduct may have proved, it is quite clear that the interdict launched against Jerusalem by the patriarch on the morrow of the day when the imperialists had just restored the Holy Sepulcher to the Christians was a mistake in itself. Such was, in fact, the later judgment of Pope Gregory IX himself when he was master of all the facts. Not only was the act of the Patriarch Gerold a cause of scandal to many of the faithful, but it was clearly not in the best Christian interests. Frederick II was deeply wounded. Abandoning the idea of putting the city into a state of defense, he set off at once for Jaffa, from whence he returned to Acre (March 21, 1229).

At Acre, Frederick II was plunged back into the atmosphere of civil war, the unhappy consequence of these Guelph and Ghibelline passions which he had disastrously imported into the Levant and which, until the ultimate catastrophe, were to bedevil the life of the Frankish colonies. In protest against the attitude of the Patriarch Gerold, the emperor, immediately on his return to Acre, summoned the townsfolk and justified his policy before them, especially his treaty with al-Kamil. With the support of his Lombard soldiers, as well as of the Pisan colony (the Pisans were passionately attached to the Ghibelline cause), he then turned to force. He closed the gates of Acre, made certain of the walls, and placed guards around the house of the Templars and even the palace of the Patriarch Gerold, who thus found himself for five days under arrest and almost besieged in his own home. Naturally, the Guelph party reacted. On Palm Sunday (April 8, 1229), in all the churches of Acre the preachers fulminated against the excommunicated emperor, whereupon the imperial satellites dragged them from the pulpit and hustled them into the streets. Frederick even tried to storm the fortress-hostel of the Templars at Acre, but the knight-monks were on their guard and he had to call it off. A similar project against John of Ibelin likewise came to naught: the lord of Beirut had wind of this new ambuscade. These escapades in which the Ghibelline monarch vented his exasperation resulted in alienating the last Frankish sympathies.

A few more ventures of the same kind and Frederick II would have found himself faced with a general revolt against which he would have been in a fairly bad way. With his usual suppleness, dissembling his rage, he changed face again. Before setting sail, he professed to be reconciled with the chiefs of the French nobility of Syria and Cyprus, even with John of Ibelin, who not only kept his fief of Beirut but was to continue to share in the government of the Holy Land. The future was to show that this was merely a piece of play acting, for the emperor had not forgiven John for having worsted him and John had not forgotten the ambuscade of Limassol. The two men were hence-forth divided by a bitter hatred, a hatred which was to disturb the life of the kingdom of Jerusalem for the whole of the next period. For the rest, Frederick left a strong Lombard garrison at Acre, charged with maintaining his authority. But the emperor and the lord of Beirut, consummate politicians both, recognizing that, for the moment, they were equally matched, had the elegance to postpone the settlement of their accounts and to take leave of each other with perfect courtesy.

A similar correctitude, however, could not be expected from the crowds; and when Frederick II left Acre for Italy, his departure was the occasion of painful scenes, so high was the feeling against him among the Guelph partisans. Aware of his unpopularity, he went aboard at dawn, almost furtively, accompanied only by the barons. But the word of his departure spread. As he passed through the market quarter to reach the port, the butchers and the market women, rushing to their doors, shouted coarse insults and pelted him with offal. John of Ibelin and the Constable Odo of Montbéliard barely had time to intervene to stop the populace from indulging in the utmost violence toward him. Full of hatred, he set sail, and after a second stop at Cyprus, was back in Italy on June 10, 1229.

Such was the lamentable epilogue to a crusade which, when all is said and done, had been a brilliant success, since it alone, of all the expeditions of its kind since 1190, had restored Jerusalem to the Christians. A paradoxical crusade, it is true, and scarce deserving of the name, when it is remembered that it was to the amity of the Moslems that the emperor owed the return of the Holy Places. There was certainly very little resemblance between the crusaders of the olden days and this strange pilgrim, who avowed that he had made the voyage to the Holy Land for the sole purpose of hearing the muezzin's call ring through the Arabian nights. His journey has already been described as a friendly visit from the sultan of Italy to the sultan of Egypt; but it was indeed a profitable visit, since the sultan of Egypt, to save him from losing face with the "polytheists" of the West, had made him a present of that Holy Sepulcher by which the Westerners set such great store.

Frederick II had therefore succeeded with the Moslems, but he had failed with the Franks, or, more precisely, with the Frankish chivalry of Syria and Cyprus, the masters of the two realms. Like other Germanic heads of state throughout history, if he had more or less successfully penetrated the Moslem psychology, he had completely failed to understand anything about the psychology of the French element. By a blend of double dealing and brutality, which had reared up public opinion against him, he had come into headlong collision with this element, so easily charmed by a little grace (as witness Richard the Lionhearted). It was here that this astute and seductive politician finally missed the mark. In spite of his devouring activity, the resources of the most supple diplomacy, his qualities of a superman, his universal culture, and the flashes of genius which, at the height of the thirteenth century could envisage the reconciliation of East and West, he departed to the howls of the mob, leaving behind him only a trail of hatred and the seeds of civil war. He had restored its capital to Christendom, and Christendom cursed him for it. Saint Louis was to come and lose all and gain nothing but respect and blessings. What was missing in this brilliant intelligence, the forerunner of modern times? No doubt a little Christian charity, gentleness, and love.

Frederick had sown the seeds of civil war in Syria and Cyprus. As soon as he left they came to harvest. In Cyprus he had entrusted the regency, with the guardianship of the young King Henry I, to Amalric Barlais and four other barons devoted to the imperial cause. These regents took advantage of their power to persecute the partisans of John of Ibelin. They tried to assassinate the leader of this party, the poet-knight Philip of Novara. Novara having escaped from this attempt, they besieged him in the Tower of the Hospitalers where he had taken refuge. The valiant knight held firm pending the arrival of help from the lord of Beirut, whom he had informed of his plight in a charming letter in verse: "I am the nightingale, and men have caged me," a letter full of quips, in spite of the serious situation, in which the poet compared his adversaries to the most repulsive animals in the fable of Reynard the Fox. At Novara's appeal, John of Ibelin hastened from Beirut to Cyprus and trounced the regents before Nicosia on July 14, 1229. Amalric Barlais, who had taken refuge in the castle of Dieu d'Amour (the modern Saint Hilarion, near Kyrenia), held out for ten months, during a siege made famous by Philip of Novara who, while wielding a crossbow, never stopped riddling the besieged, from the

foot of the ramparts, with his cruelest verses. Finally, in mid-May
1230, Dieu d'Amour yielded, and John of Ibelin remained master of
Cyprus, which he governed to the general satisfaction in the name of
his nephew, the young King Henry I.

But Frederick II could not submit to the eviction of his representatives. In February 1231, he dispatched an expeditionary force to the
Levant under the command of the marshal of the empire, Richard
Filanghieri, who took advantage of the absence of John of Ibelin to
take Beirut by surprise, with the exception of the citadel, which held
out, and then to occupy Tyre. Filanghieri then came to claim the
obedience of the assembly of barons, meeting at Acre. In the name of
the nobility, Balian of Sidon refused: the rights of the crown of
Jerusalem, on which Frederick II relied, were circumscribed by the
rights, franchises, and privileges of the barons, and Frankish Syria was
not called upon to tolerate the good pleasure of an imperial *podestà*
who permitted himself, as he had done at Beirut, to attack the lieges
without the prior judgment of their peers.

In the meantime, in Cyprus, John of Ibelin had persuaded Henry I
and the Cypriot barons to send an army to the mainland to help drive
out the imperialists. Landing on February 25, 1232, John was welcomed as a liberator at Acre and proclaimed mayor of the commune
which had been set up there. He then set about delivering Tyre. His
army had reached Casal Imbert, three or four miles south of Cape
Naqura, when he was recalled to Acre on public business and had to
leave the camp to his nephews. But they lacked the old man's experience. On May 3 at dawn, they were completely taken by surprise by
Filanghieri, who had made a secret sortie from Tyre. The Cypriot
chivalry, abandoning its camp to the imperialists, could save itself only
by flight. Filanghieri took advantage of this unexpected victory to set
about the conquest of Cyprus, which, except for a few mountain
castles, fell entirely into his hands.

But John of Ibelin was quick to restore the situation. Having
re-formed his army in Syria, he crossed over in turn to Cyprus with
King Henry I, surprised the port of Famagusta by night, and on June
15, 1232, crushed Filanghieri in a great battle at Agridi, between
Nicosia and Kyrenia. The imperialists, driven out of Cyprus and
having also lost Beirut to John of Ibelin, now kept only Tyre, where
they were virtually blockaded. In vain Filanghieri, trying seduction

where force had failed, made the most flattering propositions to John of Ibelin. The old lord of Beirut, in a speech full of subtlety and sarcastic irony, answered his guests with the fable of the deer enticed into the lion's den, and the imperial *podestà* went empty away. When John died, four years later (1236), Frankish Syria, like the kingdom of Cyprus, was virtually immune from Frederick's Caesarism. The French baron had triumphed over the Germanic Holy Roman Emperor.

The historian of the Crusades cannot help feeling a little sad at saying goodbye to John of Ibelin at this point. The old lord of Beirut remains indeed one of the most attractive figures of the Latin East. The uncle and greatly honored counselor of King Henry I of Cyprus, the elected mayor of the commune of Acre, the recognized leader of the nobility of Syria and Cyprus, he had been, since the departure of John of Brienne, the veritable chief of the two kingdoms. The perfect dignity of his life, his sense of honor, his moderation, clemency, and humanity, his skill as a lawyer, no less remarkable than his knightly virtues, his lofty wisdom, his intelligent loyalty, his flower of courtesy, his strong and fine eloquence whose echoes Novara has transmitted to us, make him the very pattern of the *prud'homme*, the perfect knight described by Saint Louis, and the most accomplished representative of French civilization in the East in the thirteenth century.

It was left for John of Ibelin's eldest son, Balian III, who succeeded him in the lordship of Beirut, and the "old lord's" nephew, Philip of Montfort, to do away with the last vestiges of Frederick's domination in Syria. Filanghieri, the imperial *podestà* of Tyre, had been rash enough to try to profit from the death of John of Ibelin to make an onslaught on the commune of Acre. The men of the commune, under the leadership of Balian and Philip of Montfort, reacted vigorously and then mounted a counterattack. On June 12, 1243, after a night march along the shore, between the sea and the ramparts of Tyre, Balian and Philip of Montfort entered the town by surprise; and the townsmen, wearied of Filanghieri's tyranny, made common cause with them. The lordship of Tyre was given to Philip of Montfort. "Thus," concludes the continuation of Novara, joyfully, "this venomous plant of the imperialists was uprooted forever from the land of Outremer."

16

A POETS' CRUSADE

Tibald of Champagne
and Philip of Nanteuil

THE DEPARTURE of the last representatives of Frederick II, if it delivered Frankish Syria from a regime which it detested, left it without a government. The ancient kingdom of Jerusalem became a round table kingdom, a sort of feudal republic, made up of small, practically autonomous lordships: the lordship of Tyre, held by Philip of Montfort; the lordships of Beirut, Arsuf, and Jaffa, in the hands of various members of the Ibelin family; the commune of Acre, where the merchant colonies of Genoa, Pisa, and Venice, self-administered under the government of their consuls, began to assume predominant political importance; and finally, the military orders, which, since the fall of the royalty, now obeyed only their grand masters and enjoyed an absolute independence in their strongholds, the Hospitalers at Krak des Chevaliers and Marqab, the Templars at Tortosa, Safitha, and Beaufort, and later at Safed, the Teutonic Knights at Montfort, to name only their main fortresses.

Disturbed by the weakening which a regime of this kind meant for Frankish Syria, Pope Gregory IX summoned a new crusade. His voice was heard by the nobility of France, whose most illustrious representatives set out for the Holy Land. Among others, mention may be made of Tibald IV, count of Champagne and king of Navarre, Hugh IV, duke of Burgundy, the count of Brittany, Peter Mauclerc, Count

Henry of Bar, Ralph of Soissons, Henry of Grandpré, Matthew of Montmorency, William of Senlis, Philip of Nanteuil, and Richard of Beaumont. Never had there been a more brilliant assembly of chivalry.

The leader of the expedition, Tibald of Champagne, was an amiable lord, generous and chivalrous who, as suitor to Queen Blanche of Castille, has left some pretty verses:

> My love is of such noble line
> That her beauty overweens me.

Perhaps, as he had shown in France during the minority of Louis IX, he was lacking, if not in clear-sightedness, at least in the minimum of strictness essential to a chief. This was to be demonstrated from the outset.

Under his command, the crusaders left Acre on November 2, 1239, to rebuild the walls of Ascalon, an important post which would have denied the Egyptians the Palestine coast. They were riding along the shore, when the count of Bar and the duke of Burgundy, accompanied by Philip of Nanteuil, a renowned troubadour, like Tibald of Champagne, decided, in order to monopolize the glory of the first blows, to give the rest of the army the slip. On the evening of November 12, they headed south at a gallop, in the teeth of Tibald's invectives, who vainly tried to hold them back.

The count of Bar, steadily galloping due south, arrived at dead of night, beyond Ascalon, at the outskirts of Gaza, where he was warned of the presence of an Egyptian detachment. The night was fine and very mild. The moon shone like daylight on the sea, the beach, and the dunes. The count of Jaffa warned the leading columns that it would be folly to advance further. Henry of Bar nevertheless persisted in pushing on among the sandhills of the coast, in the hope of a good raid. Without any precaution, without sending out scouts, the reckless French chivalry dismounted for refreshment in a sheltered hollow between the dunes. "They spread the cloths and sat down to supper, for they had been followed by a convoy laden with bread, pullets, capons, grilled meat, cheese, wine, and fruit. Some were still eating, others had finished and were sleeping or tending their horses." But the Egyptian army, informed of their march, hour by hour, had silently manned all the surrounding dunes with bowmen and had

blocked all the exits from the valley with horsemen. Suddenly, the
silence of this Oriental night was shattered by the deafening din of the
Saracen fanfares, and the crusaders found themselves surrounded and
riddled with arrows by the enemy, master of all the heights. The
knights tried to charge, but at the first pace, their horses sank in the
sand up to their fetlocks. They were massacred where they stood.
The count of Bar was slain with some of his companions. The rest
were dragged off into captivity in the prisons of Cairo. Among them
was the poet-knight, Philip of Nanteuil, who has left us a touching
plaint on this sad exploit:

> Alas! Sweet land of France,
> Accursed be the day
> So many valorous knights
> Fell into durance vile!

The main army, however, which had stayed behind with Tibald of
Champagne, was still intact. Heartbroken at this disaster, which moreover was none of his doing, Tibald drew his troops back to Acre, from
whence he moved into camp in the plain of Sephoria, in Galilee. The
mere presence of this Frankish force, without the need for any more
fighting, and by the mere fact of discord between Moslems, had the
most happy results. The Moslem empire founded by Saladin was at
this time disputed between two of his nephews, as-Salih Ayub, sultan
of Egypt, and as-Salih Ismail, sultan of Damascus. Threatened by
Ayub, Ismail had no hesitation in begging the support of the Franks.
To this end, he yielded up to them on the spot Galilee, with Beaufort
(Chaqif Arnun), Nazareth, Safed, and Tiberias (1240). For his part,
the sultan of Egypt, Ayub, to win the Franks over to his party,
abandoned Ascalon to them and confirmed their possession of Jerusalem and Bethlehem (1240–1241). At this date, therefore, the ancient
kingdom of Jerusalem, except for the Nablus region and the Hebron
region, was reconstituted almost within its historical limits.

When, in the closing days of September 1240, Tibald of Champagne
sailed home from Acre, he could therefore justly claim that his crusade,
in spite of its somewhat disjointed appearance, had yielded valuable
results, since, more fortunate than so many great politicians, the kindly
poet, merely by being in the right place at the right time, had restored
to the Christians almost all their ancient domain.

17

THE CRUSADE OF A SAINT
Louis IX in Egypt and Syria

T HE territorial restoration of the kingdom of Jerusalem, after the restitutions of 1240, did not last.   On August 23, 1244, Jerusalem was finally captured from the Franks by hordes of Khwarismian Turks.   On June 17, 1247, the Franks lost Tiberias in the same way, and on October 15 of the same year Ascalon.   To complete the menace of the situation, the Moslem Empire, so long troubled by the discord between Saladin's nephews, was once again united, after October 1245, in the hands of one of them, as-Salih Ayub, who had just added Damascus to his kingdom of Egypt.   In the face of this powerful Moslem state, Frankish Syria was now no more than a narrow coastal strip.   It was high time for a great crusade to come to its rescue.

It was then that Saint Louis appeared.

Saint Louis had taken the cross in December 1244, in the course of a serious illness.   He left Paris on June 12, 1248, and embarked at Aigues-Mortes for the island of Cyprus, which had been fixed as the general concentration point for all the troops.   He set sail on August 25.

Since no other sovereign had joined him, the crusade of Saint Louis had a purely French character.   His whole kingdom had taken the cross with him.   In the front rank were his three brothers, Robert of Artois, Alfonso of Poitiers, and Charles of Anjou.   Then came the duke of Burgundy, Hugh IV, the count of Flanders, William of Dampierre, Hugh the Brown, count of La Marche, Hugh V, Count of Saint-Paul, and lesser lords like John of Joinville, seneschal of Champagne, the historian of the expedition, Geoffrey of Sargines, Philip of Nanteuil, Gaucher of Châtillon, and a host of others whose names will recur in the following pages.

When the galleys with the noble names—*la Reine, la Demoiselle, la Montjoie*—bearing Louis IX and his army cast anchor at Limassol on the south coast of Cyprus on September 17, 1248, the French crusaders might have thought themselves back in their own country. The king of Cyprus, Henry I of Lusignan, greeted them with the most affectionate hospitality in his capital of Nicosia and gave them all the supplies they needed.

Louis IX, following the same line as Amalric I and John of Brienne, rightly decided to attack the Moslems at the heart of their power, which was at the same time their most vulnerable point, in Egypt. More than ever, in this year 1248, when Jerusalem, like Damascus, was dependent on the sultan of Egypt, the keys of the Holy City lay in Cairo. It remained to fix the date of the expedition. Saint Louis, in order to gain the benefit of surprise, was in favor of an immediate attack. It was the Syrian barons, especially the Templars, who persuaded him to postpone the expedition until the spring, to wait for the latecomers and set about conquering the delta at maximum strength. Saint Louis was in fact joined, during this hibernation, not only by the Cypriot chivalry under the orders of King Henry I, but also by the Frankish chivalry of Syria with John II of Ibelin, count of Jaffa, and moreover four hundred French knights of the Peloponnesus, led by the prince of Achaea, William of Villehardouin. Nor must we forget a corps of English knights under the orders of the valiant earl of Salisbury.

The army set sail from Limassol for Egypt in the closing days of May 1249. On June 4, in spite of a storm which separated the ships, the *Montjoie*, with Saint Louis on board, cast anchor off the coast of the delta, off Damietta, a city which, because of the 1219 precedent, had been chosen as the first objective. The Sultan as-Salih Ayub, expecting an attack at this point, had massed his army on the shore, "a host fair to look upon, for the sultan's arms are of gold, and when the sun struck upon them, they were resplendent. The noise they made with their cymbals and horns was fearful to listen to." The barons counseled Saint Louis to await the arrival of the vessels scattered by the storm before landing. He refused, rightly deeming that "to delay would put the foe in good heart." On Saturday, June 5, at dawn, the landings began, the knights bunching into the boats to gain a footing on the shore. The Syrian barons rivaled the ardor of the French. Joinville's picture of the landing of the count of Jaffa, John II of Ibelin, is a richly colored tapestry: "It was he who landed in greatest pride, for his galley came all painted, within and without, with escutcheons of his arms, which arms are of gold, with a cross of gules patée. He had at least three hundred rowers in his galley, and for each rower there was a targe with the count's arms thereon, and to each targe was a pennon attached with his arms wrought in gold. While he was coming in, it seemed as if his galley flew, so did the rowers urge it forward with their sweeps; and it seemed as if the lightning were falling from the skies at the sound that the pennants made, and the cymbals, and the drums and the Saracenic horns that were in his galley. So soon as the galley had been driven into the sand as far up as they could drive it, both he and his knights leapt from the galley, well armed and well equipped. . . ."

The Egyptians tried to oppose the landing. "So soon as they saw us land," says Joinville, "they came toward us, hotly spurring. We, when we saw them coming, fixed the points of our shields into the sand and the handles of our lances in the sand with the points set toward them. But when they were so near that they saw the lances about to enter into their bellies, they turned around and fled." The king of France had no wish to lag behind. "When the king heard tell that the ensign of Saint Denis was on shore, he went across his ship with large steps; and in despite of the legate who was with him, he would not leave from following the ensign, but leapt into the sea, which was up to his armpits. So he went, with his shield hung to his neck, and his helmet on his head, and his lance in his hand, till he came to his people who were on the shore. When he reached the land and looked upon the Saracens, he asked what people they were, and they told him they were Saracens; and he put his lance to his shoulder, and his shield before him, and would have run in upon the Saracens if the right worthy men who were about him would have suffered it."

The battle on the beach went in favor of the Franks. The Egyptian army, panic-stricken, retreated southward. The people of Damietta, left defenseless, evacuated their city as fast as they could by night, in such haste that they left everything behind them. On June 6, Louis IX made his entry into the deserted and untouched city. He found it stocked with enormous quantities of arms, ammunition, and supplies, abandoned by the enemy. When one recalls the eighteen months of effort which the conquest of the same stronghold had cost the soldiers of John of Brienne thirty years before, it must be agreed that this time the crusade had opened with a brilliant success.

Nevertheless, Louis IX did not feel that he could consolidate it by marching on Cairo. It was June. Next month the floods would start, and the king of France (who, in any event, was not yet at full muster) did not want to risk the same misfortune as Pelagius. It was therefore decided to spend the whole summer at Damietta until the end of the floods.

This delay, however reasonable, nevertheless enabled the Egyptians to recover. The sultan of Egypt, as we have seen, was at that time as-Salih Ayub, Saladin's great-nephew. The adversary of Saint Louis was indeed a strange figure. The son of a Sudanese slave girl, himself looking more like a mulatto, he in no way resembled in character the great Kurdish sultans of his father's lineage. It would be vain to look in him for the openheartedness of a Saladin, the inquiring mind of an al-Adil, or the intellectual nimbleness and culture of an al-Kamil. The Arab historians scarcely conceal their discomfort in the face of this half-Negro, hostile to letters, haughty and taciturn, harsh and gloomy, cruel and avaricious, the unexpected heir of so many great men and much more like some black tyrant of Ouadaï or Darfur. But he had one quality on his side, energy. Eaten up by ulcers and phthisis, his legs swollen, almost dying, he showed a pitiless severity in restoring the situation, massacred without a trial the troops who had given ground at Damietta, and by dint of executions and terror, succeeded in regrouping a stout army of Mameluks and opposing it to the Franks between Damietta and Mansura, to bar the road to Cairo.

Meanwhile, the flood season had passed, the reinforcements expected by Louis IX had been brought up by his brother, Alfonso of Poitiers, and the hour had come to open the campaign. The count of Brittany, Peter Mauclerc, proposed to go and take Alexandria. The naval superiority of the Franks no doubt made this a relatively easy undertaking for them. The conquest of Alexandria after Damietta would have given them a stranglehold over all the trade of Egypt, and there was a good chance that after such a blow the court of Cairo would sue for peace. But the count of Artois, who was to be the evil genius of the expedition, succeeded in getting this plan rejected, and, arguing that Egypt must be struck at the heart, carried the decision in favor of a march on Cairo. He also obtained the refusal of the proposals of the sultan, who offered to yield the Franks Jerusalem, Ascalon, and Tiberias in exchange for the return of Damietta, and, on November 20, 1249, the march on Cairo started.

Fortune still seemed to favor the Christians. At the very moment when they opened the campaign, their enemy as-Salih Ayub died at Mansura (November 23). His disappearance from the scene in these tragic hours left Egypt without a chief and almost without a government. His only son, Turanshah, was living in the heart of Diyarbekir. Until he had time to arrive, the late sultan's favorite sultana, the energetic Shajar ad-Durr ("Mouth of Pearls"), a Turk according to some sources, an Armenian according to others, was able, in concert with the eunuchs, to keep the death of her lord secret and prevent the Egyptian empire from breaking up.

Meanwhile, Saint Louis continued his march. The theater of operations was the same as in the time of John of Brienne, the triangle of lowlands, bounded on the north by Lake Manzala, on the west by the Nile, and on the south by the Bahr as-Saghir canal. At the southern apex of this triangle, at the junction of the Nile and the Bahr as-Saghir, sheltered by the canal, barring the road to Cairo, rose the central citadel of Egypt's defense, the fortified town of Mansura. To open the road to Cairo, it was therefore necessary to cross the Bahr as-Saghir, a singularly difficult operation, since it must be carried out in the teeth of the Egyptian forces massed on the south bank of the canal, their rear supported by Mansura. On December 21, Saint Louis arrived at the scene of action, on the north bank of the canal. He was able to measure the full difficulty of the problem, especially since, by secret fords, the Egyptians managed to put troops of cavalry onto the north bank, who made night raids around the French camp and cut off the stragglers. Following these alerts Saint Louis had the camp entrenched and surrounded with a palisade.

Saint Louis first tried to drain the Bahr as-Saghir by damming back the Nile waters. To protect his engineers from the arrows of the Moslem army, who harassed the work from the other bank, he installed a whole system of wooden towers and catapults. But, across the canal, the Egyptians sprayed the machines with flaming naptha, setting them alight and cruelly burning the crews. These naptha jets have been well described by Joinville: "The fashion of the Greek fire was such that it came frontwise as large as a barrel of verjuice, and the tail of fire that issued from it was as large as a large lance. The noise it made in coming was like heaven's thunder. It had the seeming of a dragon flying through the air. It gave so great a light that one saw as clearly throughout the camp as if it had been day." At each "cast" the Christians "threw themselves on their elbows and knees," and Saint Louis "would lift up his hands to our Saviour, and say, weeping, 'Fair Lord God, guard me my people!'" For the rest, as the French engineers raised their dam on the north bank of the Bahr as-Saghir, the Egyptian sappers undermined the south bank, thus widening the canal bed and neutralizing the enemy's work.

Some other way must be found. In the end, Saint Louis learned from a Bedouin or a Copt of the existence of a ford further east at a point carelessly guarded by the Egyptians. Leaving the camp in the charge of the duke of Burgundy, he led the army during the night of February 7, 1250 to the point indicated by his informer. On Tuesday the eighth, at dawn, the crossing began. The operation was slow, the ford being much deeper than had been thought, with steep and slippery sides. The count of Artois, who, with the Templars, led the van, was the first across. Louis IX had given him strict and precise orders not to advance further until the whole army was across. Disobeying this order, Robert was no sooner on the other bank than he pricked spurs, urged on his knights and, at their head, launched the assault on the Egyptian camp.

The surprise was total. The Egyptian outposts were cut down in a few seconds, the camp was taken and all that was in it overthrown, massacred, or put to flight. The Emir Fakhr ad-Din, the Egyptian generalissimo, had just got out of the bath and was having his beard hennaed when he was alerted by the cries of the fugitives. Without waiting to put on his armor, he leaped to horse and hastened to the scene of action. The Templars were like a tornado. He fell dead with a spear thrust in the side, while the Frankish cavalcade disappeared toward Mansura.

For—an unpardonable fault—Robert of Artois, after the surprise of the Egyptian camp, could not halt. In vain did the grand master of the Temple beg him to await the king. He rounded on the grand master, calling him a "poulain" and a craven. "The Templars are unaccustomed to fear," replied the old man. "We will go with you. But know you well that not one of us will come back." In vain, ten knights dispatched by Louis IX galloped up to Robert, hell bent for leather, ordering him to halt, "in the king's name." In the full tide of revolt, he replied with a blank refusal. And resuming the chase, spurring their already exhausted mounts to the gallop, without waiting for reinforcements, without any contact with the main body of the royal army, without troubling to send out scouts or to cover themselves, in isolated groups as the hazards of the charge had separated them, Robert and his knights plunged into the streets of Mansura.

At the moment when Robert of Artois was committing this supreme folly, the Egyptians had the good fortune to find a chief, the Turkish Mameluk, Baibars the Arbalester, whom all the rest of this history will show as one of the best warriors of his time. The entry on the scene of this born soldier was enough in itself to rally the Moslem fugitives, regroup them, turn the incredible error of the count of Artois to advantage, and make Mansura the starting point of an irresistible counterattack.

The count of Artois had reached the heart of Mansura, before the citadel, when Baibars, at the head of the Mameluk cavalry, charged him unexpectedly. The knights, crushed by the blow, were thrown back in isolated groups into the streets where they found themselves caught in a rat trap, since the exits were at once blocked by improvised barricades. In this Saracen city with its narrow, treacherous lanes, men, women, and children, from the heights of the moucharabies, rained projectiles upon them, while at every crossroads, the Mameluks, a hundred against one, finished off the wretches with yataghan and mace. Robert of Artois, who had tried to barricade himself in a house, was massacred there, as were Erard of Brienne, Ralph of Courcy, John of Cherizy, Roger of Rozoy, William of Salisbury, and all the other knights he had led on this death ride.

Louis IX, with the center of his army, had scarcely crossed the Bahr as-Saghir in his turn, when the Mameluks, victorious over his vanguard, fell upon him. In the face of this sudden onslaught, he found himself completely isolated, without news (for good reason) of Robert of Artois and cut off from his rearguard which, under the orders of the duke of Burgundy, had remained, with the infantry, on the north bank of the canal. The slightest loss of coolness on the part of the army commander, and all was lost.

It was then that men learned to know the king of France. Joinville, wounded at the beginning of the battle, saw him pass with his army corps, and has preserved the unforgettable sight "of the hero, towering alone above the battle." "He halted on a raised causeway. Never have I seen so fair a knight! For he seemed by the head and shoulders to tower above his people; and on his head was a gilded helm, and in his hand a sword of Allemaine."

From the joyful frenzy of the Mameluks, Louis IX divined that some misfortune had befallen the count of Artois. Calm and cool, he repeated the order to his companions to close the ranks and avoid any isolated action. But the Mameluk cavalry continued to make charge after charge without stopping. To the din of drums, horns, and cymbals, the Moslem squadrons whirled around the king, riddling him with arrows and shafts from their arbalests, and then, when their quivers were empty, wheeling about to give place to fresh squadrons.

Louis IX, seeing his chivalry weaken under this fire, ordered a charge and close combat in which his forces would regain their superiority. It is this "breakout" which Joinville refers to, still stirred, fifty years later, by the recollection of the magnificent spectacle: "And you must know that this was a very fine passage of arms, for in this battle no one drew bow or crossbow; it was a battle of mace and sword between the Turks and our people, all intermingled." In the sword-play the knights of France at first had the advantage over the Mameluks, but the superior numbers of the Turkish army again ended by crushing them.

The salvation of the Frankish army then depended on the king alone, his role of captain merging at that hour with his duties as a soldier. In the twofold role he was prodigious. "Those who were present at this battle," says the Rothelin manuscript, "afterward bore witness that if the king had not shown such valiance they would all have been killed or taken."

It was three o'clock and the battle had been going on since morning. Louis IX felt the need to maneuver. On the advice of John of Valéry, he withdrew along the Bahr as-Saghir to a point opposite the camp, to join up with the duke of Burgundy and the infantry left in reserve. A terrible march, in the course of which Alfonso of Poitiers and the count of Flanders, William of Dampierre, found themselves cut off from the main column and surrounded by Mameluks. The king's contingent itself was almost overwhelmed by the enemy masses. At one moment six Mameluks surrounded Louis IX and, seizing his bridle, would have taken him prisoner. He freed himself by mighty strokes of his sword. The battle, indeed, broke up into a multitude of single combats of which Joinville has left us a vivid picture. The seneschal had set himself the task of defending, with his cousin, John of Nesle, a secondary canal, parallel to the Bahr as-Saghir. In this grim guard, among the death cries and assaults of the Mameluk cavalry, the storm of arrows and Greek fire, the two good knights continued to jest, recalling pleasant evenings in their lands of Champagne: "The good count, in that point of danger, jested with me and said: 'Seneschal, let these curs howl! By God's bonnet'—for that was his favorite oath—'we shall talk of this day yet, you and I, in ladies' chambers.' " It was then that he saw passing the count of Brittany, Peter Mauclerc. "He had been wounded with a sword across the face so that the blood ran into his mouth. He had thrown the reins on the pummel of the saddle, and held it with his two hands."

Meanwhile, the arbalesters, whose presence was essential to counter the Mameluk archers, had remained on the north of the canal, which, hardly fordable by cavalry, was impassable for men on foot. All this infantry was condemned to stand by impotently watching the disaster of the knights on the other bank. Nevertheless, the obstinate resistance of Louis IX gave these brave folk the time to come onto the scene. At the cost of untold efforts they succeeded in flinging a pontoon across the canal, and toward evening, in the setting sun, they debouched onto the battlefield. Their arrival was decisive. When the Egyptians saw them set foot to the stirrups of their arbalests, they turned tail and fled.

The king of France was exhausted, but he had not weakened. Joinville hastened up to him, "and as we were going, I made him take off his helmet and lent him my steel cap, so that he might have air." The sun was setting over the Nile and the canals. The Egyptians were in full retreat. The army of the king of France remained masters of the battlefield. Proudly they pitched their tents near the old Egyptian camp. This terrible day therefore ended in victory, a dear bought victory, pregnant with redoubtable consequences, but still a victory, and due to the personal valor, coolness, and heroism of the king of France. The vice-master of the Hospital, John of Ronay, who came to congratulate Louis IX on his victory, had the sad privilege of telling the king of his brother's death. "He came to him and kissed his mailed hand. And the king asked if he had any tidings of the count of Artois, his brother; and the provost said that he had news of him indeed, for he knew of a certainty that his brother, the count of Artois, was in Paradise." It was then that the knight-king, the iron warrior who had withstood the shock of a whole army all day without weakening, who had faced the most redoubtable perils without flinching and mastered the most desperate situations, laid bare his heart. The great conqueror was no more than a poor man in mourning, weeping for his brother. "'Ah, sire,' said the provost, 'be of good comfort herein, for never did king of France gain such honor as you have gained this day. For in order to fight your enemies, you have passed over a river swimming, and you have discomfited them, and driven them from the field, and taken their engines, and also their tents, wherein you will sleep this night.' And the king replied 'Let God be worshipped for all He has given me!' and then the big tears fell from his eyes." The tears of a Christian hero on the evening of a victory, welling from a heart which, after Francis of Assisi, was perhaps the softest that the century had known.

But the king of France had no time to linger, either to weep for his dead or to savor the pride of sleeping on the battlefield. The morrow promised to be menacing. That very night, as Joinville, harassed and wounded, snatched a little rest in his tent, he had to spring to arms against a Mameluk cavalry patrol. "My knights came to me all wounded as they were. I got up and threw a quilted tunic over my back and a steel cap upon my head, and we drove the Saracens back, but I sent to the king to give us succor, for neither I nor my knights could put on our hauberks because of the wounds we had received."

Two days later, on Friday, February 11, the Mameluk cavalry, the Egyptian infantry, and the Bedouin irregulars launched an assault on the camp. Once again it was the king who set the example for coolness. The Rothelin manuscript describes him on this occasion as "a knight without fear and without blemish." "Not a muscle of his face moved." At one moment the contingent of Charles of Anjou was encircled and on the point of giving way. At this news, the king pricked spurs and hurled himself, sword drawn, into the thickest of the enemy battalions. He traversed the jets of Greek fire, which happily merely burned his horse's crupper, and extricated his brother. Along the canal, the count of Flanders, William of Dampierre, also wrought prodigies of valor and, by a vigorous counterattack, decisively routed the Mameluks in his sector. Further on, Alfonso of Poitiers, encircled and already taken, was delivered by the unexpected intervention of the camp servants and sutlers, the butchers and the women camp followers, who cut a way out for him with their carving knives. It may be noted, for the rest, that most of the barons had dismounted their chivalry, so that the charges of the Mameluk cavalry were shattered against a wall of knights on foot. Joinville's account makes one think of a later episode in the history of France, the battle of the Pyramids, in which Napoleon's bayonets played the same role as the lances of the dismounted knights.

This army of heroes and saints prevailed over the fury of the Mameluks. By evening the Egyptians, disheartened, and with heavy losses, were falling back on Mansura. The admirable king of France, to whom, more than to any other man, the victory was due, then assembled his barons, and in a noble discourse exalted the work accomplished, thanking God for the honor He had done them in permitting them to seize the Egyptian camp, "where we ourselves are now lodged," and to repel all the assaults of the enemy, "we on foot, and they mounted!"

After this twofold victory the wisest course for the French would have been not to hang on but to get back to Damietta while there was still time. Unfortunately, Louis IX thought that his soldierly duty would not allow him to fight a rearguard action. It was the same kind of mistake that Napoleon would have made if he had hung on in Moscow after the burning. For fifty-five days, from February 11 to April 5, Louis hugged the banks of the Bahr as-Saghir. It was a fatal immobility. A terrible epidemic, a sort of "Spanish influenza," with all the symptoms of dysentery and typhoid, swept the camp. Furthermore, the Sultan Turanshah, arriving at Cairo at this juncture, built a flotilla on the Nile which soon stopped all convoys by water between Damietta and the Christian camp, thus cutting off Louis IX's supplies. Famine was thus added to typhus in the French camp, completing the wastage of this magnificent army, visibly melting away without a battle.

Faced with this situation, Louis IX finally decided to withdraw. He crossed back over the Bahr as-Saghir and made for Damietta, pursued and soon encircled by the whole Mameluk cavalry hot on his heels. His faithful companions suggested that he should get away, either by horse, on a fast courser, or by boat down the Nile. He indignantly refused to part from his army. The charges of the Mameluks, accompanied by a storm of arrows, against all the elements of the Frankish column, which they were trying to break up, continued unceasingly day and night. The French soldiers, in a pitiable state of physical distress—general dysentery, skin diseases, mucous complaints, swollen gums—were an army of ghosts. By a miracle of moral strength, Louis IX was able to galvanize this army of sick and dying men. Himself shaking with fever and exhausted by enteritis, he succeeded in maintaining discipline in his column, which he led, bristling with pikes, intact, as far as the Sharimshah region, halfway to Damietta. But he and his companions had overtaxed the limits of human strength. On several occasions he fainted. Joinville depicts him, riding painfully with the rearguard, mounted on a little cob, beside Geoffrey of Sargines, who defended him against the Mameluks "as a good servitor defends his lord's drinking cup from flies, for every time that the Saracens approached, he took his spear, which he had placed between himself and the bow of his saddle, and put it to his shoulder, and ran upon them, and drove them away from the king."

But Louis IX, exhausted by typhus, could no longer sit his horse. Arriving at the little village of Munyat al-Khols Abdallah, Geoffrey of Sargines laid him to bed, at death's door, in a hovel, while Gaucher of Châtillon, single-handed, defended the one village street. It is a page out of a romance of chivalry. "In this street was my Lord Gaucher of Châtillon, with his naked sword in his fist. When he saw that the Turks came into the street he ran upon them, sword in hand, and sent them flying out of the village. He pulled out the darts that he had upon him and rose in his stirrups and lifted up his sword arm, and cried: 'Châtillon, knight, Châtillon, where are my good men?' When he turned and saw that the Turks had entered the street at the other end, he ran upon them again, sword in hand, and sent them flying, and this he did three times in the manner aforesaid." It was only from the sight of a Turk leading the hero's horse, the crupper red with blood, that the end of the story was known.

In the general disorder, in the absence of the king, believed to be dead, while the barons were trying to open parley with the Egyptian generals, the misunderstanding or treason of a sergeant resulted in the unconditional capitulation of the army. The Mameluks, drunk with victory, massacred some of the captives on the spot, including most of the sick. Louis IX himself was personally insulted and threatened with death, without thereby losing any of his serenity. "To these threats the king replied that he was their prisoner, and that they could do with him according to their will." This unshakable gentleness, this Christian stoicism impressed the barbarians. The Sultan Turanshah agreed to negotiate: it was arranged that the king would restore Damietta as his personal ransom and would pay 500,000 *livres tournois* to ransom the army.

The treaty, harsh as it was, had the twofold merit of liberating the French army and leaving intact the Frankish possessions in Syria. It was about to be put into effect, when a revolution heavy with consequences reopened the whole issue, in principle and in detail. On May 2, 1250, the Sultan Turanshah was overthrown by the Turkish Mameluk guard in the course of a savage drama which outshadows in horror the darkest pages of Tacitus. Chased and tracked down in a terrifying manhunt as far as the Nile, where he tried to hide, driven back into the water by great saber thrusts from the ferocious Baibars, and then "hauled out of the water with a harpoon, like a fish," the last prince of the house of Saladin expired before the eyes of the Egyptian crowd, none of whom thought of lifting a finger to save him. The Mameluks, hot from the murder of their sultan, were on the point of massacring all the French prisoners at the same stroke. But their cupidity prevailed. One of them, "le Poulain blanc," his hands still reeking with the blood of Turanshah, burst into the prison where Saint Louis lay: "What wilt thou give me? for I have slain thine enemy, who, had he lived, would have slain thee!" And the king answered him never a word. In the end, the Mameluks ratified the treaty concluded by the dead sultan.

This agreement, so painfully concluded, was nearly vitiated by events at Damietta. When Louis IX set out for Mansura, he left behind at Damietta his wife, Margaret of Provence, who was expecting a child. At the very moment of the king's capture, she gave birth to a son. An old knight of eighty, the devoted servitor of her family, was at her side in these terrible moments. The Mameluks might appear at any instant. It was then that there took place the dialogue, worthy of Corneille, reported by Joinville: "Before she was brought to bed, she caused everyone to leave her chamber, save this knight only, and knelt before him, and besought him to do her a service; and the knight consented, and gave her his oath. And she said: 'I ask of you, by the troth you have now pledged me, that if the Saracens take this city, you will cut off my head before I fall into their hands.' And the knight replied: 'Be assured that I shall do so willingly, for I was already fully minded to kill you or ever you should be taken.'" The unhappy woman was not yet at the end of her anguish. Since the departure of Louis IX, Damietta had been guarded by the Genoese and other Italian seamen. Panic-stricken at the news of the disaster, they were on the point of fleeing and abandoning the city. Their cowardice might well lead to the massacre of the king of France, for whom Damietta was precisely to stand as ransom. The behavior of Margaret of Provence was beyond all praise. It was the very day after the birth of her son. She summoned all the Italian captains to her bedside and, in a touching appeal, tried to recall them to a sense of duty: "Lords, for God's sake do not leave this city; for you see that if this city were lost, my lord the king would be utterly lost, and all those who have been taken captive with him. And if this moves you not, yet take pity upon the poor weak creature lying here (showing them the newborn child) and wait till I am recovered." In the end, the Italians settled for what they could extort: they would be maintained at the queen's expense. The energetic woman collected supplies to the value of 360,000 *livres* which were handed over to them, and Damietta was saved.

Louis IX was struggling with similar difficulties. He had to find money to make up the balance of the ransom. Joinville counseled him to borrow from the Templars, since the order conducted an overt banking business. The commander of the Temple refused. Respectful though he was of the privileges of the orders, Louis IX was deeply shocked. At his command Joinville boarded the master galley of the Temple where the coffers of the banker-knights were stowed. "So soon as I had gone down to where the treasure was, I asked the treasurer of the Temple to give me the keys, and he, seeing I was thin and emaciated with sickness, and had on only such clothes as I had worn in prison, said he would give me none of them. Then I perceived a hatchet lying there and lifted it and said I would make it the king's key. When the marshal saw this, he ordered the treasurer to give me the keys." Thanks to this forced loan, Louis IX, delivered from the Egyptian prisons, was able to embark on May 8, 1250, and on the thirteenth he landed at Acre.

At Acre, the king of France received the most moving welcome. "The whole city came in procession to meet him, the clergy in their priestly vestments, the knights, the burgesses, the sergeants, the ladies and the damsels, all in their finest attire, to the sound of the bells, which had broken into a peal as soon as his ship was sighted at sea."

Louis IX, having failed to liberate Jerusalem on the battlefields of Egypt, resolved at least to stay in Frankish Syria long enough to reorganize the country and afford it some protection against Moslem attacks. The barons, eager to get back to France, had little liking for this protracted sojourn in the East. Only Joinville backed the king. For this he was accused of being a "*poulain*," a slightly disparaging term, which, as we know, the Westerners applied to the native-born Franks. "I like better to be a *poulain* than a broken-down hack such as you," replied the good seneschal. For the rest, Louis IX allowed all who wished to do so to return to France and kept none with him but volunteers.

Louis IX stayed four years in Syria, from May 13, 1250, to April 24, 1254. He did an excellent job there. Now fully conversant with Moslem politics, he was able to play skillfully on the enmity between the Mameluks, masters of Egypt, and Saladin's family, still masters of Syria. By playing off one side against the other, he got the Mameluks

to release those of his soldiers who were still prisoners, and at one
moment, like Frederick II before him, was even within an ace of
obtaining the restitution of Jerusalem. When the Templars presumed
to thwart his policy (they made separate treaties with the sultan of
Syria, independently of him), he taught them a sharp lesson. Before
the whole army, the grand master and the high dignitaries of the
Temple were made to come barefooted and in the guise of penitents
and kneel before the Capetian to crave pardon for their disobedience.
This public humiliation inflicted on the haughty knights was tanta
mount to a manifesto. For more than twenty years, the Frankish
colonies, a kingdom without a king, had been the most anarchic of
republics. Louis IX was determined to restore the idea of the state and
discipline. During the four years of his stay he was, without assuming
the title, the veritable king of Christian Syria. The common culture of
the Capetian and the barons of Acre and Tyre, his sense of duty and
his absolute loyalty, his devotion to the interests of the Holy Land,
carried to the point of sacrifice, his kind and courteous firmness
ensured that this reform was accepted with good grace even by those
whose personal interests were likely to suffer from it.

Territorially, Louis IX placed Frankish Syria in a state of defense,
restoring or completing, with the utmost care, the fortifications of the
main towns, Acre, Caesarea, Jaffa, Sidon. In the principality of Antioch-Tripoli, he arbitrated on the differences among the reigning family
and emancipated the young Prince Bohemund VI, whom he dubbed
knight and who thereafter quartered the arms of France with his own.
He reconciled the principality of Antioch with the Armenian kingdom
of Cilicia, thus reconstituting the Christian front in the north. He had
no hesitation, against official Islam, in forming a veritable alliance with
the grand master of the Assassins, "the Old Man of the Mountains."
The chief of this redoubtable sect started by trying to intimidate Louis
with threats of assassination. When he realized that this approach was
doomed to failure with a man of the temper of the king of France, he
sent him, as a gage of friendship, "his shirt and his ring," not to
mention an elephant of crystal, a magnificent set of chessmen, and
marvelous perfumes. Louis IX responded with "a great foison of
jewels, cloths of scarlet, cups of gold, and horses' bits of silver."
Finally, Saint Louis, taking a bold initiative which shows how far he
looked into the future, sent the Franciscan Rubruck on a mission to the

Mongols to sound out these people whose intervention in the duel between Franks and Moslems might change the whole picture. If he was, for the moment, disappointed with the reply brought back by the traveler, he had nevertheless to some extent foreseen the event which, five years later, was to revolutionize the whole of Asia, the destruction of the caliphate of Baghdad by these same Mongols, the unexpected allies of Christendom.[1]

When Louis IX, recalled to France by the death of the queen regent, his mother, sailed from Acre on April 24, 1254, he had therefore wrought a recovery in Frankish Syria in every sphere, both in its internal cohesion and its diplomatic standing, which is not the least of his claims to our admiration.

[1] Cf. René Grousset, *L'Empire des steppes. Attila, Gengis-Khan, Tamerlan* (Paris: Payot, 1939), pp. 342 ff. and 426 ff. Rubruck left Constantinople on May 7, 1253, and reached the Great Khan in Mongolia at the end of December. Baghdad was taken by the Mongols on February 10, 1258.

18

EPILOGUE

The Frankish Anarchy
and the Fall of Acre

THE recovery effected by Saint Louis did not long survive his departure. His presence had restored to Frankish Syria cohesion, unity, and the idea of the state. His back once turned, it soon relapsed into its anarchy and its political and mercantile squabbles. The city of Acre, the official capital of the country, but which, since the expulsion of the imperialists had been constituted as an autonomous commune, was torn by the rivalry between the Genoese colony and the Venetian colony sheltered within its walls. A parish-pump quarrel for the possession of the church of Saint Sabas, lying between the Genoese quarter and the Venetian quarter, sparked off a street warfare between the nationals of the two Italian republics, in which the real issue was the monopoly of the Levantine trade and which ultimately spread to the whole of Frankish Syria and finally to the whole Mediterranean basin. Starting in 1256, two years after the departure of Saint Louis, the "war of Saint Sabas" compelled the various lordships which made up Frankish Syria to take sides: for the Venetians, the Ibelin family, masters of Beirut and Jaffa, the Templars, the Teutonic Order, the Pisans, and the Provençal merchants; for the Genoese, Philip of Montfort, lord of Tyre, the Hospitalers, and the Catalan merchants. This civil war, under the sardonic eyes of the Moslems, attained an unprecedented degree of violence. In Acre itself, the quarters of the different parties bristled with internal fortifications, which were constantly assaulted by the adverse party with new reinforcements of engines of war. After two years of combat, Acre remained in the hands of the Venetian party, while the Genoese withdrew to Tyre under the protection of Philip of Montfort, and Frankish Syria thus found itself cut in two (1258).

Hostilities even spread to the principality of Antioch-Tripoli, where Prince Bohemund VI had taken the Venetian side, while his vassal, Bertrand of Gibelet (Jebail), whose family was of Genoese origin, naturally leaned toward the Genoese. In the course of a clash before the walls of Tripoli, Bohemund was wounded and almost killed by Bertrand's own hand (1258). A few months later, as Bertrand was visiting his vineyards, he was slain by a peasant who offered his head as a gift to Bohemund.

So many combats, so many dramas, with the fermenting legacy of hatred they left in men's hearts, completed the weakening of this unhappy country on the eve of invasion.

The Franks were no less divided in the matter of foreign policy.

In 1260, the Mongols, commanded by the khan of Persia, Hulagu, the grandson of Genghis Khan, invaded Moslem Syria, all of whose cites, Aleppo, Hama, Homs, and Damascus, fell into their hands, while the dynasty of Saladin disappeared in the turmoil.[1] Since they were at war with the Moslem powers and since, into the bargain, some of their number, and in particular one of their generals, the famous Kitbuqa, professed Nestorian Christianity, the prince of Antioch-Tripoli, Bohemund VI, in agreement with the king of Armenia, Hethoum the Great, resolutely joined forces with them. With them, he entered Aleppo and Damascus, the inviolate cities which had never been trodden by Frankish foot, and, in company with Kitbuqa, converted several Damascene mosques into churches.

But the barons of Acre were far from adopting this policy. Alarmed at the approach of the Mongols, they did not hesitate to conclude a pact against them with the defenders of Islam, the Mame-

---

[1] Entry of the Mongols into Aleppo, January 24, 1260 and into Damascus, March 1 of the same year. See René Grousset, *L'Empire des Steppes. Attila, Gengis-Khan, Tamerlan* (Paris: Payot, 1939), p. 436.

luks of Egypt. They allowed the Mameluks to make use of Frankish territory to mount an attack on the Mongol army of occupation, and it was largely thanks to this "benevolent neutrality" that the Mameluk chiefs, Qutuz and Baibars, were able to crush and kill Kitbuqa at the battle of Ain Jalud in Galilee on September 3, 1260. The Mongols were thrown back into Persia and the Mameluks reunited Moslem Syria with Egypt.

If the Acre barons counted on the gratitude of the Mameluks, they were bitterly disappointed. The Mameluk chief Baibars, who at this juncture ascended the throne of Cairo after assassinating his predecessor, was not a man to be trammeled by his oaths. This blue-eyed Russian Turk, with his formidable stature, in whose veins may have run some of the blood which was to produce Ivan the Terrible and Peter the Great, was indeed a figure larger than life. Bought, like so many of his peers, in the slave markets of the Crimea, this prodigious adventurer, once admitted into the Mameluk fraternity, had twice saved it, and Islam with it, first by halting Saint Louis at Mansura and secondly by driving the Mongols out of Syria. Gaining the throne of Egypt by a series of assassinations—the savage murder of the last representative of Saladin's family, the murder by blackest treachery of his own chief, his personal friend, his predecessor, the Mameluk Sultan Qutuz—Baibars, once on the throne, redeemed his crimes by proving himself overnight one of the first statesman of his time, a savage and treacherous wild beast but a soldier of genius and an incomparable administrator. It was in the future against this peerless adversary—the very god of action and of victory—that the Franks would have to defend themselves.

The conquests of Baibars were like lightning. On February 27, 1265, he took Caesarea; on April 26, Arsuf; on July 25, 1266, the fortress of the Templars at Safed; on March 7, 1268, Jaffa; on April 15 the Templars' stronghold of Beaufort. In the second fortnight of May 1268, he seized Antioch and reduced Bohemund VI to the county of Tripoli. The announcement of an Eighth Crusade led by Louis IX gave the Christians some hope, but the fatal diversion of the expedition to Tunis and the death of the royal saint finally discouraged them (1270). Baibars, in all tranquility, despoiled the Templars of their castle of Safita, the White Castle (February 1271), and then won from the Hospitalers, tower by tower, *enceinte* by *enceinte*, the "impregnable" fortress of Krak des Chevaliers (March 15–April 8, 1271).

The last Frankish possessions seemed on the point of yielding. The landing at Acre on May 9, 1271, of Prince Edward of England, later King Edward I, gave them an unhoped-for respite. Edward was one of the wisest politicians of his time, a good soldier, a good diplomat, a sincere Christian. In a series of valuable expeditions he cleared the Acre region, renewed the profitable Mongol alliance, and inspired Baibars with sufficient respect for the Frankish arms and at the same time with the conviction that Europe was not prepared to disinterest itself from its colonies. On April 22, 1272, the terrible sultan granted the Christians of Acre a truce of ten years and ten months.

The Franks took advantage of this respite to reopen their quarrels. King Hugh III of Cyprus, who since 1269 had been trying to achieve a minimum of union among them, could not succeed in making himself obeyed.[2] At Beirut, the heiress of the house of Ibelin claimed the "protection" of Baibars against him. The grand master of the Templars, William of Beaujeu, systematically hampered all his efforts to restore authority. Discouraged, Henry III left to their fate these people, who seemed bent on their own destruction, and retired to his noble kingdom of Cyprus (1276). It was then that the king of Sicily, Charles of Anjou, laid claim to the crown of the Holy Land, but instead of coming in person he contented himself with sending to represent him at Acre his lieutenant, the count of Marseilles, Roger of Saint-Severin, with a derisory force. Saint-Severin's government, supported by the grand master of the Temple, William of Beaujeu, did at least restore a minimum of order to the country. It was suddenly cut short by the drama of the Sicilian Vespers, which, by recalling the count of Marseilles to Italy, put an end to this attempt at Angevin domination in the Levant (1282). And anarchy began again.

Right up to the bitter end this unhappy country was to be torn by civil strife. In the county of Tripoli the reign of Bohemund VII (1275–1287) witnessed the rivalry of a "Roman party" headed by the Princess-Mother Lucienne of Segni, and a "Poulain party" represented

[2] Hugh III of Antioch-Lusignan, king of Cyprus in 1267, nominated king of Jerusalem, 1269, died 1284.

by Bohemund VII himself. The Templars (involved in every political intrigue) and the principal vassal of Bohemund VII, Guy II of Gibelet (or Jebail), took sides against him, and a full-dress civil war—the most impious of all, when one remembers the encirclement of the country by the Mameluks—from 1278 to 1282, completed the decimation of the chivalry of Tripoli. In January 1282, Guy of Gibelet tried with the connivance of the Templars, to take Tripoli by surprise, but it was he who fell into a trap and was handed over to Bohemund VII, who had him walled up alive in a cellar and left to an atrocious death. Such was the fury of civil hatred that this savage drama was celebrated with glee by the enemies of the house of Gibelet, and at Acre the Pisans mounted a sort of theatrical show to commemorate its episodes.

For the last time, the Franks tried to consolidate themselves around the royal authority by awarding what they still continued to call "the crown of Jerusalem" to King Henry III of Cyprus. Henry's arrival at Acre and his coronation at Tyre (August 15, 1286) were welcomed with great festival; but this epileptic and effeminate youth, the plaything of his entourage and soon the victim of his brothers, "this poor Cypriot Louis XVI," as Iorga calls him, had none of the qualities of a chief. In the waters of Acre, Pisans and Genoans indulged in furious sea fights (May 1287). At Tripoli, on the death of Bohemund VII (October 19, 1287), the populace, refusing to recognize his sister, constituted themselves into an independent commune. In a curious manifesto, the burgesses of Tripoli proclaimed the forfeiture of the dynasty of the Bohemunds, listing their grievances against its tyranny and affirming their determination to govern themselves "to maintain each man in his right and reason," after which they hastened to place themselves under the protectorate of Genoa. In vain did the grand master of the Temple, William of Beaujeu, warn these haughty commoners that the moment for civil strife was past and the Mameluk squadrons were approaching. Lightheartedly, they begged him to stop trying to scare them with rumors of war.

But the Mameluks were there. At the end of February 1289, the Sultan Qalawun, with 40,000 horsemen and 100,000 foot soldiers, invested Tripoli. On April 20, the Venetians and the Genoese, whose quarrels had done so much to weaken the ancient county, left the French to themselves and took ship by stealth with all their worldly riches. Learning of this defection, the sultan ordered a general assault and took the city by storm (April 26, 1289).

The massacre, in the Mameluk manner, was terrible. "The populace," writes Abul Feda, "fled toward the port, but very few of them could take ship. Most of the men were killed and the women and children reduced to slavery. When the killing was done, the city was razed to the ground. Near the city was an islet, where there was a church of Saint Thomas. An enormous crowd had taken refuge there. The Moslems plunged into the sea on horseback, or swam out to the islet. All the men who were there were slain. I visited this island some time after and found it covered with decomposing bodies. It was impossible to stay there because of the stench." Of all that thriving population of merchants, craftsmen, doctors, and scholars, the pride of the Levant, nothing remained for months but decomposing bodies, the memory of which still obsessed Abul Feda twenty years after. A lamentable episode, but all too easy to foresee amid so much partisan feeling and political blindness.

At this juncture there arrived at Acre an Italian People's Crusade of pilgrims without military training or discipline, whose dangerous zeal recalled that of the bands of Peter the Hermit. These unbridled and exalted mobs, in the twilight of the Crusades, were to bring the same misfortunes as their forerunners had at the beginning. In 1096 they almost brought the holy war to an abortive ending in an ignoble massacre of Jews and Hungarian or Greek peasants. It was by a massacre of the same kind that, in 1291, they brought on the final catastrophe.

With infinite reason the responsible chiefs of the commune of Acre tried to calm the bellicose zeal of the People's Crusade. Prevented from matching themselves against the Mameluks, the pilgrims then scattered throughout the outskirts of Acre and set about despoiling and massacring the inoffensive Moslem peasants who were bringing their wares to market in the town. Back in Acre they organized a "Moslem Vespers," rioting through the bazaar and slaughtering all the Moslem traders who were there. In their criminal folly they even put to the sword large numbers of Syrian Christians whom they took for Moslems because they were bearded.

The Syrian barons were aghast. By this massacre, perpetrated at the height of the truce, the demagogy of the crusade had violated the law of nations, put the Christians hopelessly in the wrong, and given the Mameluks the occasion for terrible reprisals.

In effect, the Sultan al-Ashraf Khalil, who ascended the throne of Egypt at this juncture, had no mind to let slip such a favorable opportunity. On Thursday, April 5, 1291, he opened the siege of Acre at the head of 160,000 foot soldiers supported by 60,000 horsemen and a formidable "artillery" of catapults.

By assembling all the Christian forces, Franks from Syria and Cyprus, crusaders and newly landed pilgrims, Italian seamen in port, the city of Acre could muster, out of a population of about 35,000, a total of 14,000 foot soldiers and 800 knights or mounted sergeants. The military orders, whose selfish policy and quarrels were largely responsible for the Frankish decadence, proved themselves, in this supreme moment, worthy of their origins. These men could be blamed for many things, but at least they knew how to die nobly.

On the night of April 15, profiting from the magnificent moonlight, the grand master of the Temple, William of Beaujeu, and the Swiss knight Otto of Grandson, commanding the king of England's men-at-arms, attempted a sortie on the north, by the shore. With three hundred knights, they surprised the Egyptian outposts and penetrated as far as the enemy camp, but their horses stumbled among the tent ropes, the alarm was raised, and they could not, as they wished, set fire to the siege engines. In this same month of April, the besieged tried another sortie, but this time taking advantage of a dark night. At midnight, all the chivalry mustered in silence behind Saint Anthony's Gate, but the Mameluks, forewarned, were on the alert. At the very moment when the order, "To horse!" rang through the Frankish army, the whole Moslem camp was a blaze of torches, and ten thousand Mameluks also leaped to the saddle. The knights withdrew back into Acre under a furious enemy charge.

On Friday, May 18, at dawn, the Sultan al-Ashraf launched the final assault. A great battery of cymbals gave the signal. The Mameluks advanced on foot, in deep columns, submerging all before them. Penetrating between the outer wall and the inner wall, they occupied, at a single dash, the famous Accursed Tower, from which a party advanced toward Saint Anthony's Gate. It was here that the last stand was concentrated. The marshal of the Hospital, Matthew of Clermont, for an instant drove back the enemy. The Templars too withstood the storm. The chronicler of their order, who was one of the heroes of this terrible day, depicts their grand master, William of Beaujeu, running with a dozen of his folk to stop thousands of assailants. On the way, he was joined by the grand master of the Hospital, and the two of them marched to their death together: a reconciliation at the supreme moment—soon sealed by the blood of the two old men—between the two rival orders, so long separated by a wall of hatred.

What this handful of iron men was trying to do was to close the way between the two *enceintes,* save the inner *enceinte,* and win back the Accursed Tower. But "naught could avail" against the rising tide of the Moslem masses, and the two heroes seemed to be "striking against a stone wall." Blinded by the smoke of the Greek fire, they could no longer see each other. A few, in the midst of these whirlwinds and jets of flame, in the midst of the rain of crossbow shafts, where all the rest of the Franks had yielded, still resisted, foot by foot. It was three o'clock when the grand master of the Temple was fatally wounded. The arrow entered deep under the armpit. "When he felt himself wounded to the death, he fell back, and some thought he was fleeing; some crusaders from Spoleto stopped him, crying, 'For God's love, my lord, do not abandon us, or the city is lost!' And he answered them, 'I am not fleeing, I am slain, you can see the stroke!' And we saw the arrow deep in his side." His faithful followers bore him to the Temple, where he died.

The marshal of the Hospital, Matthew of Clermont, had an equally glorious end. After covering himself with glory before Saint Anthony's Gate, he drew breath an instant before the fortress house of the Temple, which could still defy assault for a long time. But hardly had he saluted the remains of William of Beaujeu, when he plunged back into the fight. "He and his companions cut down an infinity of Saracens and in the end he was killed, with all his people, like noble and valiant knights and good Christians, and may the Lord keep their souls!" As for the grand master of the Hospital, John of Villiers, he was dangerously wounded, but was saved in time by his people.

While the Mameluks, in spite of the sacrifice of the Templars and the Hospitalers, engulfed the city by Saint Anthony's Gate, John of Grailly, commanding the French contingent, and Otto of Grandson, commanding the English contingent, who had long defended Saint Nicholas's Gate and the Bridge Tower, were finally overwhelmed by numbers. John of Grailly was grievously wounded, and Otto of Grandson driven back to the port with the survivors. At least Grandson succeeded in getting Grailly, the grand master of the Hospital, and the other wounded of his entourage on board a Venetian vessel which carried them to Cyprus.

But there were not enough ships. Several foundered under the sheer weight of humanity which overcrowded them. The patriarch of Jerusalem, Nicholas of Hanapé, a Dominican of the diocese of Rheims, after sustaining the courage of the Christians with admirable zeal throughout the siege, took refuge in a boat but, in his charity, could not bring himself to set sail and continued taking newcomers on board, until finally the boat sank.

The mass of the population was delivered up to the fury of the Mameluks. "The day was terrible," writes the Templar of Tyre, "for the noblewomen, the townswomen, and the young damsels fled through the streets, some carrying their children in their arms; dissolved in tears, they ran toward the port. And when the Saracens met them, one took the mother, another took the child: sometimes they came to blows in dispute over a woman, then they would combine to slay her. Elsewhere they snatched the children from their mother's breast and flung them under the horses' hoofs."

Only the convent-fortress of the Templars still held out. Backing on the sea, with enormous walls, it was the last redoubt. After the death of the grand master, the marshal of the Temple, Peter of Sevrey, and Tibald Gaudin, the commander, barricaded themselves in with the last survivors, after collecting at the foot of the walls all the boats which were still available. All who could find refuge within this fortress, men, women, and children, were saved and, with King Henry II, sailed from there to Cyprus. "And when all those ships set sail, the Templars, who remained in their fortress, saluted them with a great cry and the vessels drew away into the distance. . . ."

For several days, the fortress of the Temple resisted all attacks. The Sultan al-Ashraf then offered the Templars an honorable capitulation, with a safe-conduct to Cyprus. The terms were accepted. The great standards of the sultan were already flying over the central keep, in sign of armistice, while an emir, with some hundred Mameluks, was

admitted into the fortress to supervise the embarkation of the Christians. But, drunk with their triumph, these Mameluks started to assault
the Frankish ladies. At this, the indignant knights fell upon them,
executed them, hauled down the sultan's flag, and closed the gates
again. And the marshal Peter of Sevrey prepared to stand a new siege.

The castle, its defenders now in desperation, seemed impregnable.
The Sultan al-Ashraf had recourse to felony. He again offered Peter
of Sevrey a capitulation in full honor. Peter was rash enough to trust
him. With a party of his followers, he kept a rendezvous with
al-Ashraf. No sooner did the sultan have them in his power than he
had them all beheaded. After that, those Templars who were still
inside the fortress, the wounded, the sick, the aged, resolved to resist
unto death. The sultan had to recommence the siege a third time, with
a great reinforcement of mines. The foundations were sapped, whole
stretches of the walls were collapsing, but the Templars still held out.
On May 28, the breach was wide enough and al-Ashraf launched the
final assault, but the weight of the Mameluk masses was too great for
the props of the saps and the whole building collapsed, burying in its
rubble the last of the Templars as well as the assault columns. The
funeral sacrifice of the "Temple of Jerusalem" was two thousand
Turkish bodies.

The remaining Christian strongholds were evacuated without a fight,
Tyre in May, Sidon in July, Tortosa in August of the same year. The
Templars kept the islet of Ruad, off Tortosa, until 1303.

It was by way of the islet of Ruad that six centuries later, in 1914,
the "Franks" were to set foot again in Syria, going on, four years later,
to deliver Tripoli, Beirut, and Tyre, the city of Raymond of Saint-
Gilles, the city of John of Ibelin, the city of Philip of Montfort.

As for Jerusalem itself, it was to be "reoccupied" on December 9,
1917, by the descendants of King Richard the Lionhearted, under the
orders of Field Marshal Allenby.

Reference and Reading List

REFERENCE WORKS

Cambridge Medieval History. Originally edited by J. M. Bury. 8 vols. Cambridge, 1911–1966. See especially Vol. IV (1936), Chaps. X, XI, XII, XIV; Vol. IV, Part I (new ed. by J. M. Hussey, 1966), Chaps. V, VII, XV, XVI; Vol. V (1957), Chaps. VI, VII, VIII, IX.

Shorter Cambridge Medieval History. Ed. by C. E. Prévité-Orton. 2 vols. Cambridge, 1952.

The Encyclopaedia of Islam. Ed. by T. Houtsama and others. 4 vols. Leiden and London, 1913; Supplement, 1933. New Edition ed. by J. H. Kramers and others; Vol. I (in 2 parts), 1950–1960, and Vol. II (in 2 parts), 1963–1965, A through G, have appeared to date.

The New Catholic Encyclopedia. Ed. by Staff of Catholic University of America. 15 vols. New York, 1967.

BIBLIOGRAPHIC WORK

Atiya, Aziz S. *The Crusade: Historiography and Bibliography.* Bloomington, Ind., 1962.

ENGLISH TRANSLATIONS OF ORIGINAL SOURCES

Ambroise. *The Book of King Richard's Expedition to the Holy Land of Jerusalem.* Translation by K. Fenwick of a medieval Latin version. London, 1958.

———— *The Crusade of Richard Lion Heart.* Trans. from French by M. J. Hubert. New York, 1941.

Anna Comnena. *The Alexiad.* Trans. from Greek by E. A. S. Dana. London, 1928.

Anonymous. *Gesta Francorum et Aliorum Hierosolymitanorum* ("The Deeds of the Franks and Other Pilgrims to Jerusalem"). Ed. with trans. from Latin by R. Hill. London, 1962.

Fulcher of Chartres. Foucher de Chartres, *Chronicle of the First Crusade.* Trans. from Latin by Martha E. McGinty. Philadelphia, 1941.

Ibn al-Qalanisi. *The Damascus Chronicle of the Crusades.* Selections trans. from Arabic by H. A. R. Gibb. London, 1932.

Joinville, John of (Jean de). Joinville and Villehardouin, *Chronicles of the Crusades.* Trans. from French by M. R. B. Shaw. Penguin Books, London, 1963.

———— *The Life of Saint Louis.* Trans. from French by René Hague. New York, 1955.

Miscellany. *The Crusades.* Trans. by Enid McLeod of *Les croisades* ed. by Régine Pernoud. New York, 1963.

The Crusades; a Documentary Survey. J. A. Brundage. Milwaukee, 1962.

The First Crusade; the Accounts of Eye-Witnesses and Participants. By A. C. Krey. Gloucester, Mass., 1958.

Philip of Novara. *The Wars of Frederick II against the Ibelins in Syria and Egypt.* Trans. from French by M. J. Hubert. New York, 1936.

Usama. *An Arab-Syrian Gentleman and Warrior in the Period of the Crusades: Memoirs of Usamah ibn-Mundiqh.* Trans. from Arabic by P. K. Hitti. New York, 1929.

—— *Autobiography of Ousama.* Trans. by G. R. Potter. Brooklyn, N.Y., 1929.

William of Tyre. *A History of Deeds Done Beyond the Sea.* Trans. by E. A. Babcock and A. C. Frey of the Latin *Historia Rerum in Partibus Transmarinis Gestarum.* 2 vols. New York, 1943.

GENERAL AND SPECIALIZED WORKS

Arnold, Sir Thomas and Guillaume, Alfred. *The Legacy of Islam.* Oxford, 1931.

Atiya, Aziz S. *Crusade, Commerce and Culture.* Bloomington, 1962.

—— *The Crusade in the Later Middle Ages.* London, 1938.

Barker, Ernest. *The Crusades.* Reprint of article in the *Encyclopaedia Britannica,* 11th ed., 1910–1911. London, 1923, 1939.

Bradford, Ernle D. S. *The Great Betrayal: Constantinople, 1204.* London, 1967.

—— *The Sundered Cross; The Story of the Fourth Crusade.* Englewood Cliffs, N.J., 1967.

Brundage, James A. *The Crusades; Motives and Achievements.* Boston, 1965.

Campbell, George A. *The Crusades.* London, 1935.

—— *The Knights Templars, Their Rise and Fall.* London, 1937.

Chalandon, Ferdinand. *Histoire de la première croisade.* Paris, 1925.

—— *Les Comnène; études sur l'empire byzantin au XIe et au XIIe siècles.* 2 vols. Paris, 1912.

—— *Jean II Comnène (1118–1143) et Manuel I Comnène (1143–1180).* Reprint of the preceding. New York, n.d. [1960?].

Coulton, George G. *Crusades, Commerce and Adventure.* London, 1930.

Duggan, Alfred L. *The Story of the Crusades.* New York, 1964.

Durant, Will(iam) and Ariel. *The Age of Faith, a History of Medieval Civilization from Constantine to Dante: A. D. 325–1200.* Vol. IV of *The Story of Civilization.* New York, 1950.

Fedden, Robin (Henry Romilly Fedden) and Thomson, John. *Crusaders' Castles.* London, 1950.

Gibb, Hamilton A. R. *Studies on the Civilization of Islam.* Ed. by S. J. Shaw and W. R. Polk. Boston, 1962.

Grousset, René. *Histoire des croisades et du royaume franc de Jérusalem.* 3 vols. Paris, 1934–1936.

Hitti, Philip K. *History of the Arabs.* London, 1937. Sixth ed., New York, 1956.

Lamb, Harold. *The Crusades; Iron Men and Saints.* 2 vols. New York, 1946.

Müller-Wiener, Wolfgang. *Castles of the Crusaders.* Trans. from German by M. Brownjohn. New York, 1966.

Munro, Dana C. *Essays on the Crusades.* Burlington, Vt., 1903.

—— *The Kingdom of the Crusaders.* New York, 1936.

Newhall, Richard A. *The Crusades.* Revised ed. New York, 1965.

Oakeshott, R. Ewart. *The Archaeology of Weapons.* London, 1960.

Oldenbourg, Zoé. *The Crusades.* Trans. by Anne Carter of *Les croisades.* New York, 1966.

Oman, Sir Charles W. C. *A History of the Art of War in the Middle Ages.* Revised ed. 2 vols. London, 1924.

—— *The Art of War in the Middle Ages.* Revised ed. of the preceding by John M. Beiler. Ithaca, N.Y., 1953. 2nd rev. ed. 2 vols. New York, 1959.

Ostrogorsky, George. *History of the Byzantine State.* Trans. from German by J. Hussey. New Brunswick, N.J., 1957.

Paetow, Louis J., ed. *The Crusades and Other Historical Essays Presented to Dana C. Munro.* New York, 1928.

Paris, N. A. *The Arab Heritage.* Princeton, 1944.

Pernoud, Régine. *The Crusaders.* Trans. by Enid Grant of *Les croisés.* London, 1963; Philadelphia, 1964.

Rice, David Talbot. *The Byzantines.* New York, 1962.

Richard, Jean. *Le royaume latin de Jérusalem.* Paris, 1953.

Rousset, P. *Histoire des croisades.* Paris, 1957.

Runciman, Steven. *A History of the Crusades.* Vol. I, *The First Hundred Years,* ed. by Marshall W. Baldwin; Vol. II, *The Later Crusades,* ed. by Robert Lee Wolff and Harry W. Hazard. Philadelphia, 1958, 1962.

Smail, R. C. *Crusading Warfare* (1097–1193). Cambridge, 1956.

Stevenson, William B. *The Crusaders in the East.* Cambridge, 1907.

Treece, Henry. *The Crusades.* London, 1962; New York, 1963.

Vasiliev, Aleksandr A. *History of the Byzantine Empire, 324–1453.* 2nd English ed. Madison, Wisc., 1964.

Williams, Jay. *Knights of the Crusades.* *Horizon* Caravel book. New York, 1962.

BIOGRAPHIES

Bohemund. Ralph B. Yewdale. *Bohemond I, Prince of Antioch.* Princeton, 1924.

Frederick II. Ernst Kantorowicz. *Frederick the Second.* London, 1931.

—— Georgina Masson. *Frederick II of Hohenstaufen: A Life.* London, 1957.

Godfrey of Boulogne. John C. Andressohn. *The Ancestry and Life of Godfrey of Boulogne.* Bloomington, 1947.

Joscelin of Courtenay. Robert L. Nicholson. *Joscelyn I, Prince of Edessa.* Urbana, Ill., 1954.

Louis IX (Saint Louis). Margaret W. Labarge. *Saint Louis: Louis IX, Most Christian King of France.* Boston, 1968.

Raymond III, Count of Tripoli. Marshall W. Baldwin. *Raymond III of Tripolis and the Fall of Jerusalem (1140–1187)*. Princeton, 1936.

Raymond of Saint-Gilles. John H. and Laurita L. Hill. *Raymond IV, Count of Toulouse*. Syracuse, 1962.

Richard the Lionhearted. Philip Henderson. *Richard I, Coeur de Lion; a Biography*. London, 1958.

———— Kate Norgate. *Richard the Lion Heart*. London and New York, 1924.

Robert Curthose. Charles W. Davis. *Robert Curthose*. Cambridge, Mass., 1920.

Saladin. Stanley Lane-Poole. *Saladin and the Fall of the Kingdom of Jerusalem*. London, 1952.

———— Charles J. Rosebault. *Saladin, Prince of Chivalry*. New York, 1930.

———— Gertrude E. Slaughter. *Saladin, 1138–1193; a Biography*. New York, 1955.

Tancred. R. L. Nicholson. *Tancred: A Study of His Career and Work*. Chicago, 1940.

Index